T0279962

DISSIDENCE

DISSIDENCE

Essays Against the Mainstream

DIMITRIOS ROUSSOPOULOS

Montréal/New York

Copyright © 1992 BLACK ROSE BOOKS LTD.

No part of this book may be reproduced or transmitted in any form, by any means
— electronic or mechanical, including photocopying and recording, or by any
information storage or retrieval system — without written permission from the
publisher, or, in the case of photocopying or other reprographic copying, a licence
from the Canadian Reprography Collective, with the exception of brief passages
quoted by a reviewer in a newspaper or magazine.

BLACK ROSE BOOKS No. V188
Hardcover ISBN: 1-895431-41-7
Paperback ISBN: 1-895431-40-9
Library of Congress No. 92-72630

Cataloguing in Publication Data
Roussopoulos, Dimitrios I.,
Dissidence

ISBN 1-895431-41-7 (bound) —
ISBN 1-895431-40-9 (pbk.)

1. Dissenters. 2. Social movements. 3. Political participation.
4. Socialism. I. Title.

HN107.R68   1992   322.4'4   C92-090361-4

Mailing Address

BLACK ROSE BOOKS
C.P. 1258
Succ. Place du Parc
Montréal, Québec
H2W 2R3 Canada

BLACK ROSE BOOKS
340 Nagel Drive
Cheektowaga, New York
14225 USA

Printed in Canada

A publication of the Institute of Policy Alternatives of Montréal
(IPAM)

This book is dedicated to
Lucia J. Kowaluk
and
Riel J.F. Roussopoulos

Other books published by Dimitrios I. Roussopoulos

The New Left in Canada (1970)
The Case for Participatory Democracy, with C. George Benello (1971)
Canada and Radical Social Change (1973)
The Political Economy of the State (1973)
Québec and Radical Social Change (1974)
The City and Radical Social Change (1982)
Our Generation Against Nuclear War (1983)
The Coming of World War Three, Vol. 1 (1983)
1984 and After, with Marsha Hewitt (1984)
The Anarchist Papers (1986)
The Radical Papers (1987)
The Radical Papers 2 (1987)
The Anarchist Papers 2 (1989)
The Anarchist Papers 3 (1990)

forthcoming
Green Politics — Agenda For a New Society (1993)

Contents

PREFACE

The last half of the 20th century is, unquestionably, the first period in human history during which the agenda absorbing our attention has been dominated by one question — the survival of the human species. This question casts the darkest shadow on all other preoccupations and concerns. Slowly at first, but quite evidently by the 1960s, we became aware that humanity could be exterminated and civilization destroyed if a nuclear war — World War III— occurred. In the last twenty years, another threat to our survival as a species (again, the awareness developed slowly), took hold: the ecological collapse of the planet.

Thus, the survival of humanity, a practical task, became for me an all embracing occupation. This task, however, required not only the questioning of the dominant institutions and the society that had put in place a system that was drifting and pushing itself towards nuclear war and ecocide, but also the formulation of how these same institutions and society could be renovated as a requirement to reversing this situation. Thus, difficult theoretical investigations and discussions could not be closed. This intellectual task could not, however, delay an immediate setting off down the road to the survival of the human species. To turn back because of the lack of a theoretical basis would mean compromising humanity's future. Hence, movement became crucial, the movement of people wanting change, in large groups or small. Movement was the condition wherein a dialectic between the practical and a reflection on experience would nourish theory. Since the 1960s, we can only be impressed at the outpouring of people into movement(s). The closest observation, analysis and interacting with this profound historical process was the rationale for the founding of the journal *Our Generation Against Nuclear War,* later to become *Our Generation,* and for my role as editor/organiser.

Such a role inevitably leads to dissent against mainstream society. The politics of dissent has the function of bringing a dissenting people out of isolation to search together and thus constitute a new community. While the forces of history — what makes history — work themselves out, there is no reason why the work of the dissenter should not include keeping alive the vista that potentially stretches before us. This sometimes modest thoughtfulness, without pretending to solve everything, must constantly strive to give human meaning to everyday life. To dissent in this society means to live simply, to keep the people foremost in mind, and to speak truth to power. To do this is not a part-time pre-occupation but a full-time occupation, so that one quits the mainstream and its dominant institutions and thus stands and works in marked contrast to them. Such a purpose

moves against the mainstream, against the official orthodoxies and intellectual fades, against the interests of those who cling to power even while
facing the abyss, and against the privileges of the secular priesthood of our
society. The task of the intellectual is to pursue with courage the logical
consequences of free inquiry. The task of the radical intellectual is to take
the synthesis of such inquiry and test it in society, to unlearn what experience finds less useful and to develop theory that will allow us to understand reality as a whole and its parts, together and separately. Experience
proves that such work requires independence, that is, the freedom and
conviction to act and thus stand against the grain, whatever the personal
cost. All this requires self-knowledge; a strong personality that withstands
the effects of solitary circumstance that inevitably follows. Dissent seems to
drive toward the building of community even in the jaws of Leviathan, and
thus, we have politics. It is conscientious objection not just to war and
ecocide, not to mention injustice, but to the whole fabric of a dehumanized
society. It is civil disobedience not just by the individual, but, hopefully by
large numbers of alienated people. Most important, this definition of dissent is not intended as a moral gesture only, but as a determined attempt
to transform society by abolishing the concentration of power as such.

Now, survival can be maintained on a temporary basis with exceptional measures by the system that is the cause of the crisis. These measures can
be either self-corrective or pressed upon the system by dissenters who
have a balance of power. This happens in particular circumstances, after
all this world-wide system of exploitation and domination wants itself to
survive. But, as we have seen time and again, these exceptional measures
are temporary. We are moving into an ever-deepening spiral, the debt becomes heavier and our only certainty is that we are not sure when the system will exhaust itself and become ready for a replacement or when we will
hit a catastrophic bottom. In the meantime, we have some space and some
more time to dwell and reflect on the experience of history.

Experience shows, notwithstanding the starkness of the question of
human survival, that no single contradiction carries within itself the seeds
of the world-wide overthrow of the system. The one fact which is new in
our era is that all the main contradictions are emerging simultaneously.
Certain people and groups experience one contradiction more sharply
than another, and become self-conscious or aware, as with feminism or
anti-militarism. These are contradictions potentially so complex that they
make nonsense of any attempt to explain why and what is happening to
the world according to one authoritative philosophy. Thus, we see daily
that a wide variety of social movements undertake one action or another
but that one loudly declared contradiction cannot replace the experienced
contradiction of another. Nevertheless, we must move from a limited
emancipation, which has failed, to a freedom movement for everybody, individually and collectively. Such a movement is a cemetery for dogma, a
formidable challenge both politically and theoretically. Along with the
basic values of peace, justice, freedom and equality that stirred the Movement activists of the 1960s, there was one overriding concern which per-

haps inspired their commitment beyond all others. It was the search for community. Community, as it was understood by the New Left, was an experience as well as a place, a shared political and social activism in open association with others who had similar ultimate concerns. By the end of the decade of the 1960s, the sense of community of "the Movement" disintegrated once "old Leftism" emerged along with a new "separatist sectarianism." The process of disintegration was fuelled first by a Black Power separatism and then accelerated by a series of other separatisms — Chicano, Native American, women's liberation and the ideology of feminist separatism, and finally, the development of gay and lesbian liberation. All of these new movements brought new issues, new vitality, and a new sense of selfhood to "progressive" politics, but none of them brought "the Movement" back together again. The particular quality of personal risk-taking and self-exposure that had attempted to build bridges and that had produced a movement which marched in the streets together, was replaced by a series of separate movements which militantly asserted their identities but lost sight of the whole.

Two contrasting interpretations have emerged regarding the final devolution of the Movement of the 1960s. The majority voice argues that the development of a spectrum of successor movements catalyzed around issues of identity has been a healthy outcome. Another viewpoint argues that the separatist politics of identity that replaced the relative unity of the 1960s Movement has marked the demise of democratic radicalism as a force in politics in our society. The development of a divided movement, this second interpretation contends, has meant not only the substitution of divisive agendas for a radical political critique that might challenge corporate liberalism in the way the New Left once did. Since the demise of the New Left as organisation as well as movement, there has not been even a radical forum where the ideas of democratic radicalism could be debated on an ongoing basis. Whichever school of thought is correct, a process of convergence is how struggling to be born politically.

The principles of democratic radicalism that inspired the best of the New Left have spread everywhere in the last few decades. Whether it is the Greens or the workers and students of Beijing, the notion of grassroots democracy and ethical politics has gained ground in many societies. A commitment to the realisation of these ideals through non-violence is a common theme as are the principles of feminism, gay liberation, and ecological awareness. These principles represent the merger in theory of an ecological and participatory-democratic politics that embody the best of the last few decades. This union, which was implicit in the Movement of the 1960s, would have continued to develop more easily if the New Left had not been torn apart by the separatist "politics of identity," (or which contradiction is primary) and adventuristic violence. The coalescing, grounded in self-conscious awareness, could have completed the new political paradigm that emerged.

The power of this new politics, and its ability to capture the imagination of virtually a whole generation was built upon a vision of a planetary grassroots-democratic and an ecologically sane future based on the decentralisation of power. One thing seems certain: the instinct of the young radicals of the New Left who framed the political debate in terms of an ethically-centred democratic political theory laid the basis of the new political discourse that will guide radical democratic experimentation in the next generation.

We need more new theory, independent of any conformity and censorship, in order to find ways of understanding and therefore, acting, which can adapt to the unprecedented problems that human society has created. Ecology in this sense is the crucial source of radical analysis and thought, as it is the exact opposite of obscurantism. Perhaps more than any other science (and because of this it steps into the realm of philosophy) it seeks new concepts to understand complexity, finiteness, movement, potential, emergence; the impossibility of reducing everything to its component parts; interaction, interdependence in time and space. It helps us grasp the dialectic between quantity and quality. It requires the greatest expansion of intellectual freedom, and hence freedom as such. Ecology, in that it is the study of the whole has the widest ramifications for the study of society and history. But while respecting most of the views of the radical ecologists it is important indeed crucial to hold the view that it is not the human species itself, but rather, institutions that are responsible for the current ecological crisis. Solutions can only be worked out and implemented *socially*, with concerned women and men remaking their society, dismantling this destructive economy, and living in careful ecological stewardship with the rest of Nature. Activists who stress that social change is the key to environmental healing usually refer to themselves as social ecologists.

A new synthesis of the acquired insights from the last three decades of struggle is emerging because it is recognized as needed. Such a synthesis which is best represented by a left-green social ecology perspective is time and space sensitive nevertheless, and will grade several philosophical and scientific traditions and new intellectual discoveries. But it must be a process, devoid of mysticism, incomplete, open to question, leaving unknown and unexplained facts honestly as they are, using the distance between theory and experience to increase our understanding by practical application. Radical theory can only be proven if applied to society. The essence of the political and social theory at the centre of this perspective runs counter to the basic premises of society at large and of the academy. The not so rigorously defined term "society" replaced "polity" as the operative category in most 19th century ideologies and this was promoted consciously as a term to mean human community. Democratic political theory should reject that inversion and reflect that political thought should be linked with ethical inquiry as the proper approach to understanding community. This contention was the basis of the reflection of the 1960s New Left which was a bold attempt to restore the political to its preeminent, Aristotelian position and, in particular, to make value-centred democratic theory the framework for discussion of fundamental change of society. A search for a deeper understanding of politics, a pre-occupation with mediated power can only bring about a new appreciation of the political philosophy rooted in classical Greece, a tradition for which "the political act, or the quality of acting rightly in the polis is the same as virtue, or the quality of right action in general."[1] It was Aristotle who argued in opposition to Realpolitik that morality and politics could not be separated and that, "The study of ethics may not improperly be termed a study of politics."[2] Politics should return to become, once again, a branch of ethics concerned with the art of creating human community in harmony with Nature. Hence, what follows is the position that it is not by words alone but also by acts that people become political and thus, public. Politics is public or civic life, and it was precisely that life which people build together through political activity that has virtually disappeared under the liberal technobureaucracy of the Atomic Age.

Thus, this collection of articles, consisting of editorials and essays, written over a period of three decades, begin and end with the politics of human survival. Straightaway the reader will note the preoccupation is not with a study of the official relationship between States or power blocs, but rather, how the weaknesses of these artificial creatures can afford opportunities for people to intervene and how a movement of these same people for peace and freedom can best be organised to revise an international system which evolved well before the Atomic Age.

The reader will find material that aimed to generate and enrich the *politics of protest* at the time of writing. Protest needless to say was and is never enough to affect a dangerous situation.

The peace movement of the 1960s soon had exhausted traditional means of protest, and soon many people became engaged in the *politics of resistance* (e.g. various forms of civil disobedience). It was recognized by sections of the Movement that while social change was needed, this effort had to be based on a majoritarian and horizontal social transformation that minimized violence, thus revolutionary non-violence became a long-term subject-matter for study and practice as a philosophy of change and the building of a type of movement where power rests at the base.

The material in **Chapter 2** attempted to place all considerations for radical change in Canada in a historical and cultural context. Notwithstanding the critique offered in these essays the basis of interest reflected a view that developments in Québec would lead one to believe that important, that is qualitative, changes were being considered. Much of the critique was more on the mark than was thought at the time, as the passing of time has shown. Besides, the national question while kicking around in other parts of the world, on this continent at least it is being absorbed into a high powered economic agenda of integrating Canada, the USA and Mexico into one trading and commercial bloc and not even Québec's nationalists are seriously opposed. Does this not mean that radicals everywhere on this continent must begin an integrative process of some sort themselves to constitute a parallel or dual power to that being established by the corporate and political elite? The European Left took forever to sort out its position on the Common Market. But now both the social democrats (who have recently formed a unitary European social democratic party regarding the parliament in Strasbourg) and the European Greens have established a continental co-ordinating body, and look at their continent's slowly emerging political institutions as an important field of work.

In **Chapter 3**, the reader will encounter some of the feature questions of the 1960s. It was a period which renewed a libertarian versus a simply democratic dynamic. This preoccupation began when some of us sought to directly participate in questions like foreign and defence policy, two of the most restricted and closely guarded domains of the State. It was realised, as the decade wore on that the natural outgrowth of revolutions was almost always a localist council system of self-government as the most authentic expression of popular objectives; that these communal forms may provide the pattern for a new kind of politics based on the power of co-operation between local units, and so ensure political freedom. A radical alternative to liberal democracy and parliamentary politics was needed. And so, two ideas became prevalent, direct democracy at the local level whereby people themselves were engaged in politics and not just "represented" and thus, alienated from decision-making institutions, and that these assemblies or councils would be federated regionally and "nationally." For us, this also meant that a country's external relations with other countries were no mere reflection of a declared public philosophy but rather reflected the prevailing values of dominant institutions. Of these, the established political institutions promoted a formal, consenting and passive form of democracy. On the other hand, a democracy of participation, sought new social forms of local or community control through which the powerless can act. Unconsciously, the generation of the 1960s, as well as that of the 1970s, picked up the long thread of the libertarian and anarchist tradition from past periods of history.

This cry for democratization and participation, in spite of its largely cultural forms, had wide repercussions. In May, 1975, the Trilateral Commission's Report of the Trilateral Task Force on the Governability of Democracies was made public. Several features of the original unpublished version of this Report are noteworthy. Pessimism and authoritarianism pervade the document, specifically Professor Samuel P. Huntington's section on America, called "The Democratic Surge of the 1960s: A Challenge to all existing authority systems." As more people became involved in public affairs, according to Huntington, their disappointment was inevitable, given the unresponsiveness of certain political institutions. The result was a rapid decline in the belief that the State and its supporting agencies were neutral. There was also an accompanying disenchantment with political parties. The Report concluded that if the system was to correct itself, this "excess of democracy" must be reduced. It argued for an emphasis on the fact that the "arenas where democratic procedures are appropriate are limited." Since the functioning of the system requires "some measure of apathy and noninvolvement," active citizens and groups should be cooled out.

The recommendations included: more economic planning, because an increase in average income encourages political apathy; stronger political leadership (read centralisation of political power); government aid to political parties and financing of elections; restrictions on the freedom of the press, for example, "...there is also the need to assure to the government the right and ability to withhold information at the source"; cutbacks in education because the democratisation of education has raised expectations; alienation attacked at its roots, therefore "a more active intervention in the area of work." Experiences in the co-management of the workplace are rejected in favour of State aid for experimentation with new forms of work organisation.

During the decade of the 1970s, notwithstanding the attempt by the mass media to convince us that the movement was dead, feminists founded the women's liberation movement, and citizen groups sprang up in various urban centres to fight not only for better housing and green spaces, but also for community control. Among the most radical of these movements the question of social change, decentralisation and participation surfaced, spilling over into debate and experimentation. In the end, however, the movement bumped against social democracy and parliamentary politics. **Chapter 4** articulated consciously determined efforts of analysis and theory to find a radical democratic and libertarian alternative.

The early 1980s witnessed a renewed and much more impressive peace movement. Initiated by the *politics of protest,* it moved into *the politics of resistance* in several countries almost at once, notably Britain and West Germany. Once again, this social movement, often a convergence for the movement(s) of the 1960s and 1970s, facing the inflexibility of the nuclear State(s), began not only to question the legitimacy of the system, but also to act outside the parliamentary order through the use of civil disobedience. It is no mere coincidence that in Britain, the birthplace of parliamentary democracy, we saw civil disobedience using peace camps, largely organised by women, initiating a new method of resistance. Alongside this campaign we also saw a new awareness of moving towards the *politics of institutional change* in the form of city councils declaring their territories to be nuclear-free zones. Other city councillors pressed for *local socialism* — that is, a form of socialism favouring a re-definition of the role of the municipality and all major questions facing citizens, including ecology, war and peace. It was no mere co-incidence that in West Germany, a society with a highly authoritarian past, the massive anti-nuclear power movement of the 1970s which began in the countryside and which stressed the importance of regionalisation and decentralisation, evolved from the politics of protest and resistance to that of political change as embodied by the Greens, who offered a synthesis of ecology, feminism and pacifism. In these circumstances, class-based insurrectionalism led by vanguard political parties were shunned. The authoritarian old Left was finally buried eight feet under, although its ghosts and ideological necrophilics continued to hang around for a while longer.

The material in **Chapter 5** outlines what has been called *the creation of politics*. It is an agenda which takes into account the nature of neo-capitalism as an analytical hypothesis from which a libertarian politics in the classical meaning of the word "politics" must be centred. Politics, in its classical sense, is defined not as parliamentarism, or Statecraft, or party "politics," but the management of our affairs as citizens in neighbour-hoods, in the city. After several decades of writing critical analysis and theory on historical and contemporary issues, appreciation and gratitude must be expressed to Murray Bookchin for having initiated this long awaited and much needed movement-building perspective conducive to the 1990s.

Almost all of these and related ideas reflected in these occasional writings are, in substance, part of libertarian socialism and the anarchist tradition, like it or not. The purpose of publishing them at this time is that we are entering the last decade of this century, where another cycle of the movement of people is being mounted which seeks to radically transform society in order to save the human species from ecocide and war, and in doing so create a new society that is both classless and warless. Hopefully, these writings may contribute to making this movement conscious of its philosophical and experiential past, as a beacon for the present and future.

Montréal, Fall 1992

NOTES

1. Barker, Ernest, *Greek Political Thought*, p. 150. London: Methuen & Co. 1918, rpy. 1961.
2. Aristotle, *Rhetoric, Book I*, C.II, No. 7.

ACKNOWLEDGEMENTS

First and foremost, I am indebted to Nat Klym for the production of this book, from word-processing to producing camera-ready copy. I also wish to thank Julia Gualtieri who did the proof-reading in a period too short for comfort. For the rest, I have over three decades of radical activism interacted with so many extraordinary personalities that it would be senseless to saddle the reader with a long string of names. But one person stands out above all others, my companion, Lucia Kowaluk. We have consistently put principles to practice, together, always ready to fight for the rights of others. Imaginative though I am, it is impossible for me to imagine this work having been done without her.

Chapter 1

THE PEACE MOVEMENT AND THE POLITICS OF PEACE

Winter 1962

INTERNATIONALISING THE NUCLEAR DISARMAMENT MOVEMENT

On our planet today, for the very first time, many ordinary people on a massive scale have begun to think internationally and are becoming involved in the growing resistance movement against war. In order to defeat the international war system, the people of the world who believe in the world of tomorrow, however, must band all their efforts together and build a world movement.

Brotherhood Not Bombs

The most important movement against the international war system has not come from any political party but from a scattered group of individuals who became aware of the danger of radiation fallout. The fear of fallout mounted protests against the testing of thermonuclear weapons and these in time developed into organised protests against the nuclear status quo. This pattern of development unfolded almost in the same way in the two countries that now have the most important, massive and well-organised anti-nuclear movements, Japan and England.

In the Western hemisphere, the mass demonstrations of Aldermaston, organised by the Campaign for Nuclear Disarmament (CND), have been an inspiration to people in every country. The influence of the CND has become widespread and its semaphore symbol has become the international symbol of resistance. Similar movements have now developed in Belgium, in the Scandinavian countries, West Germany, Canada, New Zealand, Australia, and other countries. This development has been quite haphazard without any international assistance or direction; however, it cannot continue in this manner.

It was James Cameron of the national executive of the CND, in an article in *Peace News*[1] welcoming the San Francisco-to-Moscow Marchers, who asked: "Where do we go from here?" He proceeded to answer by saying, "The arrival of the Americans is certainly not going to answer the question either, but I believe it may remind us of two things: one, that there is a pretty big world all around, and another, that we are not alone. It is possible that the time has come for the anti-nuclear fighters in Britain to think rather more internationally than we have been doing up to now..." It could well be that the coming activities of the anti-nuclear movement in Britain will involve a great deal more international liaison. As long ago as the 1960 Annual Conference of CND it was resolved to form international associations and to call an international conference. This year it was agreed to set up a Commonwealth Bureau for the co-ordination of anti-nuclear movements in the member countries, and to make contact with the government of uncommitted countries to secure their support. If these things can be realised it places the movement on a much more serious international scale and puts our entire work in a meaningful context in the 20th century.

First International Day

During Easter 1961, people all over the world demonstrated in large numbers against nuclear war. Although these demonstrations were in no way internationally or centrally co-ordinated, under the influence of the Aldermaston example, groups organised marches in support of and in conjunction with their British brothers and sisters.

The Campaigns in the US, Canada, Sweden, Norway, West Germany, Holland, Belgium, Denmark, Ghana, New Zealand, were carrying the same message. It is this which must give us hope. People no longer feel quite so helpless. The growing brotherhood, facing a common danger and having similar ideals, can lead the world to safety.

> We must march and raise our voice that mankind awakes from its thoughtlessness in which it goes on living, and realises the danger in which it finds itself before it will be too late. A thousand thanks to those who march. (Albert Schweitzer, Lambarene, March 1961.)

While many, many thousands marched the path from Aldermaston to London, in Amsterdam 2,000 people attended the final rally; in Copenhagan 2,000 people marched and 20,000 attended the final rally; a central office in Hamburg reported that some 20,000 people attended meetings in main towns and that over 8,000 took part in various marches; in the US from New York to Seattle some 25,000 people walked for peace in the largest demonstrations since the war; in Canada some 7,000 people marched in Montréal, Toronto, Regina, Winnipeg, Saskatoon, Vancouver; and, in New Zealand, after a 45-mile march began with 40 people on Good Friday, the demonstration ended with 400 on Easter Monday.[2]

The growing internationalism of the Aldermaston march can be demonstrated by the fact that the international contingent on last year's manifestation was the largest yet. Among the many countries represented were Nigeria, Ghana, Malta, Italy, France, West Germany (a large contingent of young trade unionists came all the way to Britain), Holland, Norway, the US, Canada, Ceylon, Cyprus, New Zealand, Goa, India and Australia. Many marchers came from their particular countries expressly for this march.

Recently, Mrs. Ruth Gage Colby, co-ordinator of the Women's International Strike for Peace (this group of women organised the picket of 4,000 women in Washington on January 19, 1962), announced that on March 7, women in the four nuclear countries will demonstrate in concert against the arms race and for lasting peace.

Women's Day for Peace will mark the first time since the Cold War that US and Soviet citizens have joined to demand disarmament from their governments. "Women must rise above nations on this vital matter," Mrs. Colby said.

A recent development illustrates that our thinking is moving quite rapidly towards internationalisation. A number of very important decisions were taken at the meeting of the European Federation Against Nuclear Arms in Copenhagen on January 27th and 28th of this year. It was agreed to ask all affiliated and associated organisations to mount an immediate campaign to persuade their governments to give sympathetic consideration to the Undén Plan, otherwise known as the Swedish resolution. To quote the press statement of the Copenhagen Conference: "The first fruits of this co-operation will be common activity on the Undén Plan and the co-ordination of the Aldermaston and Easter marches which will make them powerful international demonstrations."[3] A communication was sent to disarmament organisations in Austria, Belgium, Denmark, Finland, France, Germany, Great Britain, Ireland, Italy, Norway, Sweden, Switzerland, Yugoslavia, Canada, US, Japan and New Zealand. Easter demonstrations are expected in all these countries. (They will take place, in the United States and Canada, on Saturday, April 21, 1962).

The Way Forward

An elementary analysis of the world situation forces us to draw the following conclusion. The international war system is very firmly entrenched. Hundreds of years of history have meant hundreds of years of war. This system of which we speak has a hard historical basis. We know that billions upon billions of dollars perpetuate this system. We know that in involves a complex of huge military establishments. We know that this system perpetuates an archaic type of thinking. We also know that on the other hand, the forces of world peace, although armed with the greatest of all weapons, an idea that has come into its own time — the idea of permanent world peace — have a long way to go before they can effectively organise international mass resistance.

The theoretical aspect of the new thinking is slowly beginning to unfold. Recently in Sanity, the monthly newspaper of CND, there appeared an article based on a pamphlet by one of the members of its national executive, Frank Beswick, called "World Government — Let Britain Lead."[4]

Now what we need, and quickly, is a CND International to implement the new thinking. At the last general assembly meeting of the Campaign many interesting resolutions were passed showing some sort of trend in this direction, but they were not articulate enough. Mr. Francis Jude, one of the very few CND leaders who has come to Canada, went back to England convinced that some sort of International Bureau was necessary. He realised that the nuclear disarmament movements that exist now cannot continue to work in isolation from one another. The San Francisco-to-Moscow Marchers for the first time focused our work in an international context.

We need our own independent news agency, and international communications system; we need multi-lingual translations of important peace literature; we need an International Fund to assist conference delegates and movements which have difficulties; we need international co-ordinating committees on many different projects; we need a permanent United Nations lobby; we should have CND observers, if not delegates, to the UN; and we need to institute an International Nuclear Disarmament Day when people all over the world can demonstrate their resistance and protest against the arms race and the Cold War.

It is we who will bring the concepts of internationalism and human brotherhood into reality, not the national power elites with their bankrupt international relations. It is the ordinary people all over the world who are resisting nuclear weapons tests, the spread of nuclear weapons, and it is they that will play the major role in attaining world peace. We must internationalise the nuclear disarmament movement to succeed. We must all begin to work for the world as a whole, for humanity.

Notes

1. *Peace News*, London, June 2, 1961.
2. *Peace News*, London, A Peace News Publication — "Brotherhood, not Bombs."
3. *Sanity*, December 1961.
4. Press Statement of the European Federation Against Nuclear Arms issued in Copenhagen on January 27th, 1962.

> The European Federation Against Nuclear Arms, meeting in Copenhagen on Saturday and Sunday, January 27th and 28th, discussed the proposal of the Swedish Foreign Minister, Undén, which appeals to an all non-nuclear club. The Federation believes that this proposal, if adopted, would be an important step towards an alternative policy without the bomb.
> This would impose the pressure of world-wide public opinion on the nuclear powers which have been led by their nuclear policies to a dead end. The Undén proposal, furthermore, opens the way to uniting peoples to create a peaceful world, instead of playing into the hands of militarists and political adventures, leading towards genocide for all mankind.
> The European Federation is to urge all its affiliated and associated organisations to campaign during the next three months to inform the people and the press about this important plan and to persuade their Government to act in accordance with the real interests of their people by supporting the Undén Plan.

The European Federation warmly welcomes the growing strength of the anti-nuclear movements in Scandinavia. It hopes that mutual benefits will arise from co-operation between the Scandinavian movements and their counterparts in other European countries.

The first fruits of this co-operation will be common activity on the Undén Plan and the co-ordination of the "Aldermaston and Easter marches" which will make them powerful international demonstrations.

Fall 1962

"MY COUNTRY, RIGHT OR WRONG"... A DANGEROUS LUNACY

We are dealing with the subject-matter of "Nationalism and the Nation-State" in a special supplement because we believe this question is one of the most important and fundamental, if not *the* most important and fundamental, to our understanding of the mechanics of present international political behaviour.

One may ask what is the relationship of this supplement to the issue of nuclear war. The answer is very simple. Normally one thinks at the outset that journals dealing with peace have only articles studying radiation hazards, nuclear tests, disarmament negotiations — all in isolation from each other. This journal, however, has attempted from the start to demonstrate the width of peace research showing that all things are related to the bomb. Life in the nuclear situation is a complex and connected mosaic. The entire course of human history has been one which has developed the foundations of a future world community, if we survive nuclear extermination. Mankind has taken many steps backwards, but on the whole the forces that are moving us towards world unification are clear, although at present they are basically objective or material forces like industrialisation, scientific technological advances, the revolution in the communications media, to name a few. In order for our generation to achieve complete disarmament, the Nation-State system must be altered as the international war system is replaced. Some form of world community or international apparatus must emerge to maintain the disarmament framework we establish. The non-aligned and independent movements for world peace must think ahead because it is rapidly becoming clear that without them we will not achieve world peace. In turn, we will not achieve world peace unless we fight for it both nationally and internationally. For this to come about we must understand the present age of the Nation-State whose nationalist power-elites direct the missiles, hydrogen bombs and the chemical, radiological and bacteriological weapons of mass destruction.

Up until recently, the study of nationalism was barren of any serious or methodical investigation. The people in the research and academic communities who were discussing and writing on this matter were a handful. Some noteworthy philosophical writings have been contributed by left and liberal thinkers, but until the advent of Karl W. Deutch's work, *Nationalism and Social Communications,* published in 1953, very little scientific thinking was aimed at this question. In the faculties of political science, we are only beginning to deal with the material written on the issue, let alone comprehend it and subject it to scientific analysis.

Nationalism and the developing awareness of nationality have transformed the nature of international politics in a short time period. Very powerful in the western hemisphere, nationalism has now spread to the people of Asia, Africa and South America. The impact is felt in the politics, the economics, the cultural and social life of every country in the world. In this, the second half of the 20th century, no stable world community can be attained without our learning to understand these vast political forces.

We have compiled this supplement in *Our Generation Against Nuclear War* because we believe that there is a direct relationship between the issue of "Nationalism and the Nation-State" and the developments within and between the non-aligned and independent movements for world peace: the issues of negotiated disarmament and the entire theoretical base of international political relations.

We must at the outset clearly mark out intentions and attempts. We must point out immediately that this is only Part One of the supplement. In this Part One we have attempted to focus on the make-up of nationalism and the Nation-State. In the preface, one of the greatest authorities in the field, Brock Chisholm, gives us a commentary which must remain in our minds throughout a reading of the supplement. In this editorial, mercilessly hampered by lack of space, we shall give the outline of our thinking and its relevance to the peace movement.

Clearly, this supplement is *only* a beginning of a study on which we have established a permanent editorial committee. There are many important items which we would have liked to have included in this part of the supplement. But space in a quarterly format restricts us. We must point out again that this is only Part One of our study on "Nationalism and the Nation-State."

In forthcoming editions of *Our Generation Against Nuclear War* we will carry on the study and in each issue we hope to continue with an aspect of the research. We plan to define war as precisely as we can, to examine internationalism, the theory of self-determination and collective security. We hope to investigate what the ideological positions of capitalism, socialism, fascism, and religion have been on this question, and what the position of the various schools of these ideologies is now. We shall trace the rise of the theory of national-self-determination and examine the whole principle of national-sovereignty. We shall be dealing with regionalism and federalism with French-Canada as the example. We shall also study the centralised Nation-State, national independence and economic interdependence, self-determination and economic nationalism, national economic planning, national sovereignty, in relation to international economics. We shall have articles on how the peace movement is in fact the only movement for revolutionary social change, a position held by the widely respected A.J. Muste. We are convinced that it will become clearer as time goes by that deep social changes are necessarily going to take place in the sweep of the world movement for peace.

Nationalism is a pattern of interlocking habits, memories, and attitudes in the minds of human beings. It is something they learn, something they can change. Nationalism is a state of mind in which the supreme loyalty of the individual is to the Nation-State. Through ties to the soil, parental conditioning, traditions and cultural patterns existing throughout history as sentiments of varying types and strengths, nationalism began only at the end of the 18th century. Nationalism, incarnated both internally and externally by the Nation-State, had become the generally recognised emotion moulding public and private lives and thus, established itself as the great, if not the greatest single determining factor in modern history. Nationalism developed as a dominant force with the American and French revolutions which were its first important manifestations; from the western hemisphere it spread at the beginning of the 19th century to central Europe, toward the middle of the century to eastern and south-eastern Europe, until, in the first half of the 20th century, it rose up in Asia and Africa.

Nationalism and its incarnation, the Nation-State, has become a dominating force everywhere on earth.

Nationalism implies the identification of the State with the ordinary people determined ethnologically. We must understand clearly that in the age of the Nation-State, and *only* in that age, the principle that each ethnic group should form a State, and that the State should include the whole ethnic group was generally accepted. Before the age of nationalism, administered territories were not delineated by the ethnic base of a group; man's loyalty was not absorbed, the Nation-State, but by the City-State, the feudal fief and its lord, the dynastic State, the religious group or sect. Not only did the Nation-State have no basis in the real world for the greater part of human history, but it did not even appear as an ideal.

It must be perfectly clear in our minds that by nationalism we mean that sentiment and emotion developed throughout history; by the Nation-State we mean the vehicle through which this is expressed. It is of fundamental importance, in addition, to understand what elements are in control of the vehicle. In different countries, under different social systems, the make-up of the rulers is different but their national and interlocking international behaviour is the same. The Nation-State itself has its own laws of development and its own mechanics of self-perpetuation. The nature of these mechanics influences both the temperature of the nationalism and the conduct of the rulers of the State. Normally we think that society has material and non-material forces at work in its development, but what we have noticed with the Nation-State structure is that although the State rests on the basic nature of the material mode of the society, it has in reaction to other States, an independent behaviour.

The historical development of the Nation-State and nationalism has made a very great and progressive contribution to the enrichment of human life: The vast array of cultural and social traditions that have emerged, the colourful national and ethnic folklore, folk music, the whole romantic movement in the arts that flowered and is still developing in the age of nationalism. It was in this age that industrialism was born, that urbanism spread, that the revolution in communications occurred. Democracy was reborn in the age of nationalism and different peoples all over the world fought against feudalism and the concept that sovereignty was the dominion of the monarch alone; they transferred it into the hands of the people. It was in this age that capitalism was born followed by socialism.

Now, however, in the nuclear situation the idea that the supreme loyalty of the individual is due to the Nation-State is no longer progressive. "My country, right or wrong" is dangerous lunacy when you live in the shadow of the bomb.

The growth of the Committee of 100 in England and similar movements in other countries proves that men now refuse to obey the national laws and are prepared to engage in extra-legal action in order to emphasise the importance of the law of humanity. It is like the story of the German judges tried at Nuremburg. They were loyal to their country, they obeyed, and executed the laws of Germany. If they had disobeyed, they would have been heroes to the forces of democracy abroad, and traitors at home. According to the laws of Nation-States they were innocent because they followed the laws of their country, no matter how evil. They were guilty only before the developing law of humanity.

Clearly, there are two fundamental problems confronting humanity: the inter-society problem and the intra-society problem. The former is the question of how societies must live together, and the latter the nature of the society internally. They are profoundly and fundamentally connected. They react to one another and cannot be studied separately. However, in the post-Hiroshima world, the inter-society problem has vastly increased in importance over the other, because our existence is based on its solution. What we want to show in this supplement, and those to follow, is that fundamentally, the international war system is maintained by the Nation-State structure.

The Second World War marked the climax of the Nation-State, especially in the northern hemisphere. Although new nations are till emerging, they are developing far more rapidly than did the older ones. We now see trends which suggest that the present structure of international relations is going through a convulsive change. The Second World War, we hoped, was the last triumph of fissiparous nationalism, and of the ideology that the Nation-State is the ultimate political and economic unit of mankind. The *military* and *economic* insecurity of the Nation-State has been demonstrated over and over again since 1945. This institution survives only as an anomaly and an anachronism in a world which has moved and now needs new forms of political organisation.

We have posed the question in this editorial and supplement whether nationalism as an ideology and the Nation-State whose creation, preservation, or glorification it seeks, is still serving the interests of mankind as a whole. The answer to us is clear. One thing, however, must be added: nationalism, although outmoded in the industrialised world, and rapidly becoming outmoded everywhere else, will not be surrendered by those who are dedicated to its structure, the Nation-State, without a deep struggle.

The present challenge to the Nation-State system as the final and unalterable unit of human political organisation must come, both indirectly and directly, from the movements for world peace. It will come from the non-aligned and independent peace movements for *no* others will accept our position as fundamental; these others give instead such metaphysics as "the international class struggle," or the "good versus the bad," or "Sin versus Salvation," "the West versus the East," or "democracy versus tyranny" ad infinitum. We will deal with the more serious of these assertions in the supplement and in forthcoming editions.

We begin in our next issue when two editors examine what Camus states in "The Rebel," that "He (Marx) believed that through commerce and exchange, through the victory of the proletariat, barriers would fall, but that it was national barriers that brought the fall of the proletarian ideal. As a means of explaining history, the struggle between nations has been proved at least as important as the class struggle. But nations cannot be entirely explained by economics; therefore, the system (Marxism) ignored them."

It is now evident to many people, "that for basic social change we now have to look to other new social forces, and it seems to me that it is now the war issue which is the one which everyone feels poses the question of survival, for whole societies, as well as for the progressive elements in society. All this suggests that the peace movement is the spearhead of social change. The war issue is the field in which basic decisions are taken..." (A.J. Muste). In addition, the necessity for the non-aligned peace movement to become internationalised is now obvious in the extreme. The need for this lies in the fact that we must formulate and gain people's loyalty for the law of humanity, and that this is rooted in the way we campaign for disarmament and peace in different nations. All this goes to demonstrate that we have to think hard about what lies ahead.

By understanding nationalism and the Nation-State, by clarifying its influence, we will be in the best possible position to avoid whatever difficulties it may put in our way. We must utilise what creative contributions these forces have left, whenever possible, for the end of world peace and for world progress.

INTERNATIONAL PEACE ACTION

Throughout the world, the movement against nuclear war has grown and spread. Since the end of World War II we have seen the utter futility resulting from summit meetings and disarmament conferences in Geneva. We have also seen the spread of nuclear weapons to Britain and France. The despair has grown, and cynicism towards the pronouncements of national governments on world peace has reached a new high.

It is not surprising, therefore, that ordinary people have taken action into their own hands. The numbers who will be marching this Easter throughout the world will be most impressive. It is these people who have become the conscience of a world seemingly bent on nuclear suicide.

A few months ago, 1,400 people gathered in the Town Square in Copenhagen in support of the demonstrations in Britain. By the time the march reached the Danish Parliament, the numbers had swollen to 4,000. A rally of 2,000 young people was held recently in Amsterdam where Sydney Silverman, British MP, and Rev. van der Veen spoke. The Dutch Anti-Atoombon Actie has organised a leaflet campaign: 185,000 copies of their first leaflet were distributed and 250,000 of their second. In Ireland, the university students of both the south and the north have created a single organisation.

In Denmark, there are two organisations: Komiteen for Oplysning on Otomfaren, which concentrates on education work, and the Kampagen mod Atomväben which organises demonstrations and marches. They work nicely together, and organised a very effective march at Easter last year. They are now printing a million leaflets answering a government hand-out on civil defence which has been delivered to all households. A new political party which supports the policy of the disarmers was set up in 1961 and has won eleven seats in the Danish Parliament.

The Swiss campaign has been concentrating so far on a referendum on whether the Swiss army should have tactical nuclear weapons. A referendum is granted only if 50,000 citizens ask for it. The Swiss campaign collected 73,000. The referendum takes place on March 31, and they have printed a million leaflets. They publish an "Atomic Bulletin" and have brought pressure to bear on the press by setting up 100 groups which organise letters and articles for newspapers.

Activity started in Norway when the Norwegian Parliament discussed a proposal concerning nuclear arms for the army. There were spontaneous demonstrations against this. The Protest mot Atomvapen was formed. They put pressure on the political parties to organise a Gallup poll on the issue. This showed that 50 percent were opposed to nuclear weapons for Norway and only 11 percent in favour. They ran a signature campaign covering 9,000 people, of whom 4,000 signed. In 1960 they organised an appeal to the Norwegian Parliament to bring out a national constitution to prohibit the use of nuclear weapons under international law. Recently Norway's Foreign Minister told the UN that his country did not intend to produce or acquire nuclear weapons and that Norway was prepared to sign a treaty to this effect.

There are two peace organisations in Sweden. The Aktionsgruppen mot Svensk Atoombomb works mainly in the political field, campaigning against nuclear weapons for Sweden. Public opinion polls have shown increasing opposition to this: 40 percent in 1957, 51 percent in 1959 and 56.5 percent in 1961, while the number of those who support nuclear weapons for the Swedish army has gone down from 30 percent to 20 percent. The Kampagen mot Atomvapen was set up more recently, and organised the first Swedish anti-nuclear march which was a great success.

The Comitato Italiano per il Disarmo Atomoco has sponsored an Italian translation of *Fallout,* edited by John Fowler, and has promoted lectures and meetings. It organised a march in Milan a few months ago in which 10,000 people took part, and another in Piacenza. It supported a march in Assisi and a women's march in Reggio Emilia.

The West German government has recently distributed a pamphlet on civil defence, called "Everybody has a Chance," to all households. The Komitte gegen Atomrustung is producing an 8-page pamphlet in response to this, of which 200,000 are to be printed. Marches in West Germany have been organised by the Ostermarsch der Atomwaffengegner for the Easter international demonstrations.

The London Disarmament Conference

These are some of the recent activities of the peace movements in Europe, most of which were represented at the European Federation against Nuclear Arms in Copenhagen on January 27th and 28th. The meeting reflected the growth of the protest movement in Europe over the past year. Many new organisations are coming into the Federation. Plans for a much wider and more frequent circulation of information on activities, arguments and publicity material have been agreed upon. A campaign to persuade governments to support the Undén plan was launched immediately.

To quote the press statement of the Copenhagen Conference:

> The first fruits of this co-operation will be common activity on the Undén Plan and the co-ordination of the Aldermaston and Easter marches which will make them powerful international demonstrations.

A communication was sent to disarmament organisations in Austria, Belgium, Denmark, Finland, France, Germany, Great Britain, Ireland, Italy, Norway, Sweden, Switzerland, Yugoslavia, Canada, the US, Japan, and New Zealand.

Further steps have been taken in that direction recently and some bold new ones are in the offing.

It was in the autumn of 1961 that the London Disarmament Conference took place. There were representatives from Indonesia, Belgium, Austria,

Poland, Italy, Czechoslovakia, Nigeria, India, Yugoslavia, Hungary, and South Africa. All resolutions had to be passed unanimously, and some of the resolutions that were passed were severe criticisms of both Western and Eastern-bloc foreign policies. As a matter of fact, it was Llya Ehrenburg of the USSR that went on public record against the Soviet resumption of nuclear testing. This is a small indication that, given the necessary environment, the Soviet cultural leaders at any rate, will not hesitate to criticise their own government. It shows that the least promising affairs produce surprising results. It was more than two years ago that the British Campaign for Nuclear Disarmament considered the idea of a kind of cultural and political "Pugwash" conference which would be held on Western initiative and in which Communists and fellow-travellers would not be the dominant element. We should not overestimate the success of this conference however; it was a modest affair and many essential things were lacking.

In the very short time available, the conference was only able to scratch the surface of many of the most unpromising circumstances. East and West met and conducted a restrained, responsible and co-operative discussion.

Leaders of the Campaign for Nuclear Disarmament and its equivalent movements abroad flew to Zagreb, Yugoslavia, at the end of last month to plan an international nuclear disarmament conference in Accra, Ghana, this summer. The conference was instigated by Dr. Swame Nkurmah, Premier of Ghana, and Canon L. John Collins, chairman of the British CND and joint president of the European Federation Against Nuclear Arms, at the time they met last year. About one hundred "eminent and informed people who are concerned about the future of mankind and are not involved in the Cold War policies of East and West" have been, or are to be, invited.

The conferees will work in five groups, concerned with: 1) the reduction of international tensions, 2) methods of effective inspection and control in disarmament, 3) the transformation of existing military nuclear materials to peaceful uses, 4) economic problems involved in, or arising from, disarmament, and 5) examination of fundamental problems — hunger, disease, poverty and oppression — and concrete suggestions as to their solution in a "World without the Bomb" by liberating the resources now misused by the arms race.

The preparatory committee formed to plan the conference included Mr. E.C. Quaye, Chairman of the Ghana council; Professor Ritchie Calder, Vice-chairman of CND; Heinrich Buchbinder, Joint President of the European Federation; Chaman Lall of India; Professor Josue de Castro of Brazil; and the Rev. T.A. Osei of the Ghana Council of Churches (acting chairman).

The pre-conference meetings in Zagreb were attended by representatives of "CND movements" and older peace organisations in Britain (Canon Collins, Wayland Young, Robert Nield), Switzerland, India, Ghana, Afghanistan, Canada, Eire, West Germany, UAR, Belgium, Czechoslovakia, Yugoslavia, Pakistan, the US, USSR, Norway and Bulgaria.

This type of gathering, especially of people in the peace movements of the non-aligned countries, these international demonstrations, and the eventual and much needed construction of an international apparatus with its own mechanism to make it effective throughout the world is what must give us hope. People knowing these things no longer feel quite so helpless. The growing feeling of brotherhood by facing a common danger and having similar ideals, can lead the world to safety.

Spring 1963

INTERNATIONAL CONFEDERATION FOR DISARMAMENT AND PEACE

Present wars are not possible without political and strategic theories for waging them — and without mobilizing resources, armies and complex technological means. Similarly, disarmament and peace, to become a reality, need a theory of peace — and a scientific and technological implementation of this theory. Peace, like war, requires powerful organisations and these must be built immediately on a world-wide scale. An important beginning has been made with the establishment of the International Confederation for Disarmament and Peace representing the non-aligned and independent peace organisations — both pacifist and non-pacifist. It came into being in Oxford, England, in January of this year.

For many years, the movement for world peace has been Nation-State oriented. There were some groups, particularly of a pacifist nature such as the War Resisters International which were world-wide in scope, but there was no one movement linking all non-aligned organisations, although sentiment for such a movement has existed for some time. This quarterly was among the first to raise publicly the need to internationalise the peace forces.

While there was no one permanent body on a non-governmental level, meetings of an international character had taken place between those of a common orientation such as the World Federalists, pacifists, United Nations associations, as well as confrontations between the two "sides" in the Cold War. When all the pro-Soviet forces established the World Council of Peace, they sponsored a succession of world congresses.

The East-West meetings have included those of scientists (the Pugwash series), those of American and Russian intellectuals (in Dartmouth, the Crimea and Andovar), and those of parliamentarians (East-West Roundtables). Another in this series of confrontations was the London Conference on Disarmament in September, 1961. Finally, the Accra Assembly[1], held in Ghana in June 1962, brought together representatives primarily from non-aligned groups.

One of the most important meetings was the 1962 Sunnybrook Consultation of student peace movements[2] since this helped to generate the January Oxford Conference called by the European Federation Against Nuclear Arms. Very significant, too, was the Amsterdam Conference held in November 1962 which was sponsored by the Zangakurne (the Japanese student peace movement) and the British Committee of 100.

Some one hundred people representing five international and thirty-five national organisations attended the Oxford Conference which culminated in the establishment of the International Confederation for Disarmament and Peace. Proposed activities of the Confederation include a) exchange of ideas and literature, b) co-ordination of activities, such as the Easter Marches, c) representation at the United Nations and international conferences, d) stimulation of new independent peace organisations, e) promotion of international conferences.

An independent judgement of foreign policies of all countries is the basis of this new non-aligned and independent organisation. Policies must be judged by their merits — not by their origins. The Confederation must openly criticize and oppose policies of the US and SU governments when such policies emphasise military measures. It must praise governments and support them when such policies create peaceful attitudes and reduce tensions. It must honestly try to use the same criteria and principles in judging all governments. It cannot have one standard for measuring one government and another standard for judging another government. *Everything must be examined in terms of a single standard of loyalty to the principle that humanity is above all nations.*

A new era has begun in the movement for world peace. The tremendous size of the movements represented at Oxford and now entering the International Confederation means that a large body of common understanding has been forged. Ordinary people who are working throughout the world for permanent peace will find their struggle infused with greater meaningfulness in this new context. This year, International Easter Marches will demonstrate more than ever the tremendous desire of the common person for the abolition of the Cold War. The International Easter Marches will demonstrate the new strength and influence of the International Confederation for Disarmament and Peace.

Notes

1. "A Report on the Accra Assembly," *Our Generation Against Nuclear War,* Vol. 1, No. 4.
2. "International Declaration on the Student Peace Movement," *Our Generation Against Nuclear War,* Vol. 1, No. 4.

Spring 1967

THE PURPOSE OF OUR GENERATION

Readers of the journal may be wondering, after reading the various issues published since the spring of 1966, how the different questions on which we have published articles are related? One might be asking, do all the social questions dealt with represent an organic approach to the crisis facing our particular society? Have we come any closer to creating a peace and freedom movement here that is gaining ground, and which is allied with similar movements elsewhere? And how does this relate to the war in Vietnam? How do these questions connect with our pursuit of world peace?

This journal was born of a movement of passive protest against the nuclear arms race. We learned alongside a whole generation that the nature and course of the post-Hiroshima international war system is going to determine whether we *survive*. By the hundreds of thousands we urged reason and common sense to the politicians of the world, in the most massive movement of people since the end of the Second World War. Our success was marginal.

During this period we learned essentially two things: besides acquiring the skills of organising dissent and resistance, we became aware that national societies in pursing the self-interest of their elites could not dislodge themselves from the basic patterns which drift and push towards international conflict. These elites and the key supporting national institutions had themselves to undergo fundamental social and political change. This is true for societies both in the East and West. Thus, our pursuit for world peace in the atomic age forced us to face the necessity of social change, but in a new fashion. Previously, questions of social change and justice were sought as ends in themselves, with the theoretical addendum that harmonious human and international relations would result almost automatically thereafter. Twentieth-century history stood witness to the contrary. Peace must be pursued as the end in itself and social changes must accompany it to make this end possible. Looking at this hypothesis in its theoretical application we were struck at the widespread dimensions of the change required. All previous ideologies were suspect. We returned to the *roots* of contemporary human inquiry; we were referred to as the "new radicals."

As a generation we were also repulsed by the hollow cant and rhetoric about democracy in the West. In our efforts to achieve a first step in nuclear disarmament we were struck by the *completely* undemocratic ways in which decisions relating to foreign affairs and defence were made. These decisions were the ones which ultimately affected our lives the most, yet our powerlessness to affect them estrange us. From that experience we began an examination of new nations of democracy — where participation could be radically increased, where various excluded sections of society could be involved. In breaking up the facade of "experts" on the arms race, international relations, nuclear tests, which governments threw at us to impress upon us their view that only the power-elite had the ability and right to decide the issues of life and death facing all of us, we began to appreciate the fact that this paternalist "democracy" had fundamentally the same attitude towards all important decision-making.

We discovered that ethnic minorities, the large "other world" of poverty, the student, the young industrial worker, and, more particularly, people of colour in the US, and the French-Canadians in Canada were faced with the same sense of powerlessness and hence, frustration. Consequently, freedom became newly defined. It meant the fundamental restructuring of society's organisational mode. Thus, the new radicals acquired a critical perspective which allows us to look at the questions of the movement itself, Québec, Vietnam, community organising and poverty, with a different set of analytical tools. We came to the conclusion that the "dispossessed," those outside the mainstream of North American society, had to organise and learn the dynamics and exercise of power. The concepts of "black power," "student power," "national self-determination" quickly emerged under the barrage of cries to decentralise a society which was drifting toward and using greater bureaucracy.

But this new participatory democracy cannot be realised in any one Nation-State unless the new upsurge in social consciousness affects the international war system. This means that the external as well as the internal priorities of national societies must change. For this reason, the new movements must remain fundamentally *peace* movements.

The Renewed Arms Race

During 1966 we noticed a familiar drama. With the increasing cost of the war in Vietnam, the US Government was forced to reduce non-military expenditures. The main casualty of the budget pruning was the whole area of social investments for human improvement, from the "war on poverty" to fulfilment of the so-called "Great Society" programme.

As Prof. Seymour Melman states, "The Administration's requests for housing, health care, and education did not even meet by as much as 10 percent the additional national expenditures needed to bring the work in these areas up to decent standards. New research projects in the biological and physical sciences were scheduled for a cut of about one-third. The budget cutting extended to the school milk programme, where the White House ordered (and the Congress restored!) an 80 percent cut from last year's spending of about $110 million. Lyndon Johnson literally tried to finance a part of his war in Vietnam by taking milk out of the mouths of children!

> What was the reason for this unprecedented zeal by the federal government for cutting civilian spending? The principle clue is given in the following brief summary of the main Great Society budget priorities. The ordinary military budget for the next year is to be about $50 billion. The Vietnam war is approaching a cost of $24 billion a year. The space race to

the moon now requires $5 billion per year. These budget items total $79 billion a year — more than three-fourths of our tax payments — and leaves very little for everything else. ("American Needs," and "Limits on Resources.")

Add to this the great possibility that once the war in Vietnam is over we will probably be absorbed in a renewed arms race. Already the US and USSR are preparing themselves for the anti-missile race. This will cost the US approximately $40 billion, and will affect the production of some 1,000 industries in Canada and the US.

The situation is being prepared for a repetition of the arms cycle of the early 1960s, including a renewed effort to integrate Canada into a new North American "defence" system. Canada's sophisticated colonial status will be compounded. How will we respond? Will the various peace and social action groups repeat their cycle of activity? The conscious elements in Canada, for example, are still suffering from the curse of Sisyphus. This is especially so of the Student Union for Peace and Action (SUPA).

With volume 4 of *Our Generation* we discussed some of the outstanding *social questions:* an introductory analysis of the movements of the new radicals, the nature of participatory democracy, the phenomenon of youth as a possible agency for change, Québec and the new nationalism, the nature of ideology, poverty and community organising, Vietnam, the economic and political domination of Canada, the nature of technology and others. We have tried to indicate how these social questions interrelate and to suggest how their solutions are dominated by the primacy of peace.

With volume 5 of *Our Generation* we shall discuss some additional social questions, and further attempt to analyse more concretely the dynamics of socio-political movements, suggest theories of the nature of contemporary history, define more sharply the radical analysis emerging, discuss the nature of social change in our particular society and demonstrate the primacy of peace by proving the links between disarmament/peace, social development and freedom/decolonisation.

Spring 1967

TOWARDS A PEACE AND FREEDOM MOVEMENT

A strong current of growing indignation is spreading across English-speaking Canada calling for self-assertion and self-determination. This new feeling is still a subdued and subjective phenomenon, with no real form or content. What is important, however, is that in a *depressed culture* like our own, the subjective will-power to resist is being slowly nourished by a variety of individuals and groups. These include economic nationalists, anti-Vietnam war groups, lamenters, and socialists. This in it-self, though, is no cause for celebration and must be looked at with care and caution.

On April 21, 1967 in the *Toronto Star,* Messrs. Gonick, Horowitz and Sheps, the editors of *Canadian Dimension* published "An Open Letter to Canadian Nationalists." The letter called for a national independence front on the basis of a minimum programme.

The programme proposes:

1) "...to formulate a programme of specific measures, acceptable to *all* nationalists..."

2) "...to press for the implementation of this programme and to ex-pose and oppose the advocates of continentalism."

3) "...to conduct continuous research into the problems of Canada-US relations."

The programme reads like the terms of reference for a royal commis-sion. The rationale of the programme is most unclear suggesting that we shall attain independence by some magical and polite means. What kind of Canada these nationalists will work for is *not* clear. What kind of external affairs or defence policy this independence movement will stand for is *not* clear. What its position is on the *two-faced* nature of colonialism in Québec is *not* clear. The suggested style of politics will not excite the majority of Canadians — the youth. The outlined minimum programme smells of traditional "adult politics," it has no sense of drama, and underestimates the profound alienation of the Canadian people from the traditional politi-cal process. (For instance, in the recent by-elections no more than 18 per-cent of the voters turned out in one constituency.) The open letter's ambition seems to be to put old wine into a new bottle.

In addition, the open letter states that the majority of Canadians are nationalists and that most want to preserve this country's independence. It is important to realise that this statement is *not* true. This country has *never* been independent. First, we had the French empire, then the British, and now the American. To pretend otherwise is to prejudice the future course of action. We need to discover the history of this country, and to sense its texture so that what emerges anew is indigenous and not patchwork. In a word, we need to *know* as much about Canada as about the nature of exter-nal pressures.

A New Position

We must become aware of the deep crisis of almost all of our existing political institutions including the political parties. At present, all progress is hindered or actually smothered by official needs, by pressing tactical demands, if not simply by the spirit of routine. This is true for *all* parts of the ideological spectrum in this country.

We are convinced that an emerging peace and freedom movement can only be advanced through the *action* of great masses of people. The form and content of the movement must be looked at very carefully, as well as the means employed towards attaining our goals. The emergence of the new requires the overcoming of the old barriers and old dogmas. We do not believe that the traditional formulas are valid in our kind of society, be they the barricaders of old, or the conquest of parliamentary majorities. A new strategy, suited to our present situation must be arrived at which has effective action programmes which are both in and out of our political culture. In forthcoming issues of *Our Generation*, we shall be examining such strategies.

A Radical Analysis

Two essential elements characterise our analysis. *First*, we are *not* Canadian nationalists but internationalists and radicals. By this we mean we understand humanity's struggle for peace and freedom as being international everywhere it takes place, and this from two perspectives. We attempt to understand events in any Nation-State in two ways: events which indicate trends that are common to other situations, and events which arise from a particular condition.

We must put our struggle within the context of what is happening throughout the industrial/technological world. Liberal corporatism and monopoly capitalism, even in the age of the Nation-State are global phenomena. Since we have a single power elite in North America, this means we cannot ultimately separate our analysis and action from that of the new radicals in the US. In addition, we have to particularise our tactics and strategy given our historical situation in the effort to make all movements indigenous.

Second, we attempt to comprehend the global dimension and relationships in every event, because we know that nothing of any *real* importance takes place within the borders of a single country, as if each Nation-State existed in isolation. The inter-relationships, the multi-dimensional influences, and contrasts from Nation-State to Nation-State are widely varied and all are mutually conditioned. Most important, we know that modern imperialism-colonialism is exercising its many forms of pressure and intimidation, whether it originates in the West or East, it is a product of militarism, has similar political structures and authoritarian economics.

These two essential elements of a single process have condemned all of us in the Western world to subordination, exploitation and alienation, and the people of the southern hemisphere to misery, oppression and hunger. This single process has created the objective premises for an alliance, and we are deeply concerned about the need to contribute to such an awareness here. For *this* reason, in our common pursuit of peace and freedom we believe that the fight against continentalism in Canada, as well as colonialism in Québec is the *major task* facing us. We are no less concerned about this task then are others, but our constant question in the process is independence *for what*, and *for whom?*

Our objective as editors of *Our Generation,* and as internationalists, is that through a precise exchange of information, experience and analysis, and through the careful study of every situation we hope to understand the intricate international war system that penetrates every phenomenon, the reciprocal implications for all national societies, the solidarity of interests between the majority of the world's people, (namely our youth in every corner of the earth), and the urgent need for an international strategy for the new generation. Such a strategy must be flexible enough to meet each particular situation, but global in its evaluations and objectives. This end, and no less, is our task.

We believe that many of the new radicals by various means are in the process of building such a movement in Canada. We, as part of this movement are prepared, in addition to movement-building, to dialogue, consult, create working relationships with others, provided we begin with a clear understanding of the questions — *independence for what, for whom* and *by what means.*

Spring 1968

WHAT NEXT?

By the time this issue of *Our Generation* reaches you, talks between the United States and the Democratic Republic of Vietnam on the unconditional cessation of the bombing and all other acts of war against North Vietnam, will be in progress.

If the possibilities for a political settlement are to be realised, it is of the utmost importance that the peace and protest movements maintain and increase their activities and pressure, firstly for the halt to the bombing, and thereafter, for a political settlement which ensures peace and independence for the people of Vietnam.

Just as we, amongst others, have made our contribution to the actions which now seem to have forced the United States to abandon its attempts to impose its will on Vietnam, so now we must make an equal, if not greater effort, to ensure a just and peaceful settlement.

Background to the Talks

At first, the action of President Johnson in halting the bombing of a part of North Vietnam, coupled with the despatch of 13,000 more US troops, looked like just another phoney peace offensive, even though it was accomplished by his withdrawal from the Presidential election.

However, the agreement of Hanoi to limited talks created an entirely new situation.

On the basis of many talks we have had with representatives from North Vietnam and the NLF (by our travelling editors to Paris, through the International Confederation for Disarmament and Peace (ICDP), and with conversations with the Student Committee representatives of the NLF while in Montréal) we believe that there is, at last, a real possibility of a political settlement of the problems of Vietnam. There are three important reasons for this opinion:

1. It is evident that the action of the Democratic Republic of Vietnam (DRV) stems not from a sense of weakness, but from a desire to keep the initiative at all costs. Since the Tet offensive, the Vietnamese are in a stronger position, militarily and politically, than before, stronger perhaps than after the fall of Dien Bien Phu in 1954.

While attempts were made by the US Generals to write off these successes, not even Johnson believed them. The US now holds the cities only on sufferance, and many of the suburbs are still in the hands of the NLF like most of the countryside. Pacification is dead. American bases are under constant bombardment. The rice of the Mekong cannot be brought into Saigon because the roads are unsafe. One hundred thousand tons have been imported. The airport of Saigon, Tan Son Nhut, is still under rocket fire. The Saigon government is in disarray and out of hand, even threatening to invade the North with non-existent troops and weapons.

2. Most importantly, the Vietnamese people are exhausted with the savagery of the war. There is a growing refusal to fight on the part of combatants and non-combatants of both sides. This fact has military significance for both sides, but also immense political influence. The people of Vietnam in their cry for peace are resorting to those ancient methods of disobedience which terrorise the military mind. Although the Tet offensive was far more successful than the US military make out, it was not as successful as the NLF was expecting. This is understandable; it is the people who do the fighting, and when they start refusing and begin generating their own demands, the commanders better start negotiating. The war in Vietnam after all is still part of the history of human warfare.

3. The political problems in the US are enormous, even for continuing the war, let alone escalating it. The Tet offensive has transformed Eugene McCarthy and Robert Kennedy from gallant outsiders to possible Presidents. Johnson, at least for a time, is out of the running. The bankers of Europe are defecting. The dollar faces devaluation unless expenditure on the war is controlled and cut. Johnson's friends are reduced to Harold Wilson and little else. Westmoreland has been sacked. Martin Luther King's tragic death has preempted the expected summer rebellion in the cities.

4. The US has been *permitted* to relieve Khe Sanh. It is obvious that the 33,000 troops and hundreds of helicopters have met little resistance on their way through to the beleaguered garrison. "Given the nasty, rugged terrain along Highway 9," said a senior officer, "a single determined enemy infantry company could have held up a relief column for days. They have simply chosen not to fight."

Now, it may be that this is just a repetition of Giap's earlier tactics, forcing the enemy to lose hundreds of men in gaining or holding a strong point, which he then evacuates, leaving the US in control of a hill of no military significance whatsoever. But, in present circumstances, it is very significant. It is another gesture which makes the continued bombing of the panhandle of North Vietnam by the US look both brutal and stupid.

Winter 1969

THE HEMISPHERIC CONFERENCE IN MONTRÉAL

To the extent that the radical press covered the Hemispheric Conference to the End the War in Vietnam, it criticised it severely. In the Students for a Democratic Society's (SDS) *New Left Notes*, in a score of underground newspapers and periodicals the criticism was the same. The *Guardian*, for example, had former national SDS officer Carl Davidson cover the event. Among other things, he said:

> The conference, apparently initiated by elements close to the Communist party, accomplished little else — unless managing to snatch boredom from the jaws of chaos is considered an achievement. What could have been an opportunity for strengthening the anti-war movement was terribly bungled. The Canadian leaders did not appear to understand the wide range of political forces active in the US peace movement or the need to enlarge the conference leadership to encompass these views. The Canadian leaders not only disregarded the US opinion that they considered "threatening," they apparently were also reluctant to accept the view of American CP members, some of whom had earlier dropped out of active organising for the conference, because of the rigid Canadian attitude.

It can be added that many Canadian views were also isolated from the conference leadership.

The Conference brought together some 500 delegates. There was an official delegation from the Democratic Republic of Vietnam, and the South Vietnam National Front of Liberation. The Russians were to send a semi-governmental delegation but did not receive visas, partly because of the Czechoslovakia affair (August, 1968). It is important to note that the National Council of the Students for a Democratic Society (the leading new left organisation in the US), the Southern Students Organizing Committee, Youth International Party, and the whole of the underground press did not sponsor the conference, did not send delegations, in fact, they did not take the Montréal gathering seriously. The New Left present at the conference represented largely non-SDS action groups at the local level mostly from the Bay and Berkeley areas. The Black Panthers, and a few SNCC (Student Non-violent Co-ordinating Committee) people attended. It is significant that the Cubans did not attend.

The Organizing Committee of the Hemispheric Conference (OC) managed to involve a number of Québec and Canadian liberals by means of embracing the small Québec NDP. As was predicted by some, the Hemispheric Conference is now a *permanent* organisation. The OC had everything well-organised, including the control of literature sold, rigid voting procedures, and workshops with specific themes. This structure was challenged on the first day and quickly changed because of the tremendous opposition generated.

The Cubans did not come for a number of reasons. The composition of the Latin American delegations was clearly a factor as they were almost all pro-Moscow in orientation. But more important were the Cuban suspicions that the Montréal meeting was a first step in establishing a propaganda centre giving a Soviet interpretation of what was happening in the hemisphere, consequently rivalling OLAS (the political section of the Organisation of Solidarity of the Peoples of Africa, Asia and Latin America- OSPAAAL — known in short as Tricontinental, based in Havana). OLAS/OSPAAAL has a revolutionary strategy for the Third World propagating the ideas of Che Guevera and Regis Debray.

If we divide our analysis of the Conference into three parts — before, during, and after, we can begin by saying that:

The main criticism of the conference before it started came from non-aligned peace organisations and individuals, most of whom support the ICDP, and the Maoists, Trotskyists, plus other Left sects. The ICDP criticism suggested that the Hemispheric Conference was propagating a double standard. That is to say, by not allowing any mention of the Soviet invasion of Czechoslovakia at any level of the conference, it implicitly refused to acknowledge that the international situation had profoundly changed since the invasion and that it is consequently not a good thing to have one standard to judge the behaviour of socialist countries and another to judge the capitalist ones. The ICDP, unlike the World Peace Council (WPC) not only has mobilised world opinion against the war in Vietnam, but has done a lot to create pressure against the Soviet invasion of Czechoslovakia. Indeed after much representation, the Conference finally agreed to allow Mr. Alfred Hassler, a president of the ICDP to speak in Montréal about Vietnam, but also about the significance of the Soviet aggression. Two days before the conference began, the invitation was withdrawn.

The criticism of the Marxist-Leninist Party of Canada, and the Young Socialist Alliance, was that the Hemispheric Conference was not anti-imperialist and was controlled by Moscow revisionists.

During the conference several caucuses emerged: the Black Panthers who were angry at the fact that their leader, Bobby Seale, was not brought in as a speaker even though the conference publicity announced that he would attend. On Friday they stormed the stage to protest and denounce the conference organisers as racists. After much commotion the Organising Committee raised the money and Seale came with his bodyguards. The Vietnamese held separate meetings with the Black Panthers and each pledged solidarity with the other. The result was that the Panthers went along with the Vietnamese final statement of unity. Indeed, on Sunday, they guarded the stage from assaults by other caucuses.

The New Left caucus consisted of persons of various political shades, including anarchists, libertarian New Left, radical pacifists, libertarian Marxists. Their criticism was that the conference was too highly structured, the established workshops were meaningless to radical organisation against the war and to movement building, that the whole thing was grossly undemocratic, and that the conference was not anti-imperialist, including Soviet imperialism. The third caucus was called anti-imperialist, consisting of Trotskyists, Maoists, and Internationalists. They wanted the conference to denounce American imperialism, victory for the National Liberation Front of South Vietnam, Soviet aggression in Czechoslovakia, and American imperialism in Québec, Canada, and Latin America.

The fourth caucus was the Québécois who, like the Black Panthers, had national concerns, namely that not enough French was spoken, and not enough French-Canadians were present. They also wanted conference recognition for their cause and struggle. The Vietnamese met with them separately as well and came to the same understanding as with the Panthers.

It is important to note that each one of these caucuses was ready to storm the platform to press their demands. The Blacks did it first with New Left support. Consequently, the Blacks received the most publicity and met with the Vietnamese first.

The New Left was largely neutralized with pleas of unity from the Vietnamese. Some of their demands regarding conference structure were met, but none of the positive work of the workshops that the New Left established ever got to the conference plenary sessions. During the workshops a lot of constructive discussion took place about both organising and new values. The caucus pressed and a resolution was adopted which requested that all workshop resolutions be included in the Conference Resolutions book.

On Saturday the "unity statement" was adopted "unanimously," needless to say, without discussion. The next day, however, the revolutionary Left took over the spirit of the conference. For the first time, Che was mentioned, the Internationale was sung, clenched fists could be seen everywhere — all to the embarrassment of the Organising Committee. But thanks to the Vietnamese, they did get their unity statement.

The kind of peace politics that the Hemispheric Conference has introduced into North America is the kind of politics associated with the World Council for Peace. The same organising techniques were used, the same "unanimous" statements adopted. Since its founding after the Second World War, this organisation represents a genuine desire for world peace by supporting the foreign policy of the Soviet Union. It represents the views of those people who are close friends of the Soviet camp. But this is only one approach to the problems of world conflict. The World Peace Council has been, with the exception of a watery statement or two by its officers in their own name, silent on the question of the Soviet invasion of Czechoslovakia.

In profound disagreement with this approach to world peace and freedom are the non-aligned peace movements, and for additional reasons, the revolutionary New Left.

Fall 1979

ON THE NUCLEAR STATE

The Manifesto of the *Regroupement Écologique Québécois* is one of the most important statements to appear from the ecology movement. It is important because it is a radical statement going to the roots of several aspects of the ecology crisis. It states for instance: "The eco-society implies an end of the domination/exploitation system which is imposed on humanity and nature." Rarely do ecologists make the link between various issues surrounding the ecology question, like, for instance, exploitation on the one hand *and* domination on the other. These two sides of the same coin are rarely dealt with by liberals, social democrats and other socialists in the ecology movement.

The Manifesto is also valuable because it shows the growth of a radical ecology consciousness in Québec. Reviewing the recent history of ecological problems here should prove informative to non-French-speaking people. Not since the seminal ecology manifesto of the New York-based movement, *Ecology Action East*, "The Power to Destroy and the Power to Create," (published in January 1970 in *Our Generation*, Vol. 7, No. 1) have I read such a thoughtful statement. Unlike most ecology statements, the Manifesto clearly shows that a root cause of the crisis is the existence of the capitalist system itself. "Blind technology is the result of the pursuit of profit which is at the service of capitalist power. A police apparatus is more and more protecting it. We are becoming more and more dependent on it, and it is taking away from us all power. We must take it back collectively..."

The Manifesto is moving in its description of an ecological society. It reminds me of those projections into the future that the peace movement used to make of a society without war. Each successive movement of protest and resistance in the last decade, for example, the nuclear disarmament and peace movement of the early 1960s; the New Left of the late 1960s; the women's movement of the early 1970s; and now the ecology and anti-nuclear movement have added to our understanding of the limits of our society. Together, the accumulated experience of these movements have deepened our critique of capitalism and the State has well as posed an

alternative society far more revolutionary than the classical socialist movements and parties of the past. The echoes of all these movements are to be
found in this Manifesto.

The Manifesto presents a radical analysis of what must be in order to
veer away from catastrophe. "The decentralization and the participation of
all citizens in the decision-making process will be a marked characteristic
of the new society. The framework of formal democracy, parliamentary
and consultative, will be bypassed, in such a way that all will be decision-
makers, the enablers of the collective milieu, preservers of the natural environment. Ecological democracy will have abolished the hierarchical
character of political power in our society." The Manifesto goes on to say
that the new society will be classless, and not based on property nor on the
elite control of the means of economic production.

Reflecting very much the political milieu in Québec, in contrast to
what exists elsewhere on this continent, the Manifesto and the ecologists
who wrote it show the relationship of themselves and the ecology question
to the working-class by putting a series of demands and short-term objectives for change in the working-place as well as in the countryside. This is
important for other ecologists to note.

Where the Québec ecologists show their weakness in this Manifesto is
in their aspirations and demands vis-à-vis the State. This weakness they
share with most ecologists elsewhere. This reliance on the State is both
naive and contradictory. The source of this contradiction is in the way they
look at capitalist society; analysing capitalism in the way the Manifest does
is fine, but it is only half the story. We must also deal with the question of
the political organisation of society in the here and now, not simply in the
future. For surely, we have seen during the various "revolutions" in this
century that economic power might shift, but political power in the form of
the State (and hence, ultimately important economic power) has not
changed anywhere in any significant way.

What has to be raised in the current debate over nuclear energy is the
role of the State. This politico-economic question, in my view, is far more
significant in terms of actually changing the present situation than the issues of nuclear accidents at power plants, radioactive wastes, and so on. As
important as these issues are, none of them, nor the danger posed by wide
nuclear power policy, can be effectively dealt with short of a major transformation of political power.

During the post-World War period, especially, the State has grown
massively into a centralising monster across the world. This process is now
being accelerated by the birth of the nuclear State. In the past, the State had
acquired great power through its control of standing armies, military
hardware and budgets which include the increased size of a police apparatus. In more recent times the economic role of the State has grown
enormously as has been documented in *Our Generation* and other journals.
With the development of nuclear technology, the State gets another boost
in its ever growing control over society. This additional danger has barely
been touched on by the anti-nuke and ecology movement.

Born out of the armament programme of the Second World War, rather than as an energy source, nuclear power, unlike other forms of energy has always been perceived as a top security matter by the Nation-State. The possibilities of stealing various substances, either for use in weapons or for mass poisoning, and of attacking nuclear reactors are real; many attempts have been made along these lines. As these dangerous attempts are made, the dangerous State security measures are increased.

Various studies have shown that thousands of workers have been removed from nuclear operations in the US as security risks. Those that remain are heavily policed with lie-detector tests; they are asked whether they speak to journalists, belong to a union, whether they have ever been involved in anti-nuclear activities, and whether they have ever had an affair with another plant employee.

An economy based on a supply of electricity from nuclear power plants requires the maintenance and security of this technology and its sources which considerably increases the State's police apparatus. It becomes a "given" that industrial workers in this area of the economy give up free association, speech and privacy. In addition, reports of harassment abound of people who attend hearings, hold conversations with anti-nuclear militants, or who engage in similar legitimate acts. Since there are many potential attackers — organised crime, foreign interests, political groups, pathological individuals — security is impossible. A further growth in the police powers of the State becomes inevitable. Massive intelligence networks are required. The State will assume the responsibility of defining those sections of the population which it considers a challenge to the status quo.

Murray Bookchin wrote his classic statement, "Ecology and Revolutionary Thought," in 1965, some five years before "ecology" became a popular term. It clearly exposed the social roots of the massive ecological problems that have now become part of public consciousness. But he also went on to demonstrate the internal logic of this question with the anarchist critique of society. It is a classic case of co-optation then, when many liberals and Marxists freely used his analysis of the ecological crisis, finding its social implications insightful, but entirely side-stepped his anarchist conclusions. In the light of what I have noted above regarding the contradictions of the Manifesto let me quote Bookchin on this crucial matter.

> I hold that this problem cannot be resolved by appending it to an alien, economistic "class analysis" of the kind currently in vogue today. For more than capitalism and class society are at stake in the ecological crisis. Hierarchical society in its entirety as it reaches into the family as well as the factory, into domestic life as well as economic, into the psyche as well as the prevailing modes of reason — all are more fundamentally at issue than capitalism alone in resolving our breach with nature. Moreover, far more than economic exploitation is at stake in the ecological crisis. Domination in all its forms — the domination of the young by the old, of woman by man, and of man by man in all its forms — must be removed if we are to eliminate the very concept that nature is a mere "object" (to

use Marx's unhappy term) to be dominated by humanity. To recast the ecological problem in shallow reductionist terms, to diminish the historic scope of the issue to the level that "pollution is profitable" is an act of intellectual distortion of the most tragic kind.

We used much the same analysis in an editorial on the question in the above-mentioned issue of *Our Generation* in 1970, and a paraphrased summary of that statement is more relevant today than ever before.

- The ecological crisis is fundamentally a social problem, deeply rooted in the structure of society and in the cultural values that this society generates.
- The present structure of society, a product of material conditions, is based on people's domination and exploitation of nature and of each other.
- This domination is a result of the concentration of power, created by the centralisation of energy, material and human resources, and social administration.
- Cities must be decentralised into regional communal entities.
- The earth's resources must be used on a regional communal basis of mutual aid, and must be determined by the life-carrying capacity of the ecosystem in which the communities are located and,
- all social institutions of domination and exploitation, from the patriarchal family to the modern Nation-State, must be dissolved,
- that the ecology movement which includes the culture of life-style changes is an inseparable part of the liberation movements of colonised peoples, people of colour, native people, women and gays, youth and children, and all working people as a class.
- In the final analysis direct action is the only effective means that people can take to gain control of their environment, their lives, and their destinies.

Fall 1982

THE POLITICS OF THE PEACE MOVEMENT

While there was widespread sentiment for peace after World War II, it never developed into an impressive independent political force. Indeed as the Cold War between East and West unfolded, this sentiment and its principal organisational expression, the World Peace Council, (in this country, the Canadian Peace Congress) became an echo of Soviet foreign policy. In a recently published article by two Hungarians living in Budapest, Ferenc

Koszegi and Istvan Szent-Ivanyi (*New Society*, 21/28 October 1982), the authors write:

> In the People's Democracies of Eastern Europe, the peace movement had fundamentally discredited itself by the end of the forties and the beginning of the fifties. At that time, instead of the neutral term "peace movement" the expression used was "peace struggle," which was intended to camouflage the scarcely-concealed preparations in expectation of a third World War. Gradually the militant "peace struggle," lost its original meaning and became a euphemism for armament expansion and a policy of intimidation. The term further lost significance and credibility because, with the passing of time, it was used in relation to everything. Everywhere it was used in a manner which radically distorted its original meaning — a familiar example is the rhyme:
>
> *Collect your scrap, your iron send:*
> *With these too, your peace defend!*

In the article, the authors describe the recent emergence of the first independent peace movement in Hungary, in contrast to the official one affiliated with the World Peace Council.

The fifties were also a period when many countries in the Third World broke from imperial domination and sought a path in international affairs (as well, in some cases, in their internal development) that was allied to neither the Soviet Union (SU) nor the United States and their respective empires. From a series of impressive conferences held in Bandung and Belgrade starting in April 1955, Tunis in January 1960, Cairo in March 1961, and Addis Abba, 1962, a framework was developed for a third bloc. Impressive figures like Nehru, Sukarno, U Nu, Nkrumah, Mboya, who led their countries to overthrow colonialism and become new Nation-States, articulated *non-alignment.*

From about 1956, jettisoned by a combination of factors including the Franco-British military action to control the Suez canal, the secret speech of Nikita Khruschev (secretary of the SU Communist Party) denouncing the crimes of Stalin, and the interest in testing atomic and hydrogen bombs in the atmosphere by the US, SU, Britain and France, a New Left-oriented peace and disarmament movement emerged. It spread very rapidly in the form of campaigns for nuclear disarmament. The national campaigns sought unilateral denunciation of nuclear weapons by their respective governments, and an international policy of positive neutralism which meant an active North-South collaboration with the non-aligned bloc of Nation-States. Similar perspectives in the two hemispheres, it was believed, would lead to a situation in which initiatives could breakup the Cold War between East and West, and force disarmament to the benefit of all. These new non-aligned, disarmament movements federated and established an International Confederation for Disarmament and Peace in London, which was meant to co-ordinate its work, be an alternative to the WPC, and establish links with the non-aligned bloc of States.

Several factors frustrated this hope. The new Nation-States of the Third World displayed, in the end, all the contradictions of national and State power, in addition to the fact that the world economy was a one-world system dominated by the US. They slipped into their own cycle of arms build-ups, setting off an international arms trade without parallel in history. This inevitably included the spread of nuclear reactors, sophisticated delivery systems, and nuclear bombs. Another factor was the weak link that the international peace work represented. The new movement in the end fell back on the hope that a single country, Canada or Britain for instance, through pressure from the national movements, would denounce nuclear weapons unilaterally, and that this action would have a sanguine and exemplary effect on international relations. This result would be effected through a change in government policy or in government, accomplished through the system. It did not work. In the end, pressure to change Canadian foreign and defence policies came only from inside the country. The movement in Canada, as elsewhere, was not radical enough and therefore, was not sufficiently committed to fundamental social change. Its parameters were defined by the limits of the system within which its largest section chose to work. These limits did not permit such changes in the foreign and defence policies of Canada or any other country.

When the Test Ban Treaty (banning atomic testing in the atmosphere, only to have testing go underground) was signed, and when nuclear weapons were brought into Canada, without an obvious move towards nuclear war, the movement declined.

Enter the war in Vietnam and Southeast Asia which gave rise to another massive movement in opposition to this American imperial adventure. It was coupled with the emergence of a wide-ranging movement for fundamental social change: the ecology, counter-culture, women's liberation, gay and urban liberation movements. What the anti-war movement demonstrated was that it could under certain circumstances contribute to the defeat of an imperial adventure. What the movement for social change demonstrated was that a multi-issued critique of neo-capitalist and hierarchical society could affect the people who clearly felt both exploited and dominated — and there were many in our "affluent society." These two movements cross-fertilized to be sure, extending further those initial insights of the New Left counter-culture. The entire development, in ways quite different from the 1960s, broadened its base. With the Vietnam war over, the key question is: can this critical mood which became less demonstrative in the late 1970s be transformed into a renewed mass movement of opposition and resistance to the oncoming of World War III in the 1980s?

The New Conditions in the 1980s

As someone who has been directly involved in US nuclear planning, I can tell you my country has plans and forces for actually fighting nuclear war. Nuclear war is an integral part of American military planning and the US is prepared to use nuclear weapons anywhere in the world. I believe the Soviet Union is as nuclear-oriented in its military preparations as the United States. The military in both countries see nuclear weapons as a central instrument of military power. They are prepared to use them now in many contingencies.... (Rear Admiral Gene R. LaRocque, Director of the Center for Defence Information, July, 1978, *The Defence Monitor.*)

From President Truman to Nixon there is a whole history of when the US threatened to use nuclear weapons. Sources include public announcements, memoirs of Presidents and their associates, and studies based on official documents. We can assume there were instances which we do not know about. In 1946 Truman secretly threatened to use nuclear weapons in Iran[1]; in 1950 he publicly threatened to do likewise in Korea[2]; in 1953 President Eisenhower secretly threatened to use nuclear bombs in Korea[3]; in 1954 he offered atomic bombs to the French in Dienbienphu[4]; in 1958 he gave Presidential orders to secretly prepare the use of nuclear weapons for use in Iraq/Kuwait[5]; again in 1958 he gave similar orders over Quemoy, Taiwan straits[6]; in 1961 Kennedy received a recommendation to use nuclear weapons in Loas[7]; in 1961 and in 1962 Kennedy publicly threatened to use atomic bombs in the case of Berlin and Cuba[8]; in 1968 Gen. Westmoreland warned of a possible need to use nuclear weapons in Khe Sanh, Vietnam[9]; and during 1969-72, Nixon made repeated secret threats to use similar weapons in Vietnam.[10]

Over and above the conscious choice to use nuclear weapons by the political or military circles in the US or SU, the situation is additionally made dangerous by the consequences of accidents. The US for instance, has 30,000 nuclear weapons placed in different parts of the world, under the oceans in numerous countries in Europe, Asia as well as on its own soil. The US Department of Defence has admitted at least *eleven* major nuclear accidents. The US Atomic Energy Commission reports at least *four* other accidents. There is evidence that many other unreported and unconfirmed nuclear accidents have occurred since World War II. Many serious students of the problem estimate that an average of one US nuclear accident has occurred every year since 1946, with some estimating as many as *thirty* major accidents and 250 "minor" incidents during this time. (See a complete listing of 31 known US nuclear weapons accidents in World Armaments and Disarmament SIPRI Yearbook 1977, MIT Press, Cambridge, Mass.)

During the preceding decade both the US and the SU appeared to be satisfied with a policy referred to as Mutual Assured Destruction (MAD), which meant that if one side should attack first the other would always have the ability to guarantee that the consequences would be equally disastrous for both. Each side had enough nuclear weapons to kill every human being on earth many times over, and each side had roughly an equal capacity to do so. The danger of nuclear war stemmed more from some kind of human or mechanical error (which as Daniel Ellsberg notes in his "A Call to Mutiny" has happened several times during this period) than from deliberate State decisions.

What happened to change all this? Why did the European Nuclear Disarmament (END) movement suddenly come to life? Why did it spread rapidly to countries previously hardly involved? Why did a great wave of protest sweep over the US and Canada in late 1981 and into the first half of 1982? To answer these questions, an analysis of the preceding two decades is essential, which includes a knowledge of the history of the peace movements, the New Left and the movements for social change. The answers also depend on our view of the international power struggle between the larger Nation-States, and how we believe a new international movement can be built.

We can only outline the answer here. Although at first it appears to be a beginning, in fact there is a continuity. In December 1979, NATO decided to re-equip its European nuclear forces with Cruise and Pershing missiles. The SU naturally saw this as unsettling a stable balance of forces and acted predictably. These actions created widespread fear in Europe over a possible increase in confrontation between both sides, including nuclear exchanges. But the most important question was, why did NATO make this decision? And consequently, why did the US impose this new military technology on its European allies when nothing took place in Europe to justify such a turn?

One theory is that there is an inner dynamic to the arms race itself and to the Nation-State power system. This theory advanced by the New Left British historian, E.P. Thompson (with some of its theoretical roots going back to the New Left sociologist, C. Wright Mills, in his *The Causes of World War Three*) suggested that new weapons systems are always developed by the military; the period of conception and testing is usually some ten or so years. These new missiles were at the design stage in the late 60s, and became operational be the early 1980s. Why not capitalize on a major technological advance? According to E.P. Thompson, the international war system is essentially closed and follows its own logic. He states:

> The Cold War...has broken loose from its historical moorings and acquired an independent inertial thrust of its own. What is the Cold War about? It is about itself.
> We face here, in the grimmest sense, the "consequences of consequences." The Cold War may be seen as a show put on the orad by two rival entrepreneurs in 1946 or 1947. The show has grown bigger and bigger; the entrepreneurs have lost control of it, as it has thrown up its own managers, administrators, producers, and a large supporting cast, all of whom have a direct interest in its continuance, in its enlargement. Whatever happens, the show must go on. (*The Nation,* July 17, 1982)

This is an eloquent form of reasoning which we feel is as compelling as when we published a major assessment of C. Wright Mills (see *Our Generation,* Vol. 1, No. 4)

The old Left attempts to formulate its answers to the same questions, and upon these it designs its past and present response. It contends that the US has lost its monopoly of military power in the 1970s, the threat of nuclear weapons has lost its credibility, all of which complicates its ability to carry out its world-wide military commitments. During the 1970s, the US began to decline as a military power — "lost" Portugal's African colonies, was defeated in Vietnam, had the US-supported Somoza regime overthrown in Nicaragua, saw the spread of uprisings in other parts of Central America, witnessed the triumph of the national liberation movement in Zimbabwe, and in 1979 watched the fall of the Shah of Iran.

It is hard to appreciate the shock in Washington over the loss of Iran, the most important defeat to its empire since Vietnam. It was, according to this view, under these circumstances that the decision was made to deploy the new weaponry.[11] This new phase was started by Carter, and continued by Reagan who has expanded it through new enlarged military budgets. This analysis, the old Left believes, is the rationale for US nuclear policy. Simple and direct, this view holds assumptions of the nature of power in our society and in societies of Eastern Europe, and having certain consequences, which we have dealt with critically elsewhere.

The new peace movement arose like a huge giant after a nap. During 1981, mass demonstrations took place in Europe. In Canada, led by 35,000 people in Vancouver, and 15,000 people in Winnipeg, demonstrations of unprecedented size swept the country. Around the time of the failed Second Special Session on Disarmament at the United Nations, nearly one million people were in the streets of New York on June 12, while London had 250,000 and Bonn 400,000 during the preceding week. Two weeks earlier, 400,000 demonstrated in Tokyo, 100,000 in Stockholm, and 70,000 in Vienna.

These numbers complemented the similar huge turnouts last fall in Europe. In July 1982, END had drawn 1,000 activists to Brussels from 25 countries for its first continental conference. During this meeting, the debate, familiar to the older subscribers of this journal, broke out. Do we change the system through the established institutions or do we build a new movement, an extra-parliamentary opposition outside the system?

Why was the new movement so massive? Surely, it did not spring out of nowhere after the 1979 NATO decision. Contrary to what the mass media wanted us to believe, that after the 1960s everyone of that generation fell into apathy because our hopes and dreams were dashed, the movement in one form or another, as this journal showed, continued. The new radicalism of the 60s, took various new forms in the 1970s, deepening its understanding of the nature of our society and sinking firm roots in various sections of the citizenry. In Europe, the new peace movement received impetus from the squatters of Amsterdam, the urban liberationists of Copenhagen, the radical counter culture of Zurich, the ecology and anti-nuclear energy movement in West Germany. Youth and radicals from the 60s joined with the concerned people of today to give the demonstrations their scope and sweep. Once again we heard resoundingly, "No power to anyone, all power to the people."

One of the major differences between the movement of the 60s and that of the 80s is its attitude and approach to Eastern Europe. END, for instance, seeks to be a European-wide movement. Two members of the

British Campaign for Nuclear Disarmament, for example (in *Peace News*, October 15, 1982), wrote of their experiences in visiting Hungary, Poland and East Germany.

> We came back with one overwhelming message from the people we met and talked to: "tell more people to come and visit us, and learn for themselves." At a political level it is also crucial for us to print the END appeal in each of the languages of the Warsaw Pact countries and get people to take them over in small bundles for distribution: at the moment many people still confuse us with the pro-Soviet Peace Committees and until our position is clear we shall lack credibility. Once people are clear where you stand in regard to Soviet militarism as well as NATO, then they are usually prepared to talk to you, although it is the daily Soviet control which they naturally regard as a priority.

END in Britain has just published the first of a series of pamphlets called *The New Hungarian Peace Movement* by Fernc Koszegi and E.P. Thompson, which show the emergence of the first independent peace group in that country, clearly encouraged by the independent peace movement in the West. The next END pamphlet will be on the first independent peace group in Moscow (see Lucia Kowaluk's report in the last *Our Generation* which mentions it.) A similar group movement exists in East Germany (see the article in *Mother Jones*, September/October 1982).

This approach is more realistic and promising than that of the 60s with the additional perspective that peace and freedom cannot be separated. Although many of the movements of the 60s maintained such a posture, they offered nothing concrete.

The other major difference is the tendency to use direct action and civil disobedience. In the 1960s this question split the disarmament movement. One of the largest movements for example, that of Britain's Campaign for Nuclear Disarmament was severely shaken when Bertrand Russell (one of this century's leading philosophers) founder of the group left it to form the Committee of 100. This latter movement organised massive direct actions (in which British anarchists were very influential) Russell was jailed for his activities. Today, direct action in most of these movements is not controversial, and is used alongside other methods of protest and resistance.

To be sure, the ideological politics, and the political agenda of this new disarmament movement is not satisfactory to anarchists. But even though there are left-wing socialists and social democrats as well as Eurocommunists eager to influence the future of this social movement it is massive enough and has a strong independent dynamic of its own. This dynamic is profoundly libertarian at an unconscious level. While the reformists want to use it to influence this political party or that, this socialist government or that, the perception of what needs to be done however hazy is much more radical at the grass roots. Anarchists therefore have the responsibility to help make the unconsciously felt, consciously held and articulated. To sharpen a coherent anti-authoritarian critique and to suggest alternative libertarian forms is an essential contribution if we are to prevent the oncoming of another World War, the last one.

END is now planning its second convention in May 1983 in Berlin. Some 3,000-4,000 militants will be present, delegates from anarchist groups should also be present in large numbers.

What we as editors of *Our Generation* want to emphasise in the new peace movement is the need for a theoretical framework, within which tactics and strategy become more effective. Our experience from the founding of this journal in 1961 tells us, that there are very large questions underpinning the peace debate which we cannot ignore.

Industrialisation in the 19th century mutilated our society. There is less poverty now, but the same lack of true community life. Work has become less arduous in most cases without becoming more meaningful. The separation between the skilled and creative minority and the unskilled and uncreative majority remains. What was once called the proletariat has lost what culture it once had, and gained no true substitute. A facade of innocuous amusements hinders thought. Equality of opportunity produces, not a society of equals, but a society in which the class division is made more sinister by the co-optation of intelligent people into State bureaucracy and the destruction of their roots. We have a deracinated, disinherited and consenting people who lacks a concept of itself. Our socialist ancestors had ideals but no technical sophistication. We have the sophistication but we can give only a brief and denuded explanation of our ideals. The need for an overview is imperative but it is lacking. Without this overview, this larger understanding of the nature of our society and how to radically transform it into a classless and warless community, the new peace movement will sink again. Here is a promise: we shall explore it, analyse and coax it along new avenues.

NOTES

1. Senator Jackson, *Time*, Jan. 28, 1980.
2. Press Conference, Nov. 30, 1950.
3. Eisenhower's memoirs, *Mandate for Change*, Vol. 1, pp. 178-8.
4. Prime Minister Bidault in film *Hearts & Minds* and in Drummond & Coblentz, *Duel at the Brink*, (N.Y. 1960 pp. 121-122).
5. Blechman and Kaplan, *Force without War*, (Washington, 1978) pp.238, 256.
6. Morton H. Halperin, *The 1958 Taiwan Straits Crisis*, (Declassified Study).
7. Sorensen, Kennedy, (N.Y.) 1966, pp. 721-728.
8. Blechman and Kaplan, pp. 343-439.
9. R.F. Kennedy, *Thirteen Days*, (N.Y. 1971).
10. Schandler, *The Unmaking of a President*, (Princeton, 1977) pp. 86-91.
11. Haldeman's memoirs: *The Ends of Power*, (N.Y. 1978) pp. 81-85, 97-98, and *Richard Nixon's Memoirs*, pp. 393-414.

Spring 1991

NOTES TO THE READER

Too many people have bought the view dispensed by the corporate media that *because* of mass media, we are living in a brand-new world with new rules and a reality significantly different from that of the past. Personal computers, fax machines, videos, popular music, and the fall of State socialism have, alas, changed things not nearly enough.

Consider the insights of Randolphe Bourne writing in 1917, the third year of the First World War:

> They told us that war was becoming economically impossible...in these days of international economic dependence, of inextricably interlacing communications, and of financial obligations....[They told us] that the more the world became one vast market and the more each nation's economic interests became definitely implicated in those of others, just so much the more unready would be any government [to make war]....They told us that war was becoming physically impossible. The very magnitude of the armaments was making their employment hazardous. It seemed incredible that any modern government would take the initiative of letting loose those incalculable engines of destruction. The more formidable and complicated the armaments became, the safer were we in reality from their use...

This quote sounds as if it could have been written yesterday. In fact, we have seen how in a few days the same old hustles and excuses for war easily re-emerge. If, for instance, we were to read today the following words — also written in 1917 — what would be our conclusion:

> We are learning that war doesn't need enthusiasm, doesn't need conviction, doesn't need hope, to sustain it....Once manoeuvred, it takes care of itself....Our resources in men and materials are vast enough to organise the war-technique without enlisting more than a fraction of the people's conscious energy....This is why the technical organisation of this American war goes on so much more rapidly than any corresponding popular sentiment for its aims and purposes. Our war has really a superfluous quality....The government of a modern organised plutocracy does not have to ask whether the people want to fight or understand what they are fighting for, but only whether they will tolerate fighting. America does not co-operate with the President's designs. She rather feebly acquiesces. But the feeble acquiescence is the all-important factor...
>
> Responsibility lies always on the shoulders of those who failed to prevent. Here it lies upon the cowardly middle classes who failed to curb militarism.

These insights can be especially directed at the contemporary peace movement and its leadership. As soon as the Gulf War broke out a familiar cycle of protest began. The political content of this protest was as equivocal as the State authorities could have wished. What really needs to be said during these times is also nothing new. Randolphe Bourne's thoughts were part of a libertarian stream that was in a minority during his lifetime, as unfortunately it still is today. Nevertheless, it is the only substantial perspective that a peace movement can advance with honesty and intelligence.

Most of what follows is from Bourne's greatest essay, *War Is the Health of the State,* unfinished at the time of his death at age 32. It is presented here not only because of its obvious merit, but also as an example of what the peace movement *must* advance educationally and politically if the responsibility for militarism is to be met head-on.

> We have the misfortune of being born not only in a country but into a State, and as we grow up we learn to mingle the two…into a hopeless confusion.…The history of America as a country is quite different from that of America as a State.…War is the health of the State, and it is during war that one best understands the nature of that institution…
>
> With the shock of war…the State comes into its own.…The Government with no mandate from the people, without consultation of the people, conducts all negotiations…
>
> There is no case in modern times of the people being consulted in the initiation of a war. The present demand for "democratic control" of foreign policy indicates how completely, even in the most democratic of modern nations, foreign policy has been the secret private possession of the executive branch of the Government.…When the declaration of war is finally demanded by the Executive, the Congress could not refuse it.…To repudiate an Executive at that time would be to publish to the entire world the evidence that the country with an almost criminal carelessness allowed its government to commit it to gigantic national enterprises in which it had no heart.…War can scarcely be avoided unless this poisonous underground system of secret diplomacy is destroyed…
>
> For the benefit of proud and haughty citizens, [the State] is fortified with a list of intolerable insults which have been hurled toward us by other nations; for the benefit of the liberal and beneficent, it has a convincing set of moral purposes which our going to war will achieve; for the ambitious and aggressive classes, it can gently whisper of a bigger role in the destiny of the world…
>
> [But] it cannot be too firmly realised that war is a function of States and not of [countries] and nations, indeed that [war] is the chief function of States. War is a very artificial thing. It is not the naive spontaneous outburst of herd pugnacity; it is no more primary than is formal religion. War cannot exist without a military establishment and a military establishment cannot exist without a State organisation…they are inseparably and functionally joined. We can not crusade against the war without crusading implicitly against the State. And we cannot expect, or take measures to insure, that this war is a war to end war, unless at the same time we take measures to end the State in its traditional form.
>
> The State is not the nation, and the State can be modified and even abolished in its present form without harming the nation. On the contrary, with the passing of the dominance of the State, the genuine life-enhancing forces of the nation will be liberated. If the State's chief function is war, then the State must suck out of the nation a large part of its energy for its purely sterile purposes of defence and aggression.…It devotes to waste or to actual destruction as much as it can of the vitality of the nation.

This situation is very difficult to change. But we must remember that human beings and history bear witness to the most incredible and unpredictable upheavals. No one is justified in the arrogance of hopelessness. We should be ever watchful for shifts and eddies in the political, economic, and historical circumstances surrounding current movements and be prepared to intervene creatively. As a start, concerned people should have a sense of the *real* underlying reasons for historical events. A war like the one in the Persian Gulf is naturally surrounded by clouds of State propaganda from all sides, echoed by an army of priests (journalists, academics, and self-appointed experts).

Hence, we publish in this issue interviews with Noam Chomsky, who with an independent mind probes the real causes of the Middle East crisis. It should be added that an essential background document to this discussion is Chomsky's book, *The Fateful Triangle,* about Israel, the United States, and the Palestinians. (It is a book that many booksellers have refused to carry, as in general this caste belongs to the same priesthood of apologists.)

The fine article by Paul Marshall on Chomsky's basic philosophy is published here not only because of its obvious reflective merits, but also because it is useful to know the fundamental values which guide an independent mind. Our first book review also deals with Chomsky's work.

Fundamental change is difficult at best, and the theoretical thinking required can be arduous. However, with the traditional Left in upheaval and the libertarian Left sensing new opportunities, it is clear that we must think again about the key items on our political and social agenda, especially such principles as *radical democracy*. In "Socialism and Ecology," a sweeping review of the recent courtship between red and green, James O'Connor argues, among other things, that local-level direct democracy is a necessary outcome of the marriage of these converging movements. His attempt is perhaps marked by certain gaps and incompletions, including some unexamined assumptions about social ecology. Murray Bookchin's essay on confederalism fills in some of the holes, giving a concrete social and organisational expression to the principle. Likewise, Frank Harrison and George Woodcock take up real social forms in their essays, but this time from an historical point of view, looking at past intersections of community and structures of democratic participation. Woodcock, in particular, draws the distinction between formalistic and liberatory democracy, insisting on the *content* as well as the form of direct rule. Bookchin, Harrison, and Woodcock all come from the libertarian school and all are at pains to sketch the outlines of a democratic society which will know neither political domination nor economic exploitation and, thus, will have eliminated the roots of war.

All three authors press for a democracy which goes far beyond the limits of traditional representational parliamentarism; i.e., one that includes citizens' initiatives, referenda, proportional representation, recall of elected persons, shorter tenures in office, and so on. Participation, democratic control of local institutions from community centres to schools to municipal councils — these are essential features of a radical agenda and the creation of a political space towards the transformation of society. Further, two of our books under review are also concerned with the localness of politics and urban planning, and how we might open up space both figuratively and literally. We would do well to remember the libertarian origin of these ideas and to re-examine them in their original context as a means of protecting them and ourselves from co-optation.

We have, then, a substantial double issue of the journal, one which counts as two numbers for subscribers. Publishing the material in this way permits us to catch up to our twice-yearly production schedule, and you should have the next number in hand by summer's end.

And a final word as we again become deeply involved in anti-war movements: let us take a few moments to re-read Brian Martin's essay, *The Limits of the Peace Movement*. You will find it in *Our Generation*, Volume 17, No. 2. It is worthy of our attention.

Chapter 2

THE NATIONAL QUESTION —
LOOKING AT QUÉBEC AND CANADA

Fall 1966

ON QUÉBEC

The analysis and position taken in this editorial is the result of discussion, research and dialogue over a period of three years. From the vantage point of an English-language journal in the heart of Québec, which we believe gives us particular qualifications, we submit to you this perspective viewed from the one moral and political criterion we hold essential — that of world peace and freedom.

This is not a definitive analysis of position. The social developments in Québec are going to be a permanent feature of the journal from now on. Next to the African-American revolution in the US, Québec society is the homogeneous dynamic in the North American technological complex. A realistic policy on Québec is integral to the programme of the *new radicals* in Canada, just as a correct policy addressing the demand of the blacks in the US for their human rights is for the New Left there.

Finally the interdependence of these questions is manifested in the interdependence of the triple revolutions of cybernetics, weaponry and human rights on this continent and throughout the world.

The Primary Context — The Planet

The *future* of man in peace and freedom is both the principle and framework within which we base our analysis of the question of Québec and the crisis of Confederation.

We realize the intricate interdependency of man and nature, as well as between these two issues. Solutions must be sought which are based upon the understanding of the *limitations* of our situation. Our planet has *limited* human, natural and financial resources. These are unjustly distributed. We must also realize that given the atomic age, the time is *limited* within which we can solve this major crisis of modern man.

There are some one hundred and seventeen Nation-States on earth, all trapped within the international war system. The thrust of these Nation-

States and the drift of the system combine in making every conflicting embrace the most costly in the history of man. Each Nation-State is in a profound situation of stress and strain generated by the numerous contradictory internal social forces. Each internal crisis is placed in relief by the happenings of the international war system which is caught up within its own upheavals. It is these upheavals, cumulatively and qualitatively different from the strictly national ones, which will determine the fate of man before the end of this century. If humanity is to prevail, then this international system must be radically renovated and this in turn, for the most part, can only be ushered in by fundamental social changes in the societies of the East and West.

All other objectives are dwarfed by this single task. It is at this level that human society is basically moulded and determined, making this *revolution* the essence of this generation's agenda.

The Crisis of National Power

Within our *present* historical period, certain Nation-States have the *power* to determine the course of the future more than others. The contemporary definition of this power is essentially spelled out in industrial and technological terms. First in power-political importance is *military* technology. "The world's stockpiles of atomic weapons are now believed to total the equivalent of 16,000 twenty-megaton bombs. The power of a single twenty-megaton bomb is equal to the effect of a thousand bomber raids of World War II, repeated day after day for fourteen years." (*Unesco Courier 1964*.) This power is distributed amongst the "great powers": the US, SU (the Soviet Union), Britain, France, China. During this present historical period the US is *the* most powerful Nation-State on earth.

Other forms of power are reflected in these facts: a small group of highly industrialized Nation-States, with 16% of the world's population, control 70% of the world's wealth. The US comprises 6% of the world's people, controls nearly 60% of all natural resources, and enjoys more than 40% of the world's income. The US per capita income is over $3,000 per annum. The per capita income of the forty poorest developing countries is $120. All outstanding economists are indicating that the gap is increasing between rich and poor nations. Population growth rates, often as high as three percent, promise to double the population within a single generation in countries least able to provide for their inhabitants. The absolute number of illiterate as well as starving people is greater now than ever before in history.

In assessing national power it is important to note that the ability to withhold or furnish economic necessities, in many instances, represents power quite as effectively as do armed forces and atomic bombs.

This non-military aspect of power enters in various ways into the political evaluation of food stuffs and raw materials. If X country is the sole or principal source of a key raw material — say, industrial diamonds — this fact is an element to be weighed in the international balance of power, both military and non-military. Conversely, if X country must depend wholly or primarily upon another for some essential raw material — say, hydro-electric power — that fact too has weight in the scale both of diplomacy and military potential.

Though chemical synthesis plays a large and increasing role in freeing the great states from precarious dependence upon external supplies, the geography of food stuffs and raw materials is still very important. If X-country depends heavily upon external sources of supply for certain of these resources, that fact may portend inconvenience and temporary loss of power, if not disaster. Or such dependence may reveal weakness in a Nation-State's negotiating or bargaining capacity with other states, and therefore lessen their ability to attain desired national objectives without recourse to war.

That does not mean that the only material resources that count are those inside a State's own territorial frontiers. The vast nickel deposits of Canada, for example, may be presumed for the moment to be accessible to the US. The US imports about 80% of its nickel from Canada, which is the most important additive to the production of stainless steel. But what of manganese from Brazil, or copper from Chile, or oil from the Middle East? *These facts underline the strategic placement of the middle powers vis-à-vis international power.*

Nature and Function

The operations of international power and the operations of world peace are overwhelmingly antithetical. National power, no matter in what friendly hands it is held, given the nature of the international war system, especially in the atomic age, is inevitably misused and attracts to it large measures of suspicion and distrust. Take the power of the super-states: we are suspicious of it, worried about it, anxious about it. There is a crisis of national power in the world nowadays because, as we can see by observing the relationships between Canada and the US, these feelings of anxiety have been given a much sharper edge during the last few years than ever before. The power in question is now the power to destroy absolutely, to destroy whole cultures, to destroy the species. When the nature of national power has been transformed so radically, it is only natural that there should be a similar escalation in the anxieties felt about it, especially when we are so totally unable to share in its exercise.

The United States

The US emerged after 1945 as the principal national power on our planet. To consolidate that national power, the US needs more than its own resources to maintain the technological heights of its present industrial-military complex. Having such power, the US can be the chief restraint and cause of a thermonuclear conflagration. What are some of the elements in this drift, thrust and restraint from world war?

Every structure has its self-imposed limitations; so with the present international structure and its distribution or power. Looking at it outside the context of its dynamics, it allows us to drift into relatively the same restricting situations. "The immediate cause of World War III is the continuous preparation of it. The indispensable condition for this kind of preparation is the fact of the sovereign State as a continental economic domain. International events are increasingly the result of the decisions and the lack of decisions of men who act in the name of these nations and with the means of action made available by their economic, military, and political institutions. The international centralization of decisions and the internal development of the super-states, we have seen, means that history-making is less a matter of some overwhelming fate than of the decisions and the defaults of two power elites." (C. Wright Mills.)

The United States and Canada

The US power elite, for one, needs more and more the resources of other countries to maintain its imperial position. The 1952 US Presidential "Material Policy Commission" reported that non-US sources are needed for every significant resource except molybdenum and magnesium. With particular reference to Canada, a recent issue of *U.S. News & World Report* stated, "The Big Rush is on to Tap Canada's Wealth: The natural riches of Canada are going to play an increasingly important role in the world, especially in the US Oil, uranium for atomic power, and fresh water are only three of many basic resources Canada has in abundance. All are sought in growing amounts by the US and others. Upshot: an expanding race to gather Canada's treasure." In the post-war period, Canada has been carrying out a defence policy geared to the interests of the US, at a cost of $27 billion. While this enormous amount has been diverted from the development of this country, $17 billion of US capital has flowed in and together with reinvested profits has taken the controlling percentage of the Canadian economy. It is thus understandable that over 60% of Canadian exports go to the US as raw materials and semi-processed commodities in return for US manufactured goods. Almost 26% of all imports into the US come from Canada. In short, external dependency is at the root of contemporary national power. Dependency in itself is not objectionable; the planet is indeed becoming more interdependent, but when *this kind* of dependency helps to express the barbarism of the Vietnamese war, then it must be fundamentally redefined.

Purpose for Canada

If the thesis in the primary context is correct, then in order for world peace to be realized in this century it is essential that major social revolutionary developments take place in middle powers, particularly Canada. These developments will not happen in isolation from what is occurring in the "third world," but in interaction with them. This will affect the rivalry of the "great powers." It is at this level that the future of the international war system will be heavily determined.

In previous issues of *Our Generation* we have analysed the nature of the Third World. This group of national powers, both for reasons of survival and because of the nature of the path for survival, play a restraining role vis-à-vis the super-states. In recent years, their independence of action has been undermined because of the powerful attraction of the bi-polar world. With the breakup of NATO, the shake-up of the Warsaw Pact, the Vietnam war, and finally the emergence of Gaullism, new vigour is imbuing independent political action against the Cold War. An indirect way this can be illustrated is that both the military and the bloc attitudes toward Gaullism have had an impact, which was reflected (Romania for example) in the recent Warsaw Pact conference in Bucharest. The pact nations, far from strengthening the organisational competence of their alliance, instead committed themselves to its dismantlement if NATO would take the same steps. Romania has let it be known that should France leave NATO, it would leave the Warsaw Pact.

In the economic sphere, Romania and Bulgaria have both responded with enthusiasm to French proposals for industrial co-operation. In the few years since Romania began buying industrial equipment in western Europe, the West's share of its total trade has jumped from 20 to 30%. The Soviet Union still tops its trading list. But West Germany has just become a remarkable second.

Increasingly, the Balkan states are doing what General de Gaulle has envisaged for everybody in a "renewed Europe." They are more and more "acting on their own" in a "new Balkans."

During the month of August, General de Gaulle embarked on a world-wide trip of Africa and South-East Asia appealing to those countries to strengthen their national independence by remaining unattracted by the process of bi-polarization, and counting on France for support. Granted this is "altruism" in the French State's interest; all the same, it will have an effect on the nature of the Cold War.

Canada has a similar choice. Either it will continue in its *particular* colonial status and thus accept the historically disproved "balance of power" theory and be integrated more thoroughly into the American Empire, or it will choose to act as a restraint on US aggrandisement and declare independence. The natural first-step consequence of such a declaration will be to aid and strengthen the independence of other middle countries including those presently in the Soviet bloc. The prelude to such a declaration for world peace would mean fundamental social change.

Canada's Task

Fundamental social change for Canada means essentially two things: a political State declaring a policy of positive neutralism (leaving all military alliances, working closely with the non-aligned nations in the UN, a prerequisite of which will be to move into an era of political and economic self-determination from all external powers, particularly the USA) and a major reconstitution and redistribution of social power within Canada, beginning with the constitution of a bi-national Confederation. Both of these necessities are intertwined, and no progress will be made towards them short of a major social upheaval. The objective must be freedom from outside restrictions and the realisation of internal freedom; this is one and the same task.

The First Internal Question — The Crisis of Confederation

It is doubtful whether any concrete policy position can be worked out on Canada's domestic crisis if it does not first begin with a correct and just position on the Crisis of Confederation. Indeed, any social analysis of the country's outstanding problems would begin in a distorted manner unless that analysis begins at the beginning — Québec.

Souviens-Toi

The official motto, *"Je me souviens"* is a phrase that we see in many places, from signs marking the town limits of many a village in the Gaspésie to books, editorial pages and official government documents.

What is it then, this inescapable motto? To what does it refer, and what is its significance? According to historians it has a two-fold reference. It harks back to the glorious past of New France, but also carries bitter memories of what in Québec is called the Conquest — the victory of Wolfe over Montcalm on that summer day of 1759 that left a lonely 70,000 French-Canadians isolated in the midst of an alien people and under alien rule in North America. It is a slogan that conjures up the struggle for survival, both physical and cultural, that forms the major portion of French-Canadian history. It has reminded generations of Québecers that they belong to a people that have had to fight hard for privileges and rights. In so doing, it has also reminded them of their cultural identity and recalled the debt to their forebears. It has reminded them of their duty to maintain this culture that has been passed on to them at the cost of so much sweat, determination and hardship. (Thomas Sloan, *The Not-so-Quiet Revolution*, p. vii.)

The persistence into the present of the historic grievances of the vanquished is a fact of life. Were it not so, the repeated surges of French-Canadian nationalism would constitute nothing more than the synthetic, subjective-emotional outbursts that supporters of the status quo assert them to be. But if such a comfortably complacent explanation were well-founded, it is hardly likely that the whole state structure of the country would be so profoundly shaken, so gravely strained, as it evidently is today.

There is a kind of mythology of the *Bonne Entente*, of the amicable agreement between the national communities, that calls for a critical re-examination. According to hallowed legend, the inconvenience and curbs on liberty occasioned by the British Conquest and Occupation were eliminated by the granting of Assemblies to Lower and Upper

Canada in 1791; or if not then (since an armed insurrection for independence *did* occur within less than a half-century of that event), the
problem was solved with the granting of Responsible Government and
the Baldwin-Lafontaine coalition of 1848; or if not then, at least by Confederation...The effect of this version is to obscure a cardinal fact. While
it is true, and a matter of major significance, that *bourgeois democracy* (in-
itially the gift of the great English Revolution of the 17th century) was
secured by the British North American colonies, and later under *Colonial
self-government* 1847-67 — both involving the solidarity and joint efforts
of French and English-Canadians — the problem of *National inequality*
was left unsolved. This inequality was not only social and economic, but
political. And, as a general persistent condition of national inequality, it
has passed through a number of phases without ever receiving an effective solution. As the condition has been operative within the framework
of a social structure, of class relationships that have evolved, it has been
radically modified, but never fundamentally changed in the past two
centuries. The bloc of ruling social forces of 1763 is the historic
progenitor of the bloc of ruling social forces of 1963. (Stanley B. Ryerson,
French Canada: A Study in Canadian Democracy.)

To substantiate this point, Québec's leading historian, Prof. Michel
Brunet of the Université de Montréal writes in his *La Presence Anglaise et les
Canadiens* (p. 221):

> Starting with the decade of 1780, the fur trade, imports, exports, and a
> large share of the internal market belonged to the English mer-
> chants...At this time the English numbered no more than 5% of the total
> population of the St. Lawrence valley. Although the Canadiens then
> formed the immense majority of the population...they lived under the
> economic domination of foreign capitalists.

This domination was assisted by certain sections of French-Canada itself. Coupled with the high clergy of the Roman Catholic Church was a
small French-Canadian plutocracy. As Prof. Brunet states: "The French
Canadians acquire the marginal profits of a prosperity that is not the outcome of their initiative...[Their] lawyer-politicians were richly rewarded
as necessary intermediaries between the Anglo-Canadian bourgeoisie and
the mass of French-Canadian electors. Sir George Etienne Cartier is the
model of the species." (p. 223) This bears repetition — that it was these elements in French-Canada *plus* the British imperial administrators, and the
rising English-Canadian industrial power elite — that helped create
Québec's past and contemporary status.

The Situation of a People

> French Canada did not drop its guard at the time of Confederation, and
> subsequent events convinced it that the dice, all along, had been loaded
> against it. Polite talk about the partnership of the two founding groups
> meant little when bilingualism was an everyday fact only in Québec and
> only, to a great extent, among French Canadians, when it required years
> of agitation to achieve such a trifling "concession" as French terminology
> on federal government cheques, so many years that the final decision

was greeted in Québec with more cynicism than jubilation; when English-language Protestant schools were supported by taxes in Québec while Catholic schools in most other provinces were cut off from tax support and English was legislated as the only official language of instruction; when bilingualism in the federal civil service applied only to French Canadians, when in brief, English Canada let nature take its course in an English-speaking continent making many special efforts to provide for its special situation." (Peter Debarats, The State of Québec, p. 185)

But bilingualism and biculturalism are essentially used to cover politico-economic questions. In a survey of foreign ownership in November 1962, the *Financial Post* of Toronto called the 1950s and 1960s the "age of the Big Takeover." It claimed that in 1960, foreign owners controlled almost 70% of the assets of Canada's big manufacturing, petroleum and natural gas, and mining enterprises. According to the *Financial Post's* statistics, 38% of the capital employed in the pulp and paper industry, Quebec's biggest, was controlled by United States interests in 1959, not to mention British holdings. The ratio for mining, another major Quebec industry, was 53%.

Although statistics such as these are a constant source of irritation in Canada, English-speaking Canada at least has the consolation of owning what the American, British, and other foreign investors have left. By the time the English-speaking Canadians have helped themselves to these left-overs, there is not much food, except for thought, on the French-Canadian plate. (Peter Debarats, *The State of Quebec*, p. 157)

According to Prof. Leon Dion (*Globe and Mail*, Jan. 14, 1962), while French Canadians make up over 80 percent of the population in Québec, they control less than 20 percent of its industry. To the Quebecer, his economic domination is simply perpetuated by *"les anglais,"* especially when he sees that the statistics above have created only irritation in English Canada, whereas in recent times he has created and participated in movements for self-determination.

Today, these people do not understand what the new nationalism is about. Just because nationalism is traditionally reactionary does not mean that it has be reactionary. The new nationalism is not reactionary, at least in most respects. It is part of our coming of age.

It is hard for a French Canadian over forty to understand that the typical young French Canadian wants to free himself from foreign economic control, from capitalist control, and from Church control — all at the same time. People like Trudeau identify nationalism and separatism with a tendency toward revolutionary means and autocratic government. I think that he exaggerates. (Father Lévesque, Université Laval.)

Canada as a Bi-National State

Former Liberal Cabinet Minister René Lévesque once said:

A lot of people can find their places anywhere in the world but there is only one place that we can call home and that's right here. Quebec is on a road on which there is hardly any way back, a road leading very quickly to a full measure of self-determination as can be allowed in the world today to a small, compact and very resistant group of people.

This requires a sort of life-and-death dedication because there is not another single spot in the world for us. Lévesque is not talking about Confederation. He is talking about survival. "If Canada disappears, what does the English Canadian lose? He trades an imperfect system. He gives up British legal practices, the CBC, the Queen, the National Film Board and his treasured and traditional right to consider himself warmer and more aggressive than the British, colder and more dignified than Americans. If Quebec disappears, what does the French Canadian lose? Everything. (Peter Desbarats, January 1964, *The Montreal Star*)

If citizens of the Canadian Confederation wish to preserve a political presence on the continent of North America other than that of the USA, then this Confederation must be based on the equality of the two founding nations of Canada. *This equality is not an end in itself but a means to an end.* The *end* being a common struggle towards substantiating what "independence" there is left from the USA *in order to contribute better to world peace!*

Historically, the French-Canadians have found themselves dominated by English-Canadians. The injustices have crystallized around the particular denial of constitutional recognition of the full right of national self-determination.[1] The right of a people to arrange its affairs as it pleases must include the right to choose its own form of State, whether separately or in voluntary union with another nation. Full national equality for Québec requires the unequivocal recognition of its right to self-determination, up to and including separation should its people so decide. Such a position offers the only equitable basis for a lasting voluntary union within one federal State.

The only acceptable basis for such a bi-national State is one which recognizes the above within the primary context we described earlier, which itself will further the eventual dissolution of the Nation-State system. The initial phase of this process is a foreign and defense policy of positive neutralism for Canada. This reconstitution and rededication is unlikely to be created by the present mainstream institutions of our society. Only a massive social and political movement proceeding toward fundamental social change *and* world peace can do this.

Should this not prove possible, it would be with great sadness that we will experience the creation of another Nation-State, but it may be one which because of its historical roots, will be more oriented towards taking concrete action for world peace. The people of this upper half of the North American continent have a *last* chance. Can we together and separately reconstruct and reconstitute the Confederation on the basis of a non-aligned external affairs policy, a truly bi-national voluntary union with full self-determination for both language groups, including full human rights for every other human being and ethnic group?

"Québec Wants Peace"

Few Canadians are aware that the principle reason we do not have a garrison State military in Canada, including the draft, is because of Québec. "Constitutionally" the Federal Government cannot introduce conscription unless Canada is officially at war with another country, and this cannot be done without an act of Parliament. French Canada, largely for survivalist reasons, fought against war preparations and conscription on several occasions in its history.

There was the resistance by the French Canadians against conscription and involvement in the British military campaign during the American revolution for independence between 1775-77. Local actions against mobilisation broke out at a number of towns including Terrebonne, Verchères and Berthier. Conscripted militias in Trois-Rivières, Ile d'Orléans and the region south of the St. Laurent river below Québec City refused to march against the Americans. "Illegal" town meetings were held in many areas including Québec City.

French-Canadians resisted conscription and involvement in World War I, 1914-18. A great deal of violence occurred during this struggle, reaching near civil war proportions at one point. The significant fact however, is that the method of violence failed to stop conscription. It was only after the passage of conscription, when people adopted a policy of non-co-operation, that conscription was defeated to a very large extent.

The non-co-operation took the form of hiding the called-up youth and resisting the man-hunts waged by the militarists; 40.83% of the draftees were never found by the man-hunters! And this does not include the many more who had not registered and were therefore not listed in the government records.

The French-Canadians resisted the conscription to World War II. Although not on the scale as that of World War I, the most serious occurrences were fights between civilian youth and men in the armed forces. The 1942 referendum on conscription showed the population of Québec to be 72% opposed. The percentage among the French-Canadians alone was estimated to be 90%.

The Mayor of Montréal tried to initiate a campaign of civil disobedience by calling upon the population not to register for Selective Service. He was interned for four years in Ontario.

After the passage of conscription, a goodly number of youth took to the forests again. Government statistics indicated that the men fleeing military service in Montréal and Québec were more than half the national total.

There was also some resistance to the Korean war. During the campaign against nuclear bombs for Canada, both Québec trade union movements, all important voluntary associations, including youth and student groups, all major newspapers, and the official provincial parliamentary opposition, categorically supported it. The defeat of this popular campaign was a significant factor in the growing estrangement and resentment of young Québecers towards English Canada.

The well-known author, Miriam Chapin, in her book, *Québec Now* (1955) concludes with these prophetic words:

> Québec wants peace. It refutes those who think that because it is anti-Communist it should be eager to plunge into war with Russia or China. It spoke through the voice of the old Archbishop Desranleau when he said, "As well as praying for peace, we shall struggle with all our force and without ceasing against the crime which is the ideology of war. The war of today, serviced by atomic forces and scattering of bacteria, destroying cities instead of arms, killing men for the sake of raw materials and markets, this warfare which has already half-ruined the world, and which would complete the work for the advantage of a few arch-capitalists, it is absolutely necessary that it disappear from the earth."
> Québec wants peace, and it wants freedom, freedom from the bonds of the past and unjust burdens of the present, freedom to make its own synthesis of industry and human values. Québec is what makes Canada different from all other countries. It is the mustard plaster on the chest of the body politic, it is also the salt in the soup. It is Gargantua struggling to be born, it is Banquo's reproachful ghost at every political parley. It is funny, it is pitiful, it is exciting, it is magnificent. While Québec cannot in isolation realise its great future, it is likewise important to the rest of the world that the forces of progress win in Québec.

NOTE

1. The word "nation" in French means a culture, race or people. Colloquially in English it is assumed to mean a Nation-State, a sovereign political entity. Much misunderstanding has arisen because the two people use this word differently.

Spring 1972

SOCIAL CLASSES AND NATIONALISM IN QUÉBEC

In two major articles entitled, "Classes sociales et idéologies nationalistes au Québec, 1760-1970" published in the Montréal journal, *Socialisme québécoise*, No. 20, and a subsequent version, "La Structure nationale québécoise" in *Socialisme québécoise*, Nos. 21-22, both by Gilles Bourque and Nicole Laurin-Frenette, the raging debate on this question begun in the early 1960s was joined in a significantly new way. The two articles and Bourque's preceding book, *Classes Sociales et la Question Nationale au Québec 1760-1840* (Éditions Parti Pris) deserve careful study.

This debate, which has important political consequences for the future of Québec, has been contributed to by Alfred Dubuc, Gérald Fortin, Michel

Van Schendel, Marcel Rioux, Jacques Dofny, Fernand Dumont, among others. It has been largely discussed in the disciplines of sociology and history, as well as among the Left. Why is it so important, and how can it be instructive to people outside Québec?

This question can be answered in the following way. The outcome of this debate will determine what kind of *organising strategy* will be utilised in order to mobilise much larger numbers of the popular classes. Can the working population be reached by means of "class politics" or "nationalism" or a combination of both? What does "class politics" mean in this instance. Is there a "nationalism of the Left"?

Bourque and Laurin-Frenette insist that the only correct way to begin answering these and other related questions is to develop a satisfactory theory of the nation. Otherwise, they maintain it is impossible to emerge with a sound analysis of Québec reality, and a proper examination of the national question.

"Classes sociales et idéologies nationalistes au Québec 1760-1970" does essentially two things in this regard. It presents a theoretical framework with which to evolve a theory of nation, and then attempts to apply this structure to the history of Québec. The theoretical framework also involves a critique of the Rioux/Dofny thesis, the essence of which we shall present further on.

In this article, we shall attempt in turn, to address the following. We shall present in translation the substance of the Bourque and Laurin-Frenette theory of the nation, on which we shall make an *initial* commentary as to its limitations. We shall then outline their analysis of the class structure of contemporary Québec and its relationship to nationalism.

The aggressive and often bitter tone of Bourque and Laurin-Frenette's criticism of Marcel Rioux, Jacques Dofny and Fernand Dumont need not preoccupy us here. The position under attack is to be found in Rioux's "Conscience nationale et conscience de classes au Québec" (*Cahiers Internationaux de Sociologie*, Vol. 38, 1965, and *Recherches Sociographiques*, VI-I. 1965), as well as Rioux-Dofny's "Social Class in French Canada" (*French Canadian Society*, Vol. 1, 1964, edited by Rioux and Martin) and can best be summarised by the following:

> At this point I would like to clarify and nuance the hypothesis that Dofny and I have proposed on the relationship between ethnic consciousness and class consciousness. We have said than in every political crisis, it has been the ethnic which has prevailed and also prevented the development of a class consciousness among French Canadian social classes. In each of the following, the ethnic consciousness dominated: the Riel affair, the Boer War, the conscription crisis of 1918, the economic crisis of the 1930s and the conscription plebiscite of 1942. Even the economic crisis of the 1930s, which produced strong anti-capitalist sentiments in English Canada and a growth of class consciousness among certain elements of its working class, did not succeed in breaking this national consciousness. Even though the social and class structures of French Canada are not too different from those of English Canada, its system of values and its culture have remained much more homogeneous. It is this

factor which has delayed the development of class consciousness in Québec and particularly among the working class. (Marcel Rioux, *Cahiers Internationaux de Sociologie*, Vol. 38, 1965.)

Bourque and Laurin-Frenette have a completely different interpretation of Québec history. They see class antagonism throughout, particularly from 1760 onwards.

Bourque and Laurin-Frenette set forth their theoretical framework as follows:

The scientific concept of nation,....refers to certain characteristic features of a capitalist social formation. By social formation we understand, in the manner of Althusser, a particular mode of articulation of the economic, political, and ideological instances, determined in the final analysis by the economic. The capitalist social formation rests on a mode of production involving private ownership of it and free labour. It implies a principal contradiction between the productive forces and the relations of production.

The national features of the structure of a capitalist social formation are a) the existence of an economic unity, b) of a territorial, juridical, and political unity, c) of a cultural and linguistic unity of all the groups engaged in capitalist-type relations of production underlying the domination of one class, d) the ideological domination of this unity, in the form of "national," "national community," "national interest," "national will," and other such images. The nation is thus the specific effect of these aspects of the structure of the capitalist mode of production on its supports. Accepting Poulantzas' definition of the term support, it refers to the agents of a mode of production, who are constituted into classes by "the effects of all the structures together, of the matrix of a mode of production or of a social formation."[1] This implies that the nation exists objectively in the sense in which we have defined it, and must be brought back, contrary to what Fernand Dumont believes, "to objective factors of structure." We cannot simply consider the nation to be a reflection of, as Nadel and Dumont would have it, "whatever theory its members make of it."

In fact, during its formative phase, the capitalist mode of production absolutely requires the existence of these national features of the structure, of this type of economic, political, and ideological unity. The rising bourgeoisie creates and profits from this unity by using and transforming the political formations. More precisely, we can enumerate the following features: the creation of a national economy, a centralized national state, increased political, juridical, and customs unity within the territory, the abolition of local dialects and linguistic uniformity within national frontiers, the creation of various national symbols, etc. [2]

Bourgeois, nationalist ideology (or the nationalist elements of bourgeois ideology in general) is a deformed image of that unity necessary for the set-up and function of the capitalist mode of production and exploitation; a representation that clearly reveals the structural necessity for this national unity and, accordingly, its class character.

We understand nationalism to be an ideological formation with the nationalist strand dominating. This means an ideological formation whose principle theme represents a particular conceptualization of the nation, i.e. of the national features of the social formation.

At first glance, the definition which we have given of the nation as the specific effect of certain aspects of the structure of the mode of capitalist production on the supports of this mode, may appear tautological. Such an impression would be a natural consequence of the confusion generally surrounding the Althusserian-Marxist concepts of the mode of production, social formation, and social classes. It is not the definition of the concepts in question which is the source of difficulty, rather the absence of a specific concept allowing us to make a connection between the structures (mode of production) on the one hand, and practice (the social classes) on the other. The concept of social formation fails to do this, because it only indicates the specific articulation of instances of different modes of production. Accordingly, it characterizes structure and not practice, albeit at a concrete, real level. We can, on the other hand, correctly define social classes as the effect of the structures of a mode of production (or of the articulation of the structures of the different modes of production in a social formation) on its supports. The agents of a mode of production are constituted into classes by the effects of the structure of a mode of production, but it is also the structure of this mode of production that constitutes them into a whole, or totality, at the level of practice. We can only understand the concept of *class as effect* of the structure of a mode of production and its supports if we adopt a complementary concept which speaks of the whole or the unity of practice as an effect of the structure. At the level of practice, the structure of the mode of production constitutes the agents into a whole divided into classes. The existence of this class division, of antagonism between these classes in their diverse practice, implicitly assumes a "global field" of antagonistic class practices. This global field represents the effect of certain aspects of the structure of the mode of production; this same structure, but under other aspects, also has the effect of constituting the agents into classes.

We have seen in the case of the capitalist mode of production that certain features in the structure of this mode tended, in practice, to constitute the agents of this mode into a nation. Here, the nation is a particular type of whole or global field of class practice; a particular type corresponding to the capitalist mode of production in the same way that corresponds to this mode....What we wish to stress, however, is that the concept of nation in the capitalist system is derived from a more general concept, referring to what we can call the whole, the unity or the global field of practice as the effect of the structure of a mode of production.

Variations in National Structures

At later stages in the development of the capitalist mode of production (viz. the state of monopoly, imperialist capitalism), the nation and its ideological representation undergo certain transformations which we cannot analyse here in any detailed manner. The essential structural elements which have been enumerated above remain, but the need for greater cohesion and interdependence among the dominant classes of different social formations may modify or even render these elements obsolete. This cohesion often takes the form of domination of one national bourgeoisie over another, or the domination by an international bourgeoisie over several national bourgeoisie. The creation of blocs and economic, political and military alliances among nations...the abolition of customs, tariffs, and other barriers among certain countries, illustrate this evolution. Notwithstanding these modifications, the essential aspects of a capitalist type of social formation remain because they are vital for the maintenance of the domination of the national bourgeoisie in these countries, and therefore, for the reproduction of the mode of production. We can even state that in the final analysis, the existence of a national bourgeoisie is essential for the existence of the international bourgeoisie and its imperialist domination through international monopolies for a number of technical, political, and administrative reasons. Africa, where the imperialist countries have established national structures, is a strident example of this. These considerations, moreover, lead us to note the absence of a specific concept to designate the articulation of the economic, political, and ideological instances of a given mode of production at a level embracing different social formations of the same type...

Until now, we have been discussing national characteristics, including the evolution of these characteristics as a function of the development of the mode of production. We must, however, add to this first category a number of situations showing particular conditions. We can distinguish two types of situations.

a) A particular group (whether it be territorial, linguistic, or cultural) which exists within a nation and believes itself capable of constituting a nation by itself, as in the sense defined above; this is the case of Brittany, Flanders, and the Basque country.

b) The deformed or truncated nation which experiences a partial territorial, political, and cultural unity based on a regional economy, as the result of conquest or partial annexation by another nation. An example is Québec.

In these particular cases, the nationalist ideology will take complex forms. We will not attempt to analyse all the possible ideological representations resulting from different types of national situations. It is, however, important to note that this representation is, in the last analysis, determined by the economic situation of the dominant faction in a) the particular group and b) the dominated nation. Without entering into a detailed analysis, we observe that it would be possible to explain the fluctuations of Basque, Breton, and Flemish nationalism, by making use of this hypothesis.

It follows from the preceding that the national question is always tied to the specific articulation in the three instances of the capitalist mode of production. In saying this, we reject any definition of the nation which makes use of the cultural or ideological as the sole or principal criterion. In effect, there are a number of groups that define themselves as "cultural groups," but which have no special national traits at the economic or political level. This is the case, among others, of the Acadians and Ukrainians in Canada. We can explain these phenomena by the periodisation (rhythm of change) particular to an ideological or cultural instance, and by the specific autonomy of this instance in relation to others and its effects on a group arising from an earlier (Acadia) or external (Ukraine) social formation. We can now further elucidate the nature of nationalist ideology, by examining the question of social classes. It follows from the definition of the concept of nation that we have given above, that the nation exists as a function of the dominant class in capitalist type social formations, and of its economic, political, and cultural interests. The bourgeoisie requires the nation in order to dominate all the spheres of social activity: economic domination through the framework of the national market, political domination through a national state centralized on a juridically homogeneous territory, cultural domination through the national language, the culture, and so-called national symbols. The role of the ideological representation of the nation in bourgeois nationalism is precisely to mask the connection between bourgeois domination and the national features of the social formation that the bourgeoisie dominates.

We now have Bourque and Laurin-Frenette dealing with the question of *Classes and Nationalist Ideologies*. The section moves lightly through the classical Marxist position on the issue. This "position" was one of the weakest features of the work of Marx and Engels, and we shall deal with it later. However, the authors of this essay do make some important clarifications from a Marxist point of view which indicate some new insights. These insights are worthy of study in Québec and elsewhere:

> Must we logically conclude that nationalism is, by definition, a bourgeois ideology, whose essential function is to produce an inverted image of the real economic, social and political relations (the relations of domination and exploitation, i.e. class struggle)? Or can non-bourgeois nationalist ideologies exist, linked to the interests and situation of other classes within the social formation?…
>
> …The working class, because of its interests, may modify these national features of the structure; the State will be used by the proletariat and eventually disappear…But to realize these objectives, the proletariat must seize control of the nation and use it for its own ends. The national territory, the national State, the national language, the national heritage, can only be national "in the non-bourgeois sense of the term," serving the interests of the dominated classes, if bourgeois domination has been abolished.
>
> We are now in a position to state that a "non-bourgeois" nationalism…can exist. For the nation does not exist outside classes, but as a function of classes. It could not be otherwise because the nation is the effect of the structure of a capitalist social formation on the supports of the mode of production, and these supports, in the capitalist mode of production, are contrived classes. The significance of these national features varies with each class, in relation to the situation and practice of each class. Marxist analysis generally concerns itself only with the significance of these national features for the bourgeoisie which allows it mistakenly to identify nation and bourgeoisie, leaving the national interests of other classes to one side. We have clearly admitted that in its origins the effect of the structure of the capitalist mode of production is constituted "by and for" the bourgeoisie, but these structural features (economy, territory, national language, etc.) also affect other classes, corresponding to certain of their interests.
>
> We can now better understand the deforming character of bourgeois nationalist ideology. This ideology appeals to diverse national elements which it uses for its own ends, interpreting them in terms of its own interests, although they also correspond, as we have shown, to the interests of other classes. For example, both the workers and the bourgeoisie have an interest in defending the so-called national language when it is threatened, but given the real position of these two classes within the relations of production, this interest in defending and preserving the language is different for each of the two classes. This language is a tool for work and creation, for the workers as much as for the bourgeoisie, but the content and significance of this work and creation varies for these two classes as a function of their respective situations as exploited and rulers.

We can conclude as follows:

1) Nationalism (the particular importance placed upon the national features of a social formation) is by definition a class ideology.

2) Nationalist ideology does not have a single structure and content.

3) There are (or can be) as many ideologies containing nationalist elements as there are classes in a social formation.

4) Each class is capable of attaching a particular significance and value to the national features of a social formation, thus, of incorporating nationalist elements that are a function of its class position into its ideology.

It is clear that when nationalist elements are present in the ideology of the working class, this is generally linked to a situation of national domination. Even in this case, these elements are not the dominant theme in the revolutionary ideology into which they are incorporated. The revolutionary struggle of the proletariat is by definition international, especially at the level of imperialist monopoly capitalism. This internationalism, however, does not put into question the national character of the class struggle to which the nationalist elements of the working class's ideology are linked. It corresponds to the necessary linking of the national struggles of the working class in different social formations.

5) Culture is always a class culture, and the notion of a "national culture" is fictitious and ideological.

There is much with which we can agree in this presentation. What concerns us here, however, and this is the crux of our *initial* commentary in this article, is what is *omitted*. The omissions, which lead to serious distortions are a result of the narrow methodology used, which in turn, is a result of the most limited view of a materialist interpretation of history — the confusion of economic determinism with dialectical materialism. Only the fullest materialist view of historical phenomena can help us in this matter.

This methodological narrowness is a result of an attempt to return Marxism to the "new orthodoxy" by the French Marxist philosopher Althusser (whom it appears Bourque and Laurin-Frenette support) and the resulting departure from the new developments in neo-Marxism. Some of these developments include a fundamental re-examination of the relationship between "structure" (the economic mode of production) and "superstructure" (the State, science and technology). This can be an extremely important examination with wide-ranging consequences. By now, most revolutionaries working in industrial/technological societies assume as self-evident that the nationalisation of property and the means of production does not fundamentally alter the basic inequality between those who exercise power and those who are subject to it. That is, we are beginning to understand anew the relationship, and difference, between the realities called exploitation and domination, and that social revolution today must mean not only the end of exploitation of one person by another, *but also* simultaneously, the end of domination of one person by another. We no longer believe that "bureaucracy," "the State," will "wither away." The dogma that the "superstructure" merely reflects the economic mode of production is no longer supportable in the face of the assertion that the phenomena constituting the superstructure shape history separately and decisively. Thus, Rudolf Hilferding, a noted Marxist economist has written: "It is the essence of a totalitarian state that it subjects the economy to its aims…the Marxist sectarian cannot grasp the idea that present day state power, having achieved independence, is unfolding its enormous strengths according to its own laws, subjecting other social forces and compelling them to serve its ends…" Even the question of what today constitutes "the mode of production" is being re-examined, also from *within* the Marxist tradition.

Also, our concern with the "problematic" is that many of its ultimate political implications are not apparent in this essay. Such unstated implications can always emerge in practice at a later period and can be used by some "vanguard group" of intellectuals and politicians to justify this or that political line of action or programme. To us, the past and present Marxist methodology which attempts to deal with such social realities as "nation," "community," "culture," "nationalism," "national self-determination," "State," "superstructure," is important, *but strictly limited.* Indeed, the use of this methodology is very much dependent on its practitioner.

We will deal here with some of the contradictions in this methodology, and its consequent social theory.

We shall demonstrate as succinctly as possible, in this our initial commentary, that *first* Marx and Engels had no theory of the nation, and a very limited understanding of the origin and function of the Nation-State and nationalism (Horace Davis); *second* that the traditionally dogmatic analysis of the relationship between the "superstructure" and "structure" of society leads to the reduction of the significance of the "political principle;" *third* that historical phenomena must be viewed more dialectically and as a whole (Murray Bookchin); *fourth* that there is no mechanical cause and effect between economics and politics (George Lechtheim); *fifth* we shall pose an alternative hypothesis as to the origins of the Nation-State, and that it was not simply the creation of the bourgeoisie, but rather that the basis of the nation and national consciousness was laid down by the dynastic use of State power (Boyd Schafer and Rudolf Rocker); *sixth* that the superstructure's most political form, the State, has an importance which reaches back into history (Kathleen Gough); and *seventh* that Bourque and Laurin-Frenette blind themselves to the role and function of the State in particular (Peter Kropotkin, Colin Ward and Martin Buber), not only in history, but since this study is omitted from the "orthodox Marxist" methodology it forces them to neglect the "political principle" and the question of the superstructure today with the result that this will have the most unfortunate consequences for their recommendations to the Québec Left.

> *Nous pensons aussi, et sur ce point on ne peut qu'être d'accord avec A. Orr, qu'un malaise (est) ressenti par de nombreux socialistes révolutionnaires face à adopter sur "le problème national."* (From the introduction to the May/August issue of the Marxist journal *Partisan*, which is the first issue of a projected two issue study on "Le Domaine National")

Horace B. Davis in his *Nationalism and Socialism — Marxist and Labor Theories of Nationalism to 1917* (Monthly Review Press, 1967), indicates that the Marxist position on nationalism and the national question is filled with contradictions. Marxists thus start with the disadvantage that on an important question like this one, Marx and Engels never worked out a theory of the nation. Indeed their understanding of the rise of the Nation-State was limited, and their understanding of nationalism was even more limited.

As a young Hegelian, Marx was influenced by the concept of the State and community as being one and the same thing. Later, he concluded that the system of private property cannot be held together by the State "which is itself the creation of the bourgeoisie and does its bidding." (Davis, p. 5). Marx foresaw or hoped for the creation of a classless society within which a true community (Gemeinshaft) would exist, thus making the State unnecessary. It is in this way that he hoped for the State's disappearance and *not* through its outright abolition during and after social revolution which was the view of his contemporary, Bakunin. Marx never dealt with the *separate* but interrelated evolution of the State as a social organization. Thus, the relationship between this dominating social organization and its dynamics and effects, let alone its causes, were not clearly worked out with the forces and relations of production.

It is no wonder that Davis poses the question — "Did Marx think of the nation as identical with the State? Sometimes it seems so, since he occasionally used the term "nation" to refer to the Nation-State of his era." Davis puts it thus, "It is not even clear that Marx intended any theory of the nation at all. But it is surely high time that Marxists face up to the question, which was barely touched on by Marx and Lenin, of what is supposed to remain when the State withers away. If not the classless nation, then what?" (Davis, pp. 6-7.)

> When they [Marx and Engels] abandoned their early pro-imperialist line and sharply criticized the exploitative activities of the colonial powers, this shift represented progress and is surely commendable. But on some points, such as self-determination, the future of the South Slavs, the permissibility of offensive wars, the protective tariffs, and so on, we have observed contradictions and inconsistencies in their treatment. The unifying thread, as we would expect, was in general opposition to exploitation and a vindication of the rights of the underdog; but even this guiding principle is not always adhered to.
>
> The real problem of interpreting the attitude of Marx and Engels on nationalism arises when the several strands of their thought on nationalism clash, or when events fail to bear out their predictions, so that we are left to wonder which of several suggested alternatives they would have chosen. These problems began to arise already during the lives of both men. (Davis, p. 79.)

Finally, Davis notes, and we concur, "Marxist writers on nationalism too often think that when they have found an economic explanation of the phenomena, their task is finished. Actually, there is more to it than that, as our discussion should have made plain." (Davis, p. 213.)

This plainly stated is also one of the main contradictions in the Bourque and Laurin-Frenette thesis under review here. Without a broader materialist approach to historical phenomena, the rise of the nation as a *political* organization is never clear, the dynamics generating nationalism are not clearly understood, the State as the dominating social organization is not studied separately nor is its historic role and evolution. Indeed, the whole question of social organization and its accompanying effects of social domination, hierarchy, bureaucracy, as these are influenced by the mode of production and in reaction to it, remains vague. Without such a comprehensive approach, the social realities constituting "nation," "national consciousness," "class culture," and "community" also remain lacking in concreteness.

The essence of a radical analysis of society must be that it must be viewed *historically* and must be viewed as a *whole*.

For us, Murray Bookchin puts it most aptly:

> ...The great historic splits that destroyed early organic societies, dividing man from nature and man from man, had their origins in the problems of survival, in the problems that involved mere maintenance of human existence. (By "organic societies" I mean forms of organization in which the community is united by kinship ties and by common interests in dealing with the means of life. Organic societies are not yet divided into the classes and bureaucracies based on exploitation that we find in hierarchical society.) Material scarcity provided the historic rationale for the development of the patriarchal family, private property, class domination and the State; it nourished the great divisions in hierarchical society that pitted town against country, mind against sensuousness, work against play, individual against society, and, finally, the individual against himself. (From the introduction to *Post-Scarcity Anarchism*)

George Lichtheim makes the point succinctly in another way, that (a) the modern socialist movement was born in France, (b) that it was England and Belgium where industrialism was most advanced, (c) that this is an argument against those who argue simple *mechanical* cause and effect between economics and politics.

Looking back into history, change can be explained as much by means of change in the forces and relations of production as by changes in the nature of social organization whose highest form is the State. In antiquity, the main dynamic determining developments in the forces of production was the degree of external commercial intercourse, and the main dynamic determining the development of social organization was militarism. In both cases the main motive was *property* and *control*. During some periods of history, the first set of factors played the dominating role (merchant capitalism moved feudalism into the industrial revolution), during other periods the second set of factors played the determining, although not exclusive role (as with the change from tribalism to the city-State). There are still other periods when both sets of dynamics played an equally important role, constantly intertwined.

Nationalism and the nation are not static social realities, but are factors in evolution. The nation is as much a creature of the State (at certain stages of its development) as it is the creation of the forces and relations of production historically specified. That is, when royal dynasties of early modern times controlled the State, the Henry VIIIs and Louis XIVs, their predecessors and their successors for power, land, and wealth, *were* major forces in nation building. Nationalities like those of Yugoslavia, Romania, Hungary, and above all, Russia, came into being *without* a strong bourgeoisie and, in the latter case, found strong assistance for its national ambitions in the nobility of the land, the court aristocracy, as well as the orthodox clergy. Nations and nationality developed from the 12th to the 18th centuries. *The nation slowly became the people,* as opposed to the ruling class, between 1715 to about 1815. (See Rudolf Rocker's *Nationalism and Culture.*)

Therefore, a clear distinction has to be made between the rise of the *nation, national consciousness* (which had emerged by the 18th century) and *nationalism* (which had evolved by the end of the 18th century). Nationalism was that abstract liberal democratic notion that identified the nation as most of the people.

> It was primarily statism not nationalism, which characterised the governments of the Bourbons and Tudors and most other dynasties. (Boyd C. Schafer, *Nationalism,* p. 68.)

It is during this period that the *basis* of the Nation-State was born, and it was the *dynastic use of the State,* more than the changes in the mode of production *in this instance,* that laid the groundwork for future developments.

> ...they were establishing the governmental as well as the territorial foundation of the modern nation. In order to gain and retain power they had to obtain money through centrally levied and collected taxes, to establish a royal army and navy, and to erect a superior court system. And to carry out their will and government they had to have a great number of loyal officials. While the taxes, armed forces, courts, and officials were not national at first, they would become increasingly so.
>
> As the royal central government became more extensive and powerful, the governmental bases of the nation were being laid down. (Schafer, p. 68.)

> The State...in the economic as well as the political spheres, now combatted the "medieval combination of universalism and particularism." As it did so, it tended to centralise and unify the internal economic activities of each country, and, at the same time, to divide and set off the interests of each nation from every other nation. Though the end was state power, the means had to be national. The State had to strengthen the nation economically to be strong itself, and it had to try to weaken the other like Nation-States so as to be comparatively stronger. The result was stronger national States and a greater stress upon national interests. (Schafer, p. 76.)

This brings us to the common Marxist assertion, which Bourque and Laurin-Frenette also maintain, that the bourgeoisie created the Nation-State. This is simply not correct, the bourgeoisie created a *specific kind* of Nation-State, and helped unleash nationalism, the basis of which was laid, as indicated above, by means of State power. The means of production were throughout in a process of development. This development changed *qualitatively* at a certain point which gave the rising bourgeoisie the leverage to create a new kind of Nation-State, along with nationalism.

> It is clearly a mistaken view that the bourgeoisie was the agent of the modern national State. The western European bourgeoisie came to share or to obtain full political power in the eighteenth century in the name of the nation, and a national patriot was he who favored a government providing liberty and protecting property. The nation was no longer a king, his territory, and his subjects. It was now composed of citizens, propertied citizens usually, who inhabited a common territory, possessed a voice in their common government, and were conscious of their common (imagined or real) heritage and their common interests. (Schafer, p. 104.)

It is now even clearer why the omission of this historical dimension to the rise of the nation, the State, and national consciousness has profound implications for the revolutionary project of today, and contributes to the resulting confusion as to the relationship of nationalism to class, and to internationalism. Again, let us labour this important point at bit further. It is essential for a radical analysis to study *both* the political economy and its social organization, its dominating structure being the State. Both these features are intertwined, interdependent, sometimes one being more important than the other in the historical short-run, as far as the ultimate outcome of the revolutionary project. Anthropologist Kathleen Gough once explained it like this:

> Man, as distinct from his ape-like ancestors who lacked speech and other forms of symbolic representations, has probably been on earth for about a million years. The first States arose about 5,500 years ago, in Egypt and Iraq. Somewhat later — at various times between 3,000 B.C. and about 200 B.C. — States also developed independently in North China, North India, Peru, Mexico, and possibly, on the Niger in West Africa. It is interesting to notice that most, if not all, of these "primary States" appear to have developed on the basis of extensive irrigation works in arid regions near great rivers. That is, it was irrigation as a technological form which first allowed the productive surplus necessary to support a specialized government. Furthermore, it seems probable that it was the co-ordination of large labor teams, needed to maintain interconnected irrigation works, which fostered, and eventually required, a central government. It is probable that other States have been offshoots from one or other of these six or seven primary States. The State as a social form has therefore only existed for about one-two-hundredth part of man's history. It is important to notice this, because many people today probably think of the State as eternal. Quite the contrary — it may be one of the shortest-lived forms of human society. (Kathleen Gough, "The Decline of the State," in *Our Generation,* Vol.2, No. 1.)

Peter Kropotkin in *Modern Science and Anarchism* adds the following to our understanding,

The state organization, having been the force to which the minorities resorted for establishing and organising their power over the masses, cannot be the force which will serve to destroy these privileges,

and,

The economic and political liberation of man will have to create new forms for its expression of life, instead of those established by the State.

He claimed that we will be compelled to find new social forms of organization for the social functions which the State fulfils through bureaucracy, and that "as long as this is not done, nothing will be done." And finally, Colin Ward wrote:

What is it, Buber asks, that gives the political principle its ascendency? And he answers, "the fact that every people feels itself threatened by the others gives it its definite unifying power; it depends upon the instinct of self-preservation of society itself; the latent external crisis enables it to get the upper hand in the internal crisis…All forms of government have this in common: each possesses more power than is required by the given conditions; in fact, this excess in the capacity for making dispositions is actually what we understand by political power. The measure of this excess, which cannot, of course, be computed precisely, represents the exact difference between administration and government." He calls this excess the "political surplus" and observes that "its justification derives from the external instability, from the latent state of crisis between nations and within every nation. The political principle is always stronger in relation to the social principle that the given conditions require. The result is a spontaneity. (Martin Buber, in "Society and the State," *World Review,* May, 1951.)

The conflict between these two principles is a permanent aspect of the human condition. Or as Kropotkin put it, "Throughout the history of our civilization, two traditions, two opposed tendencies, have been in conflict: the Roman tradition and the popular tradition…" There is an inverse correlation between the two: the strength of one is the weakness of the other. If we want to strengthen society we must weaken the Sate. Totalitarians of all kinds realize this, which is why they invariably seek to destroy those social institutions which they cannot dominate. So do the dominant interest groups in the State……

Shorn of the metaphysics with which politicians and philosophers have enveloped it, the State can be defined as a political mechanism using force, and to the sociologists it is one among many forms of social organization. It is however, "distinguished from all other associations by its exclusive investment with the final power of coercion." (Kropotkin) And against whom is this final power applied? It is ostensibly directed at the enemy without, but it is used upon the subject society within.

This is why Buber declared that it is the maintenance of the latent external crisis that enables the State to get the upper hand in internal crisis. Is this a conscious procedure? Is it simply that wicked men control the State? Could we put things right simply by voting good men? Or is it a fundamental characteristic of the State as an institution? It was because she drew this final conclusion that Simone Weil declared, "The great error of nearly all studies of war, an error in which all socialists have fallen, has been to consider war as an episode in foreign politics, when it is especially an act of interior politics, and the most atrocious act of all." (Colin Ward, essay in "The Case for Participatory Democracy," 1971, p. 283.)

We would like to register our agreement with Bourque and Laurin-Frenette that culture is a class phenomenon and that the culture of a Nation-State is fiction. Equally, we would add that culture and nationalism are not coterminous; indeed, the former is a much sounder basis for new social forms than the latter.

Only such a *dialectical* analysis of the political economy (a view particularly relevant to our kind of society) that includes a study of the forces *and relations* of production, the structure *and superstructure,* ownership *and direct popular control* of the means of production, can enrich the poverty-stricken vision of the socialist project and transform it into a contemporary revolutionary project. All this is missing from the Bourque and Laurin-Frenette theoretical framework.

In summary, we might say that our *initial* commentary on the Bourque and Laurin-Frenette thesis under review here, looks sympathetically on several aspects of their attempt at a theory of the nation but bristles at the omissions, the wrong emphasis on what is primary and when, and on the lopsided view of historical phenomena which reflect a methodological poverty and an a-historical attitude.

To propose a new analysis of the origin of the Nation-State and thus nationalism, or at least a more enriched analysis (as Horace Davis suggests is needed) is synonymous with an invitation to be misunderstood by the traditional Left. The revolutionary project must be devoid of misrepresentation of reality, and new ideas must not be painful experiences but greeted eagerly and examined carefully provided they emerge out of the revolutionary tradition. This tradition however, is much wider than simply Marxism-Leninism, and in its "successes" it temporarily buried some of the important libertarian revolutionary traditions that are now returning at least in industrial-technological societies.

Québec's National Structure

Bourque and Laurin-Frenette now apply their theoretical conceptualization of the question under investigation in a fascinating and very useful manner. They deal with the specifics of Québec's national structures.

> We shall now try, making use of the theoretical approach outlined above, to study the specific case of social formation that is Québec. We shall attempt to explain the structural factors that give Québec a double class structure.
> Québec is a province inside the Canadian Confederation. On this basis, it has a state apparatus with certain powers, concentrated principally in the cultural and social domains. On the economic plane,

Québec constitutes a regional economy characterized by a double phenomenon of colonization:

1) Following the founding of the Canadian Confederation, Québec's economy came to be based on a type of industry using cheap labour: the dairy industry, textiles, shoes. In the pan-Canadian schema, Québec's economy is defined by its relationships to the Ontario economy.

2) Starting with the 1920s, principally because of her wealth in non-ferrous metals and water resources, Québec became a source of primary materials for American imperialist capital. Since the last war, American investments have tended to invade many different sectors of production.

With respect to the national question, Québec is therefore doubly interesting. In it we can study, a sort of structural condensation, the two forms which national oppression has assumed in the development of the capitalist structures of the mode of production: internal domination resulting from the ascendency of one nation over other nations occupying the same territory; external domination (colonialist or imperialist) resulting from the exploitation of one or several collectivities by a nation not itself interested in populating the subjected country or countries. In its first phase, the creation of national states marks the ascendency of the capitalist mode of production in different social formations. Within this construct, we can study not only the national characteristics of the class struggle resulting from the rise of the capitalist mode of production, but also the phenomenon of national domination which may result from one nation (and a dominant class within it) gaining ascendency over other weaker nations within the same territory. Québec is thus a dominated nation, within the Canadian national structures.

Bourque and Laurin-Frenette then deal with the Conquest, and Confederation in some detail. This is followed by a new section called, *Classes and Nationalist Ideologies,* and the first sub-section, "The Types of Nationalist Ideologies" is a renewed attack on the Rioux/Dofny thesis:

1) The notion of ethnic class explains no period of Québec history. Since 1760, a diversified class structure has existed within the two nations, present in Québec's social formation. We witness opposition between classes, or factions within each of these structures: the struggle between the administration and the English-Canadian bourgeoisie from 1760 to 1800 and the struggle between the urban and rural factions of the French-Canadian petite bourgeoisie from 1840 to 1960. The existence of this double structure does not prevent alliance between the ethnically differentiated classes: seigneur cum high clergy with the colonial administration from 1760 to 1800; seigneur cum high clergy, colonial administration, and bourgeoisie and English-Canadian bourgeoisie from 1840 to today. Even though the most fundamental conflicts oppose ethnically different classes (French-Canadian petite bourgeoisie / English-Canadian bourgeoisie from 1800-1840; French-Canadian working class — English-Canadian bourgeoisie 1945-70), the structure does not prevent collaboration on the one hand, between those members in the majority who are from different nations, and class struggle on the other hand, within each nation. The concept of ethnic class, therefore, cannot explain Québec history, and merely serves as ideological coating for the independence struggle led by a new faction of the petite bourgeoisie.

Rioux and Dofny define French-Canadian society as a nation and consequently, claim that French Canadians can be considered as an ethnic
class. It is clear that the concepts of nation and ethnic class are mutually
exclusive. The nation, as we stressed above, is the effect of certain
economic, political, and ideological features of the structure of the
capitalist mode of production. It therefore follows that when we make
use of the concept of nation, we are referring to a class structure characterized by a certain type of domination, that of the capitalist mode of
production, even when we are describing a dominated nation. An ethnic
group forming a single dominated social class cannot therefore constitute a nation...

Using this framework, the authors then go on to analyse in detail the
first two kinds of nationalisms:

2) Within a nation, there does not exist, as Dofny and Rioux suggest,
class consciousness and an ethnic consciousness that can transcend the
different types of class consciousness. Nationalist ideologies can only be
class ideologies. A nationalist ideology only makes sense when fun-
nelled through the class which becomes its propagandist. It is in this
sense that we stated earlier that several types of nationalist ideologies
can exist within a social formation. In Québec, we can thus delineate
three types of nationalist ideologies, which we can only explain by referring to their class origins:
    a) A conservative nationalism, defining the French- Canadian na-
tion as an entity with cultural peculiarities, enjoying certain rights that
protect these peculiarities, even while participating in Canadian political
structures. Within this ideology, we can distinguish two sub-types,
depending on its economic vision. The first was held by the seigneur and
high clergy from 1760 to 1840 and by the rural-based petite bourgeoisie
from 1840 to 1960, and was an ideology more or less immune to
capitalism, insisting on the agricultural vocation of the French
Canadians. The second was held by the urban faction of the petite bourgeoisie who, while stressing French Canadian particularism, insisted on
French-speaking Québécois participating in the Canadian capitalist
economy and on the possibility of their succeeding.
    b) A dynamic nationalism, oriented toward independence. We can
here recognize the ideology of the French-Canadian petite bourgeoisie
from 1800 to 1837 which sought to obtain political independence with
the aim of controlling capitalist development. We can also think of the
new faction of the petite bourgeoisie which was formed in the 1950s, and
which is now making an independentist thrust through the Parti
Québécois, with the aim of making Québec a kind of neo-capitalist State.
We shall return to this theme.
    c) A nationalist ideology which links national liberation to the es-
tablishment of a system of socialist self-management. This ideology, put
forward by working class militants and intellectuals, tries to reflect the
aspirations of the working class and to formulate the conditions for its
liberation.
    We observe that these three nationalisms, though all refer to the
three instances of the social formation, emphasize different features of
the Québec nation. The first type insists on the juridical and cultural features (recognition and protection of cultural rights and peculiarities).
The second, essentially emphasizes the political, seeking the transformation of political relationships in order to promote the economic and

cultural interests of the nation. The third type stresses the need to transform relations of production in order to abolish all forms of domination
(economic, political, and cultural).

There is, therefore, no nationalist ideology common to all classes in
the same nation. A nationalist ideology, in and of itself, cannot mask the
class consciousness of dominated classes. Rioux and Dofny forget that it
is precisely the character of any dominant ideology to cover up the
relationship of domination. Nationalism is only one element in a larger
whole tending to fulfil the same function. We do not intend to deny that
nationalist ideology can help mask the exploitation of dominated classes
in a specific way. We do, however, wish to avoid the confusion which
leads some to attribute this role exclusively to the nationalist character of
the dominant ideologies in Québec. It follows from this theoretical position that we can only come to grips with the nationalist character of an
ideology:

1) by relating it to other elements in the ideological formation into
which it fits;

2) by pinpointing its specific effects in the area of the class struggle;

3) by relating ideology to other instances in the social formation
(political and economic).

Bourque and Laurin-Frenette follow this up by dealing with
"Nationalism and the Clerical Aristocracy" and "The Nationalism of the
"Patriots'" and "The Nationalism of the Traditional Petite Bourgeoisie."
These need not preoccupy us here, since they are outside the limits of our
main purpose.

In dealing with "The Quiet Revolution or the United Bourgeois Front"
1960 to 1964 and followed by a period 1965 to 1970, Bourque and Laurin-
Frenette illustrate the rise to political power of the urban French-Canadian
petite bourgeoisie for the first time. This rise is paralleled with a new class-
based nationalism. From 1965 to 1970, however, this petite bourgeoisie split
into two, first at an ideological level followed by a political one. One section
from this split founded first the *Mouvement Souveraineté-Association (MSA)*,
which was followed by the founding of the Parti Québécois.

The Quiet Revolution in effect reflected the collapse of the hegemony
of the traditional class that had lost its economic base during the industrialisation of the 1950s, but whose influence still permeated through
"Duplessisism," the State, the Church, mass media and the educational
system.

There was, during this first period, an absence within the new urban
petite bourgeoisie, now the "ruling bloc," of any important ideological or
political struggle. This was the period of the consolidation of its 1960 victory. As time went on, however, two new factions began to slowly emerge.
This new split reflected what the authors call the "technocratic" faction of
the urban petite bourgeoisie and the "neo-capitalist."

In Québec, as in several other countries, these technocrats have come
into existence as a direct effect of certain features of the structure of the
capitalist mode of production in its advanced stage (capitalism of large
private and state-run monopolies). The appearance of a "technocratic"
faction reveals the existence of new developments and functions in the

capitalist production process. These new functions correspond to new kinds of managerial, administrative, organisational and planning needs of the production, as well as the consumption of material and symbolic goods. They connote a greater sharing of power and a greater complexity of the former direct relationship of exploitation by the private capitalist owner of the means of production of the salaried worker. We must add to this extension of functions, a change in one of the features in this relationship; the replacement by the State — collective capitalist entrepreneur — of the private capitalist, in certain cases. We suggest that this change in the structure can explain the existence of this technocratic petit bourgeois faction. In Québec, they are a French-speaking majority, concentrated in the public sector (Hydro-Quebec, the CBC, government ministries, universities, and trade union organizations).

The other faction of the petite bourgeoisie is based, on the one hand, on private (rather than state) ownership of the means of production, and on the other, on the more classical functions of property and property control in the modern capitalist enterprise. This faction of the French-Canadian petite bourgeoisie is numerically small; it consists of entrepreneurs (in industry, commerce, and services), financiers, and upper-echelon executives in large private corporations, usually Canadian or American. For lack of a better term, we can call them the "neo-capitalist" faction.

We have described the opposition between these two factions in Québec and over the means each would use to promote its economic and political interests within the system of capitalist relations. The technocratic group, has interests as a French-speaking group which, to a certain degree, place it in opposition to the French-speaking neo-capitalist faction and to the English-speaking bourgeoisie. It uses the State as the main instrument of economic development through its role of entrepreneur-employer; hence its insistence on strengthening the Québec State through political independence from Canada. (Obviously, only the Québec State can be this entrepreneur-employer State for the French-speaking technocratic petite bourgeoisie.) The main purpose of this drive is to strengthen the economic functions of the State: its role as capitalist entrepreneur on the one hand, the development and "rationalization" of the economy on the other through planning, social security, industrial relations. Pushed to its logical conclusion, the aim of the technocrats is to establish their hegemony over the bourgeois bloc which would become possible under a system of State monopoly capitalism.

We see once again that each nationalist ideology has a class origin. The technocratic character of this faction of the petite bourgeoisie explains the form of nationalism. Its independentism is only possible insofar as it entails a modification in the other instances of the structure of the capitalist mode of production, a modification which is this faction's specific effect, as we have seen above. This structural modification took effect in the years 1950-1970 analogous to those brought about in the arena of the class and national struggle by the economic and political transformations which we described in the period 1800-1837.

In the same way, the technocratic petite bourgeoisie is now trying to push further the tendencies to State capitalism inherent in the present stage of imperialist monopoly capitalism. It is doing this because this tendency can promote its interests as a dominated French-speaking petite bourgeoisie within a double class structure. The existence of a phenomenon of national domination in Québec explains this tendency, (unique in North America but common to a number of European capitalist countries) to displace the index of the political structural domination and to increase the importance of the economic, cultural, and ideological functions of the State.

We can thus understand the possible conflict of interest between the technocratic and neo-capitalist factions, as well as between this technocratic faction and the English-speaking big bourgeoisie. This contradiction remains secondary, insofar as the technocrats do not for a moment question the fundamental structure of the capitalist relations of production. But this contradiction does exist insofar as the strengthening of the State and its economic functions (the technocratic faction's objective) can harm the interests of private capitalism in certain cases (and only in certain cases).

The national situation, however, makes the contradiction between these two factions especially complex in the case of Québec, for it pushes the French-speaking technocratic faction into increased support for a State capitalist economy. In fact, the class interests of the French-Canadian neo-capitalist faction may be threatened insofar as the French-speaking technocratic petite bourgeoisie can only promote its class interests by strengthening the Québec State (independentism), i.e. by making Québec into a real nation. The French-speaking neo-capitalist faction also needs the Québec State in order to improve its precarious economic position vis-à-vis American and Canadian capitalists' all-powerful interests. The General Investment Corporation is an example of how the State serves its interests. But the French-speaking neo-capitalist petite bourgeoisie also needs the federal State which controls some of the main economic mechanisms and looks after the integrated functioning of the whole Canadian economy. It has as much of an interest in the maintenance of the federal State as does the English speaking bourgeoisie. However, the French-speaking neo-capitalist petite bourgeoisie needs the support of the English-speaking neo-capitalist petite bourgeoisie, to whom its economic interests are closely tied. It performs the role of a ruling class at the federal, and especially provincial, levels of government in the interests of this big bourgeoisie.

All these factors help explain the neo-capitalist petite bourgeoisie's opposition to the technocratic faction's independentist project.

Now at last Bourque and Laurin-Frenette deal with "The Working Class and Nationalism." But before we go into this, we must note, and with enthusiasm, that this early detection of the "technocratic faction" and its proposed use of the State not only is a great help in making us vigilant as to the present and future role and function of the State in Québec, but also (as is the case in some other industrial countries) has helped open and is considerably enriching the discussion of a society of workers' self-management: in a word, the whole anarcho-syndicalist perspective is brought back into consideration.

The authors believe that the working class and farmers of Québec have not as yet developed their own nationalism, just as they have failed thus far to develop their own revolutionary ideology.

We could say that the working class and farmers in Québec were completely impervious to the petite bourgeois nationalist ideology right through the period of the Quiet Revolution. On the other hand, they had to bear most acutely the consequences of the reforms which the petite bourgeoisie initiated in its own class interests; the dominated classes had, in large part, to pay for these reforms; increase in income and sales taxes, the upsetting of their traditional way of life. Insofar as the measures realized did not go directly against their interests, they failed to meet their most important needs and aspirations (employment, housing, debts, working conditions). Lacking their own political organization, independent of the bourgeois parties, the working class and farmers could only express their political opposition, by modifying the equilibrium between the bourgeois parties electorally. Thus, acting as supporting classes for the Union Nationale, they brought about the defeat of the ruling party in 1966. We must, however, note that this ability to modify the political equilibrium does not mean that the dominated classes have political power. The proof is that the party that comes to power will continue to serve the interests of the dominant class and its factions.

The technocratic faction of the petite bourgeoisie is now in the process of altering the political and ideological equilibrium between the petite bourgeois factions in its favour. This faction felt "strong enough" to found its own political party (the PQ) and engage in full-scale electoral battle. The effect of this was to leave the Liberal Party in the hands of the neo-capitalist petite bourgeois faction. However, like all political formations, the Parti Québécois can only come to power through the support of a large proportion of the working class and farmers. Everything seems to indicate that this party can count on such electoral support, in the intermediate and long term (though to what extent is difficult to say). Need we therefore conclude that the dominated classes would be prepared to adopt the nationalist ideology of the petite bourgeoisie, and more particularly its technocratic faction, for the first time since 1960? We do not think we should interpret the support of workers and farmers for the Parti Québécois in this way.

As the editors of *Our Generation* have indicated elsewhere, the urban working class will likely support whatever "solutions" are thrown into the air during the psychological frenzy of elections, provided the political party offering them can manipulate the discontent and the mental depression that often result from the domination and exploitation this class endures.

There is, therefore, no nationalist ideology or ideology with nationalist elements emanating from the dominated classes in Québec.[3] We can only discover a number of interests, of economic, political, and cultural aspirations specific to the dominated classes and linked to their situation; it might be possible to express these interests as national elements integrated into these classes' own ideology. We have noted the absence of such an ideology specific to the dominated classes, i.e. not integrated into the dominant classes' ideology, but opposed to them. By definition, such an ideology would be revolutionary, resulting from a situation where the struggle of the dominated classes against the dominating will have reached the revolutionary stage. We cannot analyse such a revolutionary situation or its eventuality within the framework of this article. We can only state the possibility that an ideology specific to the dominated classes in Québec may come into existence, and that it would contain non-bourgeois nationalist elements, linked to the economic, political, and cultural interests of the dominated classes.

We maintain that Québec workers can only accomplish their liberation from economic exploitation, the seizure of political power, cultural
affirmation, in short, the global revolution, if they can overthrow the
triple domination that stands in the way: that of the petite bourgeois
classes, of the colonialist Anglo-Canadian bourgeoisie, and of the
American imperialist bourgeoisie. The revolutionary ideology of
Québec's dominated classes will thus probably be anti-bourgeois, anti-
imperialist, and nationalist. Through its integration into a revolutionary
ideology, this nationalism would focus on the economic, politico-juridi-
cal, and cultural features of the nation at the same time, quite unlike
preceding nationalisms which tended, as we have seen, to stress political
features.

Clearly, this liberation of the dominated classes in Québec society is
linked to that of the North American proletariat as a whole. This double
character, national and international, of the proletariat's struggle, is a
specific effect of the structure of the capitalist mode of production. Any
attempt to deny one or the other, in analysis as in practice, will only hold
back the liberation of the working class.

Bourque and Laurin-Frenette completed the article under review here
several weeks before Québec's general election of April 1970. Thereafter
they added an appendix where they state and correctly so, that these elections in no substantial way reversed their analysis. The behaviour of the
PQ, for all the parliamentarisms elected from working-class districts, (Waf-
flers[4] please note) bears this out.

The impetus of economic (the general crisis in capitalism, unemployment, strikes and the forthcoming wave of strikes) and social developments
(the radicalisation of the trade union movement) since the fall of 1971 will
likely force the PQ to become more of a social democratic party.

The authors end with this sharp warning that others besides the
Québécois should note:

It would be disastrous if Quebec's revolutionary militants allowed themselves a useless and costly waste of time and energy, blindly ignoring the
experience of all revolutionary movements since the nineteenth century, and their own political experience in Québec (inside the RIN, Parti
Socialiste du Québec, etc.). These experiences have decisively proved,
we would argue, that the structures and political institutions of capitalist
society, like all other institutions in this society, are established, maintained, and used by the dominant classes as a function of their class interests. Whatever group uses these institutions and mechanisms will
only help to maintain and perpetuate them. It is absolutely impossible to
modify the capitalist rules of the game if you have not first destroyed
their *raison d'être*.

This class analysis of Québec, especially its contemporary one is brilliant, as is the description of the resulting various class-based nationalisms.
But the relationship between the analysis and the theoretical framework of
the "problematic" is a tortured leap, because it is ahistorical and omits the
larger "political principle." The resulting shortcoming of this programmatic
may mean a rush at some point to embrace "l'État paternal socialiste," in one
form or another. And the avoidance of discussion of the possible nature of a

working class "nationalism" is also disturbing. We do not think that it is a question of imposing from above a "new working class-based nationalism" on the exploited and dominated powerless in our society. It is simply that this question must be investigated by us systematically immediately (here the earlier mentioned issue of *Partisan* is a welcome development. It does not hesitate to discuss seriously the ideas of Bakunin or Luxemburg).

Finally, talk of socialist self-management fills the Left-wing Québec air, as well as the socially conscious population as a whole, in one form or another. A key dilemma which has not been faced as yet is where the bureaucratically degenerate State ends, and where self-management begins? This dilemma will not likely be confronted from within the Bourque and Laurin-Frenette "problematic." Theirs is a major essay whose significance has made an impact on us. It is, we believe, an analysis that has no pre-determined (again, except by its omissions) political line of action.

In discussing Lenin's classic, *State and Revolution,* Daniel Guérin states, quoting the text, that Marx and Proudhon were as one in desiring "the demolition of the existing machinery of the State." "The opportunists," Guérin quotes Lenin as saying "are unwilling to admit the similarity between Marxism and the anarchism of Proudhon and Bakunin." Let us be bold enough to apply ourselves to these important questions with the experience of the *entire* revolutionary tradition. We may make some startling new discoveries, and reach the exploited and dominated in our society with an enriched vision of liberation, that is freedom.

NOTES

1. Nicos Poulantzas, *Pouvoir Politique et Classes Sociales*, Paris, F. Maspero, 1968, p. 69.
2. We can thus see how the establishment of the nation itself results from the combination and articulation of the actual effects of the different instances of the capitalist mode of production. For example, the creation of the State which considers itself a Nation-Popular-State is a direct respond to the need to regroup the agents, conceived as isolated individuals in production. We know that what characterizes capitalist relations of production is the separation of the direct producer from his means of production; i.e. that the latter has no control over his conditions of labour and over the product of his labour. At the level of socio-economic relations this separation is legitimized through law (contractual law) and through ideology (liberal individualism). Poulantzas notes: "The institutionalized power of the capitalist State embodies juridical, territorial, and cultural conditions inherited from the preceding social situation and its own unity in its relations to socio-economic relationships — the economic class struggle — insofar as it represents the unity of the people-nation composed of agents installed as "personal-individual political" subjects; i.e. to the extent that it represents the political unity of the economic isolation which it itself produces. At the level of the relationship between the State and the political class struggle this leads to a seemingly paradoxical result, which is, in fact, the secret of this National-Popular-Class-State: the institutionalized power of the capitalist class State reveals its class-bound unity precisely to the degree to which it cannot pretend to be a National-Popular-State, a State which does not represent the power of one class or of determined classes. Rather, the State is seen as representing the political unity of private agents, caught up in economic antagonisms, and its function lies in surmounting the latter and unifying these agents into a "popular-national" corps." (Poulantzas, op. cit., pp. 300-301).

3. In this regard, we must not identify the ideology of movements claiming to "represent" the dominated classes with the ideology and real aspirations of the classes these
claim to represent. We can explain the Parti Québécois-oriented nationalism of a good
number of Québec union leaders, in the Confederation of National Trade Unions or
the Quebec Teachers Corporation, or the Quebec Federation of Labour, by the fact that
many of these leaders belong to the technocratic faction of the petite bourgeoisie, and
by the clear affinity that exists between the economic and political ideology of the Parti
Québécois and trade union ideology. For the business unionism, with a participatory
tendency that prevails in Québec union headquarters, mixed or pure State capitalism,
which in the last instance also constitutes the technocratic faction's political-economic
project, is their true ideal.
4. The Waffle was a temporary left-nationalist formation within and around the social-
democratic party in English-speaking Canada, the New Democratic Party.

REFERENCES

Benjamin Akzin, *State and Nation*, Hutchinson University Library, 1964.
Daniel Guérin, *Anarchism*, Monthly Review Press, 1970.
Dona Torr, *Marxism, Nationality and War*, 2 Volumes, Lawrence & Wishart, 1940.
Louis L. Snyder, *The Dynamics of Nationalism*, Van Nostrand, 1964.
Nationalism, A Report by a study group of the Royal Institute of International Affairs, Cass
    & Co., 1963.
Alfred Cobban, *National Self-Determination*, Oxford University Press, 1944.
V.I. Lenin, *State and Revolution*, International Publishers, 1932.
Rudolf Rocker, *Nationalism and Culture*, Freedom Press, 1937.
Murrray Bookchin, *Post-Scarcity Anarchism*, Ramparts Press, 1971, Black Rose Books, 1986.
Peter Kropotkin, *Mutual Aid*, Porter Sargent, 1959.
Peter Kropotkin, *The State, its Historic Role*, Freedom Press, 1969.
Horace Davis, *Nationalism and Socialism: Marxist and Labor Theories of Nationalism to 1917*,
    Monthly Review Press, 1967.
Boyd, C. Schafer, *Nationalism*, Gollancz, 1955.
Colin Ward in *The Case for Participatory Democracy*, Grossman Publishers, 1970, edited by
    Benello and Roussopoulos.

Spring 1972

MAY 1972 — QUÉBEC'S GENERAL STRIKE

Québec has probably lived through the most dramatic and intense week
of its history...never...has Québec risen to such heights of liberty...never have Québécois in such numbers shown their commitment to
liberty and their rights...Something has begun which nothing and
nobody can stop: a taste of real democracy. (Editorial in *Québec-Presse*,
May 14, 1972.)

The May general strike marks a decisive change in the development of social forces in Québec. It is essential to grasp what happened, so that when

the upsurge swells again, people across the country will know what forces are at play and will also know how to push it still further.

The strike was no mere protest against the imprisonment of labour leaders. The imprisonment and the repressive Bill 19 was the pretext for action because these acts embodied everything that working people here have learned to hate: lay-offs, high unemployment, exploitation, deceit, violence, and reactionary decision-making by a handful of men at the top. The workers' instinctive reaction was to strike at the only locus of power available, their place of work, and to fight militantly against lies and manipulation and other instruments of State violence which tried to break them.

In the midst of the strike, the commercial mass media said that there must be a conspiracy behind the popular actions, for without "goons" going around from factory to factory "forcing them to shut down," how could thousands of happy workers conduct the same kinds of struggles around the same basic issues in a dozen towns and cities?

Of course, everyone who participated in the May revolt knows there was no conspiracy behind it, not even a centralized leadership; rather, the strike was a spontaneous and elemental response to contemporary life in Québec. Yet the nature of a general strike will be difficult to understand, not only for those in power who believe that when the people act there must be a conspiracy behind them, but also by those on the Left who believe that only a centralized organization can lead mass struggles.

The strike represents a type of struggle which has not been seen in Canada for a very long time. The most important thing about it was that it was "out of control;" there were no leaders who controlled it — which is to say, the people who acted on their own controlled the strike.

We will not describe here in detail the whole range of actions that took place during the general wildcat strike, or assess its impact on this society. What we hope to do briefly is to outline the significance of this general strike as a revolutionary and democratic weapon for social change. It is a realistic alternative to various other forms of social and political action.

The outward appearance of the upheaval had to do with the fact that this spring 210,000 teachers (public school, high school, CEGEP, and university), maintenance workers, liquor board employees, public electricity workers, civic servants, hospital workers, and nurses had their collective contracts up for renewal. To strengthen their bargaining power against their common boss, the Québec State, they formed a Common Front which brought together the three main trade union federations — the Confederation of National Trade Unions, the Québec Federation of Labour, and the Québec Teachers Corporation. This working relationship, unprecedented in North American labour movement history, took place in a social atmosphere filled with a new social and political consciousness which had developed slowly over the last three years, but more intensely in the last eight months.

The demands of the Common Front included, a minimum weekly salary of $100 for all workers, equal pay for similar work for men and women, and an improvement in working conditions and job security. Social and industrial conflicts can transform themselves from minor to major revolts. And although the Common Front demands are the visible tip of the iceberg, its submerged bulk encompasses all the issues that workers feel affect their daily lives — the fact that they do not direct their production, that what they do is directed against their advantage in the short-run and in the long-run, in a way that tries to restrict their income, their working conditions, and a very authoritarian context in which they work.

After several weeks of delaying tactics by the Liberal Party government, the Common Front called for a generalized strike in the public sector.

The State responded with institutionalized violence by imposing injunctions to end the walkouts. Local labour leaders were fined and sentenced to six months prison terms, and unions were fined up to $50,000 each. This did not stop the strike. The State then imposed its infamous Bill 19 which slapped penalties of $250 per day per worker on strike, and $50,000 per day per union. The Bill also will impose a government-designed settlement by June 30th, takes away the right to strike in the public sector for two years. The Common Front categorically refused to negotiate under these conditions and the workers voted sixty percent in favour of continued strike action in defiance of Bill 19, although the percentage of those who voted was small. For a time the three leaders of the Common Front — Marcel Pépin, Louis Laberge, and Yvon Charbonneau — urged the workers not to return to work. Although they later changed their minds because of the small vote in favour, they were charged with contempt of court and received the maximum one year jail sentence. They refused to appeal and cheerfully went off to jail.

For the first time in the history of Québec or Canada, more than 150,000 workers in over a dozen cities and towns, without direct orders from above embarked on a general political and economic strike which began on May 9th and ended officially on May 17th defying Bill 19 and the State structure. Starting with 210,000 striking workers belonging to the Common Front, the number soon swelled to 350,000 workers. Workers spontaneously seized control of several towns and occupied radio stations which broadcasted revolutionary songs and messages. For the first time, organized labour directly challenged the status quo in its totality by defying State injunctions and propelling the demands of ordinary people into the political arena. There can now be no doubt that the "social question" has assumed the same, if not greater importance than the "national question" in Québec.

With the class-conscious slogan, *NOUS: contre le gouvernement* we witnessed day after day the closing down of mines, schools, newspapers, courts, construction sites, ports, and a whole variety of industries. Workers had set up councils which administered entire towns, and in other cases workers established control over the institutions in which they worked.

We shall now examine some of the revolutionary actions that took place, and then discuss the significance of the general strike.

Tuesday, May 9

Pepin, Laberge, and Charbonneau present themselves to their jailers. Head of the Policeman's Union asks his men not to take them into custody, and he is threatened with dismissal. Two thousand longshoremen (who have very good contracts by current Labour standards) strike at the Montréal port of Trois Rivières, and in Québec City. Teachers, maintenance workers, and hospital workers strike in various parts of Québec.

Wednesday, May 10
Fifty thousand (80 percent) of Québec's construction workers strike, paralysing all construction.

The mining town of Sept-Iles is taken over by workers and the local radio station is under workers' control for 12 hours. Mines and the port are closed and highways are barricaded. Non-essential commerce and all bars are closed. Food services and stores are warned not to raise prices.

Two thousand teachers in Joliette and Victoriaville strike.

Municipal workers strike in St. Lambert, and Becancourt.

Sporadic walk-outs in Montréal from hospitals, universities and CEGEPs.

Canadian Broadcasting Corporation's technicians in Montréal and Québec walk out for 24 hours.

Thursday, May 11
Eighty thousand (85 percent) of construction workers now strike.

Hospitals and schools remain shut down across Québec.

Workers from private and public sector occupy town of Thetford Mines and take over local radio station. A demonstration of 10,000 workers is held.

Thirteen hundred workers at the State-owned Hydro Quebec strike in the Laurentians. The hospital and radio station are occupied.

Workers control the city of Labrador.

Workers close down Wabush mines in Point Noire.

Quebec Cartier Mining, an affiliate of US Steel in Manicouaugan and Fermont is closed down.

Five thousand miners in Thetford Mines, Asbestos and Black Lake strike.

Twenty-five thousand workers in St. Jerome close down twenty-three factories, schools, hospitals, construction and public services.

Two bombs explode in Montréal's Metro electrical section, three bridges into the city are blocked for several hours, striking mechanics of Montréal Transportation Commission (city bus line) try to block garages, and demonstrations take place at the radio station CKAC which is owned by Power Corporation.

Friday, May 12
St. Jerome, St. Hyacinthe, Joliette, Murdochville, Sept-Iles, Hauterive, Thetford Mines, Lévis and Baie Comeau are occupied by workers.

Parti Québécois leader René Lévesque calls upon union leaders to appeal their cases and calls for renewed negotiations with the government.

Some 40,000 unionized workers (85 percent) strike in the North Shore area closing down among others, Québec North Shore Paper, and Canadian Reynolds and paralysing Chibougami, Murdochville and Hauterive.

Two thousand workers close the down General Motors assembly plant in Sainte Thérèse.

All daily newspapers (French and English) do not publish today as a result of the strike action by their workers.

Eight thousand city blue-collar workers strike in Montréal.

CBC (English) newsroom personnel strike for 24 hours.

Four hundred Post Office workers in the Main Office strike in Montréal.

Three thousand workers from the warehouses of the largest food chains, Steinbergs and Dominion strike.

Longshoremen strike in Montréal harbour.

Rally of 4,000 workers and students at Paul Sauvé Arena in Montréal.

Hospital workers expel administrators and set up workers' control at the psychiatric Albert Prévost Institute.

Saturday, May 13

By now some 18 radio and television stations across Québec have been occupied in one form or another for certain periods of time.

Ten thousand workers strike in St. Thérèse closing down large factories like General Motors, ITT, Secord, BMK, Hydro Quebec, Coronation Foods, Konnulu, Secant, Regent Knitting, and the Quebec Liquor Board.

The pulp and paper plant of Domtar is shut down in Trois Rivières.

Eighty percent of the teachers strike in Québec City.

Davie Shipbuilding as well as Canadian International Paper are closed down with 2,000 workers on strike.

Provincial Courts are shut down with 2,000 workers on strike.

Provincial Courts are shut down by civil workers and friends.

Eighteen hospitals are on strike in Montréal.

Joliette, Firestone, Abesc, Imperial Tobacco, Independent Cement and Vanchessa are shut down.

Sunday, May 14

Three thousand people camp outside Orsonville prison where the three Common Front leaders are imprisoned and hold a "Woodstock Orsonville."

Hydro Quebec workers come out against taking strike action.

The public sector in the Gaspé Peninsula goes on strike.

Monday, May 15

A Common Front of citizens' committees, food co-ops, community medical clinics, womens' groups, is formed to organize protest action against Bill 19 and government repression in Montréal.

The demands of the Trade Union Common Front are enlarged to include the demand to have the minimum salary in Québec at $100 a week for all workers.

The city of Sept-Iles (27,000) remains under worker control.

Tuesday, May 16
Five thousand, five hundred hospital workers at 11 hospitals remain on strike.
Thirty-four local hospital union leaders who were fined and sentenced to prison and who were out on bail, surrender to prison authorities and go to jail.
Thirteen arrested in Lévis while occupying a radio station.
Four thousand, five hundred aluminum workers in Arvida vote against strike but support Common Front.
Five hundred and fifty Hydro workers strike in defiance of union no-strike vote on North Shore.
One thousand, five hundred teachers strike in the Gaspé Peninsula.
One hundred workers are arrested during various demonstrations in Québec City, the port is paralysed by 2,000 striking dockworkers and 650 elevator operators.
Four thousand, three hundred Canadair workers strike in Montréal, bus and Metro drivers vote against strike action, strikes take place at Weston, Christie, Toastmaster, Robin and General Bakeries.
Striking workers at A&P bakery department in Montréal throw products into the streets before police arrive on the scene.

Wednesday, May 17
The Common Front calls for a "truce" period and a temporary end to the generalised strike.

We have given a most brief outline of the actions taken throughout Québec. What was the significance of the general strike?
First: a mass strike in the public sector, was joined by an equally massive strike in private industry.
Second: The sentiment for strikers always exists in one form or another among most working people because of the day-to-day conflict and tension at the workplace, the sense of insecurity due to inadequate wages and a resentment against subordination. Whether triggered by a small incident or moderate demands, a strike can quickly mushroom into an action that both at the conscious and sub-conscious level symbolizes the revolt of the alienated and the exploited. In the course of strikes, as in the case of the May general strike here, the ordinary life of workers broke out of its confines of boredom, and they had to think, act, and co-ordinate their activities for themselves. This experience can never be forgotten, and it will come into play again with fuller maturity next time.
Third: Once the self-activity and self-reliance of a strike breaks out, and as it grows into a mass strike, the emerging solidarity transcends the greatest divisions in the working class. Workers in completely unrelated industries and trades demonstrated solidarity for each other. Once the dimensions of social transformation become clear, other forms of divisions between working people, such as language and race, are also swept aside. One of the most important reasons why this strike was so extensive and so militant

was because of the large percentage of women involved. Thus, yet another division in social movements was overcome during the strike action.

Fourth: Because this mass strike challenged in no uncertain terms the real power-holders of our society, capital and the State, and because if it had continued to its end it would have replaced this authoritarian power, it can be considered a revolutionary action.

It was not simply a struggle between two groups or classes.

The very essence of a general strike is the development, out of necessity, of the skills of human solidarity, mutual aid, and self-reliance and self-management, which carried forward to their fullest. These skills are in fact the principles of a radically different form of society.

In our workplace and in our community life we are pounded by passivity and manipulated by authoritarian personalities and structures. Whatever group sense survives our early socialisation and schooling is systematically destroyed in the present structure of the workplace. During mass strikes we witness a gradual transformation of people and their relationships from passivity to participation in collective forms.

From participation follows the need for a radical redefinition of power, that is for popular and direct control. People thus begin directing their own activities in small and large groups. At one point in the strike this process of control or self-management arises out of the immediate needs of the strike, without which it cannot grow and expand. At another point, mass actions become an attack on the authoritarian organization of the management of the economy of government and social life.

Needless to say, expanding the experience of participation and control are not the only tendencies in mass strike. Within the strike movement itself there are those who in the name of "reality" wish to take over the leadership and direction of this activity coming from below.

Fifth: Besides having experienced the *reality* of directing and managing things themselves, the workers of Québec experienced an unprecedented solidarity with each other.

Sixth: Although most trade unions in North America are bureaucratic and hierarchical structures which allow next to no meaningful participation of rank-in-file members, in Québec this is significantly less so. The May generalized strike here was actively supported by the Common Front member unions — the Confederation of National Trade Unions, the Québec Federation of Labour, and the Québec Teachers Corporation, combining a membership of 750,000 workers.

Seventh: This was by far the largest worker action in the history of Canada, originating in the self-activity of the workers themselves with the active support of many others. It shows the potential and the dynamism of the social movement in Québec, and the possibilities of social revolution. The successes and militancy of the actions were directly proportional to the radical context of the history of each region (Thetford Mines, Sorel), the degree of recent New Left type organizing (St. Jerome), the presence of the most advanced elements of the new working class (Albert Prévost Institute, the CEGEPs and other schools) and the high degree of US imperialism (Sept-Iles).

The commercial and liberal mass media reacted with predictable hysteria. The Toronto newspapers in their fearful reaction correctly saw that the general strike posed the greatest threat to the established order to date. In Québec it has now become quite clear that the Parti Québécois is but one factor in the mosaic of social forces working for political and social change. Indications are that the Confederation of National Trade Unions will emerge even stronger and more influential after the spin-off of its right-wing group. The new trade union proposed by the moderates will take a minimum of 10 percent and a maximum of 15 percent of the current membership of the (Confederation of National Trade Unions (CNTU). The main body can then become even more radical. No wonder the commercial press urged the moderates within the CNTU to stay in rather than to set up a new trade union in order to prevent this further radicalisation.

In summary, we have tried to give a sketch of only some of the actions that took place during the generalized strike, and to outline its significance as a preparation for a future more complete general strike. No doubt the various old left sects in the country will have already rushed to print to indicate the weaknesses of this kind of revolutionary struggle. They will try to demonstrate that without a centralized leadership, without a Leninist vanguard party of professional revolutionaries who can orchestrate a social upheaval, a revolution cannot take place. Needless to say, we profoundly disagree.

> That the Leninist party is incapable of serving as a means to the kind of revolution we want has been proven by historical experience. When such parties have played a revolutionary role — in the underdeveloped role — in the underdeveloped world — they have produced societies controlled and directed by the parties acting as the state, rather than by the people. And in the industrial capitalist nations they have been condemned either to insignificance (e.g. USA, England) or to functioning as liberal reform parties (e.g. Italy, France). (From the introduction to *Workers Councils,* by Anton Pannekoek, a Root & Branch pamphlet.)

The goal of any revolutionary movement must be direct control of all social institutions by those who are engaged in them. The effort of any organization to substitute *its* control of society for this is a distortion of the social revolution.

Finally, there is a kind of convergence between the ethos of May 1968 in France, and May 1972 in Québec. It is not accidental that the most popular slogan in Québec is *"Ce n'est qu'un debut, continuons le combat,"* a slogan originating in May 1968.

THE CANADIAN ELECTIONS

The June elections have had a depressing effect on many of people. The range of reasons begins with the fact that many people took the elections seriously enough to work extremely hard at campaigning and canvassing. Yet the most sympathetic of the political parties, the New Democratic Party, made no substantial gains, indeed it was routed. At the other end, people like ourselves were saddened by the fact that so many took the electoral game seriously without understanding its true function and limitations.

The NDP put forward a good liberal democratic program of social reform, addressing itself squarely to some of the outstanding issues facing this country, pleaded reason with the electorate, and expected considerable parliamentary gains, but instead received a setback.

The Conservatives based their principal strategy on their analysis that the rising tide of nationalism in Québec could be channelled, with the help of the Union Nationale, into a "responsible dynamic," into a kind of "Duplessisism" and consequently, taken out of the hands of revolutionary nationalists as an instrument of mass agitation and constituency building. This strategy failed to do so; Québec nationalism can still theoretically go right or left, in the short-run.

The Liberal Party under the leadership of Pierre Elliott Trudeau won the game by playing it with extraordinary skill. The Liberals generated a façade of "popular participation" and with their immense financial resources plus a communications medium which by the very nature of its art becomes enraptured by "style," "form," "technique," "skill" and conse- quently, cannot deal with content, used all the modern Madison Avenue tricks to "win" the day.

With these techniques of persuasion, the Trudeau Liberals managed to manipulate the creation of a coalition of opposite tendencies from coast to coast, plus the dreams of the first pan-Canadian generation of youth who believe in bi-culturalism and bi-nationalism and who constitute an important percentage of the electorate, into a significant victory. Even so, the "image of participation" did not increase the voter turnout from that of the last election. The average across the country remained the same as in 1965: it increased in English-speaking Canada and dropped to about 60% in Québec.

Pierre Elliott Trudeau who has succeeded in staging a "palace revolution" within the Liberal Party and within the Canadian electoral system is a genuine liberal democrat but an aristocratic elitist. This may appear to be a contradiction on the surface, but it is not when one examines the implications of modern liberalism. Trudeau is an intellectual, the first in this country's history to become Prime Minister. He has a precise theory of politics. For many years he tried to persuade Canadian socialists to accept his theory of federalism (see "The Practice and Theory of Federalism" in *So-*

cial Purpose for Canada, M. Oliver, ed.) embellishing his sense of political strategy by quoting ironically from Lenin and Mao Tse-Tung. His notions of liberal democracy are Jeffersonian, expressed in 18th and 19th century imagery. Since he failed to persuade the socialists, he could only realize his ideal by running intellectual circles around the "non-ideological" Liberals supplemented the latest techniques of management, administration and manipulation. *Coups d'états,* palace or cerebral revolutions, however, do not succeed in changing very much. But then again, Trudeau is only a reformer.

The columnist Peter C. Newman recently wrote about the "business administration" types that Trudeau has surrounded himself with, along with an assortment of computers. The Prime Minister is certainly going to introduce technological management into mainstream politics, and Jacques Ellul's nightmare will unfold a little faster in this country — all this in the name of realising liberal democracy, but then again, this is the logical consequence of liberalism.

The Nature of Electoral Politics

The majority of people in this country have a "feeling" of tremendous distance between themselves (voting) and genuine political representation (elections) in this parliamentary bureaucracy. For the moment this "feeling" has no political expression, although the anger, despair and frustration are expressed in many acts of violence. Present day political institutions were developed at a time when a far less bureaucratised and centralised society existed within a competitive *"laissez-faire"* economy. Power today is monopolized in immense bureaucracies which have become political institutions due to the effect and role they perform in society. The power of the gigantic corporations is *informed,* to be sure, but there is little doubt that the attraction of real power from the formal political institutions makes a hollow chant of the sung virtues of "pluralism." Couple this development with the density of power at the top of the parliamentary pyramid, and both the legislature and the electorate are reduced to ritual.

This concentration of power, plus the new manipulative methods of conditioning public attitudes and motivation through the mass media which celebrates the "values" of a compulsive society of consumption, cause us to question the electoral system per se.

The issues dividing the political parties in this country are artificial: questions of *management* rather than *basic policy.* Electoralism is fundamentally ritualistic. The important questions of the day — the nature of growing liberal totalitarianism, the growing distance between government and people, the lack of content in our lives and the purposelessness of our society, racism, the arms race and so on — are not usually put before the people. This is a phenomenon characteristic of our type of society.

The profound crisis of our society is not, and cannot be explained to the people by our political parties, because it cannot be set within a programme for the "democratic" seizure of administrative power which has no room for changing the nature of power politics. Even when fundamental social questions are put forward, electoralism forces them to be put according to a traditional pattern, to be applauded not because they are worth applause but because applause has always been accorded them.

The electoral system in a consenting neo-capitalist society serves the purpose of creating a sense of identification and excitement but in this largely fails and seeks to do so. Politicians and opinion-makers exert strenuous efforts to fix attention on the ritual act itself, in this case, the casting of the vote. Voting as a result becomes an isolated, magic act set apart from the rest of life, and ceases to have any political or social meaning except as an instrument by which the status quo is conserved. Electoral pageantry serves the same purpose as a circus — the beguilement of the populace. The voter is reduced to voting for dazzling smiles, clean teeth, smooth voices and firm handshakes — playing the role of a shaking puppet manipulated by the party image-makers.

If we could vote for those who in fact control the country, for example, the directors of the Royal Bank of Canada, the governors of universities, social welfare agencies, of industrial corporations and the shadows behind the ministries, the trappings of liberal democracy would be understandable. The real power centres lie far beyond the people's influence at elections. These remain constant *whatever* Party is "in power" as long as the system remains the same. In terms of this type of centralized "democracy" the only possible argument to justify participation in electoral politics, or voting during general elections, is that *marginal* benefits may be gained. The *raison d'être of the Nation-State and its power elite is to keep itself* intact, the rest is incidental. Its main concern is its relative power in relation to other sources of power in other States, and this finds its most perfect expression in defence and external affairs, matters *most* inaccessible to the electorate.

On the other hand, radicalism — used in its root sense here — is a strong and central concern with the *fundamental* questions, the essential problems of our social existence. These questions lie beyond the conventional confines of government institutions or established public values.

In the period of primitive capitalist accumulation, it was the socialists and the labour leaders who spoke most directly to the issues of industrial democracy and social security — the terminal issues of the time. The changes these movements demanded of the structure of 19th century bourgeois society were so far-reaching that only revolution (or severe dislocation of world war and protracted depression) could bring them about. Both for what they demanded of the social order and for the methods which they developed (unionization, the strike), the socialists and their allies could genuinely be regarded as radical.

What turns yesterday's radicalism into today's conventionality is, ironically, a combination of compromise, success and the development of the fundamental problems into new forms. It has been a long, uphill fight for the labour movement and its allies, but isn't it clear enough that *that* battle has been superseded in our society, making it politically safe, so that the official politics of the last twenty-five years has been to consolidate that victory.

The difference between Liberal, Conservative and NDP parties is no longer one of conflicting visions of society. What distinguishes the parties are a great many scattered and random technical proposals as to how best to finance and manage the welfare state. The difference between the political parties is one of managerial technique — but is this a conceivable difference worth analysing, or deciding upon? It is not a difference that is intellectually liberating or morally compassionate. This is very obviously a serious conclusion to reach and to recommend, or at least sanction. For it implies that the political parties — *all of them* — are not operating within the province of *deep political concern*. This is not to say either that objectively "it makes no difference" who wins an election. It is rather to say that the "difference" is so slight in degree or exists in such relatively trivial areas that one might very well bypass the area of electoral politics as being irrelevant to any fresh and profound issue of political circumstance in which such questions might more naturally be confronted.

The Poverty of Existence

The new radicalism on the other hand, concerns itself with the boredom and conformity of life in the midst of the cybernetic economy; with the human need for creative work in the midst of societies of abundance; with the continued restriction of inner and outer freedom; with the absence of compassion and community and purpose in the midst of a highly industrial technology which ultimately feeds the military machines.

It centres itself around the necessity of transcending territorial allegiances, and dismantling the genocidal war machinery that now contravenes not only the people's interest that it is supposed to defend, but also man's basic biological existence as a species — issues the socialist parties, not to mention the others, lost touch with in 1914. Clearly, the revolution in North America is going to have to be the type of revolution which by the very nature of our technological level of development forefronts such revolutions to occur throughout the rest of the world.

In the face of this need for revolution, electoral politics are meaningless, for elections are not won at these terminal points; they are won amid tried formulas, old slogans and the familiar. They are won by proposing changes of degree, not of kind, by working for adjustment, not transformation.

Towards a New Democratic Movement

Assuming the above analysis to be essentially correct, what do we do? We must begin with a new political sociology which gives us fresh insights into the process of social change. In Canada, unlike the United States, we have a clearer barometric reading of people's dissatisfaction with the status quo. Of the seventy to seventy-five percent of the electorate that voted in June (7,880,434), 17 percent (1,360,330) voted for the New Democratic Party. Without embellishing this percentage of the electorate with protest votes given to other political parties in particular circumstances, the NDP voters, however myopic most of their understanding is of the dynamics of neo-capitalism, do represent an important indicator of people's desire for some kind of social and political change.

The conventional weaknesses of the NDP as a political party are compounded by its aura of unreality. It lacks all social and cultural reality. Besides the work of its professional politicians and party organisers, little goes on in the organisation at the constituency level in between elections. The people who voted for the NDP do not feel themselves part of an ongoing movement of social action. The populist roots of this organisation have evaporated. It is at the complete mercy of the commercial press, our corporatist educational system, and our lobotomized cultural institutions. At best is "prays" for fair play within the process of established power politics and rarely gets it. Despite its hard work at electioneering (never has the NDP worked harder at winning than this June) the mass frustration that is sublimated in between elections is given no form or substance. In between elections there is no way to act directly on a particular issue except to write to your MP, or to form an *ad hoc* action group.

We wish to briefly state that there appear to be two positions amongst us. Both have particular weaknesses and strengths. There are those among us who believe that parliamentary democracy as a system does not permit fundamental change and we would, therefore, move out of the whole process of electoralism and party politics into the area of creating a non-violent revolutionary movement for peace and freedom which challenges the established order at its base. There are others among us who believe that the genuine liberal democrats and socialists within the NDP can be given maximum leverage within the electoral process only if we have in this country a mass populist social action movement that far more profoundly involves its supporters. Whether one school of thought or the other is correct will largely be determined in future debate, and by the course of events. The debate cannot be dealt with within the confines of this editorial. The important point to understand, however, is that the mass of people must be vitalised and involved in a movement for a democratic society over and above a electoral political party.

What do we mean by a social movement? We mean the creation of a movement of people who participate on a day-to-day basis in changing the society around them by changing the meaning of their work style and their life style. Wherever we are working, in school, office, factory, the arts, we must challenge daily the meaningless and purposeless nature of our work, its dehumanizing and bureaucratic nature, its automatic absorption of American values with the object to create a process of liberation and to develop new constituencies. In our personal and public life we must embody the notion of struggle as the *only* means of achieving freedom. Commitment must take on a new and fresh meaning. A new life style will involve debunking any established piety — in thought, dress, speech patterns, art forms, social and sexual behaviour, even in stimulants. In our life styles the values of spontaneity, experimentation, individual style and free expression must again be celebrated. Our revolutionary times demand no less than a revolutionary personal and cultural transformation. This movement must *build* the alternative institutions of change, and *resist* directly and militantly the injustices of this pathological society. It will, in many respects, be a collective act of *civil* disobedience.

But in addition to this, what do we mean by a social and cultural reality for a movement? A radical movement cannot wait to change society "when it comes to power." It must do so from the beginning of its existence by building counter-institutions. This includes everything *from* strengthening and radicalizing the co-operative movement, whether in housing, food purchase, legal and medical aid, insurance, and capital borrowing *to* the creation of new primary, secondary schools and free universities. Such a movement could challenge the status quo with its own values and its own resources. It would not be dependent in the pathetic way the NDP is dependent with its 18th century rationalist approach in an irrational system.

Consider the immense resources of the establishment. In contrast dissent and social criticism in this country have the strength of a twig in a thunderstorm. In Montréal alone, to give but one example, a local hot-liner with a salary of $85,000 a year dominates the most listened-to English-language program while haranguing against the NDP consistently for several weeks before the elections. The example can be repeated a thousand times across the country in a thousand different ways.

Such a social movement as we propose would bring together all our resources to create a massive internal and public educational campaign. It would generate a movement which is decentralized in small face-to-face groups engaged in common work. A publishing company would be established so that the manuscripts which are now being rejected by commercial corporations would be printed and widely distributed. Radio stations would be established, and eventually television programmes. Daily, weekly, and monthly periodicals and newspapers would be created. Research and training institutions would be established.

Such a programme of building the institutions of a new society and the technical apparatus of contestation and education makes the possibility of radical politics common sense. It is a truism to say that we live in a time of social revolution, and we are either in or out of that process, there is no in between. Only such a social and political movement will give us the fair opportunity of radically improving the classical pattern of revolution — that is to say, revolutionise revolution. Only such a movement whose dimensions we have barely outlined here can create a classless and warless society where there is direct democracy and where, as a consequence, people have a firm control over the decisions that affect their lives.

CANADIAN INDEPENDENCE AND THE MARXIST LEFT

> When the revolution is far off, the difficult task of the revolutionary or-
> ganisation is the practice of theory. When the revolution begins, its dif-
> ficult task is more and more the theory or practice. (Anonymous)

The relationship between US imperialism and Canada raises the question
of the relationship between the development of Canada since its founding
as a Nation-State and its socio-economic system. These two aspects are part
of the same process of history. A complete analysis of colonialism and imperialism north of the 49th parallel cannot in turn be separated from the
question of the relationship between Canada and Québec on the one hand,
and the relationship of these two principal cultures within their territories
to other racial and ethnic minorities. In other words, the pattern of exploitation and domination has many overlapping features. All are interdependent, one feeding on the other. This system of relationships cannot
be abolished without a wholesale sweep from the bottom to the top.

What has the Canadian Marxist Left to say about all this?

We will not deal here with the multitude of Marxist-Leninist sects,
whether they be Stalinists, Trotskyists or Maoists. With the exception of an
issue of the *Progressive Worker* produced in Vancouver, devoted to "Independence and Socialism in Canada — A Marxist-Leninist View" which represents a sophisticated view of this ideology, our efforts in obtaining the
positions of the other vanguard workers parties met with little success. We
can only come to the conclusion that they do not have a developed position
on imperialism and the national question in Canada. We do not deal either
with the "arrivistes" or "nouveau-marxists" in Ian Lumden's confusing
book, *Close the 49th Parallel — The Americanization of Canada*. Instead, we
choose to deal exclusively with the best of the independent Marxists.

In an edited collection of important writings, *Capitalism and the National
Question* by Gary Teeple[1], a number of essayists assert some basic positions
with which the editors of *Our Generation* can only agree. The book has the
natural weaknesses of any collection of essays and it is noted by the editor
that not all the contributors will necessarily agree with either the entire contents of the book, or some of the fundamental positions taken by him or his
colleague Tom Naylor with whom Teeple shares a great deal. But the book, as
the sum total of its parts does not clearly put forward that no country's social
problems are the basis upon which any independence movement should be
built. These social problems must be set in their cultural setting which entails
an understanding of the specific mould of these problems in Canada.

In his contributions to the book, Teeple maintains that Canada "has
the political trappings of independence but not reality because politics
under capitalism are ultimately subordinate to the amassing of capital by
individuals and corporations, the most powerful of which in this country
are American." Teeple further maintains that there is no Canadian ruling

class as such, distinct from American capital. The capitalist group here is basically an extension of US multi-national corporations and has no collectively expressed desire of its own to establish anything different. He writes:

> Most of the large concentrations of capital today, perform complementary (or at least non-contradictory) roles in relations to US capital — the form of which is more powerful because it dominates the sphere of production, while Canadian capital prevails largely in circulation, that is, in transportation, communication, retailing and finance. The Canadian capitalists who accumulate the capital in the area of "circulation" invest it in turn in sub-imperialist activities, e.g. the Caribbean, Brazil. This is a privilege they are accorded by metropolitan US imperialism.
>
> The central fact of the Canadian ruling class before and after Confederation was, and is, its foundation in mercantile capital. (A thesis attributed to Naylor, the editor.) This form of capital is accumulated in the process of circulation of goods; that is, money is made by buying and selling articles (raw materials or manufactured goods) — not by producing the article, this latter process being the basis of industrial capital. It is this central characteristic of the Canadian ruling class which explains why, even to the present time, Canada has not become the industrial nation with a large population that it might have been. The point is, as Marx argued, that "wherever merchant's capital still predominates we find backward conditions."

This thesis is supported with an impressive argument found in Tom Naylor's "The Rise and Fall of the Third Commercial Empire of the St. Lawrence."

In it he contends that:

> ...conventional liberal studies have failed to give explicit consideration to the peculiarities of the Canadian capitalist class and Marxist studies have misinterpreted its character. By comprehending this class as a mercantile one, accumulating wealth through circulation rather than production, one realizes that the dominance of a few staple trades leads not to independent capitalist development, but to the perpetuation of colonialism and underdevelopment. Canadian Confederation results not from the inability of the Canadian bourgeoisie to find a new dependency. The National Policy was one of mercantilism, of consolidation and expansion within a strong state structure.

Naylor's Harold Innis-inspired thesis which is offered as a neo-Marxist perspective clashes with the traditional Marxist thesis *Unequal Union*, by Stanley Ryerson. Ryerson suggests that Confederation was the result of a drive by growing industrial capitalism to harmonize tariffs among the various British North American colonies; in other words, that there was a direct lineage between the old mercantile and the new industrial ruling class. Naylor, on the other hand, writes, "Finance capital emerges, not from industrial capital, as usually supposed, but from merchant capital, through the pooling of merchants' resources and their development of a banking structure, and through the earnings of the entrepôt trade. Corporation capital in its American form thus merged industrial capital and finance capital never became a potent force on its own."

Teeple sees the "new national consciousness" as a product of certain sections of the middle class professionals. He asserts that without fundamentally challenging the established order, "compromise and accommodation will be used to mitigate the nationalist complaints of professors, teachers, artists, lawyers, engineers, government functionaries, and other technocrats...But what has not been so subject to appeasement is the struggle between labour and capital — in the main, American capital."

What is important to underline here is that both Teeple and Naylor repeatedly make clear that there is no independent capitalist group either English- or French-speaking, which has national interests as a class that are in contradiction with those of the US power elite and ruling class, or with their multi-national corporations. Although in the last few years since the Canadian centennial celebrations many people have been caught up in "a feeling of being Canadian," the process of integration into the American empire is so far advanced that nothing short of a social revolution can reverse the tide. The previously mentioned middle-class professionals do not have the stomach for initiating such a struggle as a group nor do the Canadian capitalists feel their interests clashing enough with those of the Americans to justify allying themselves, however cautiously, with any radical departure from the status quo.

Unlike Québec where the awakening and active resistance of a small group of cultural workers had an enormous impact in a society which was isolated by its language, the problem in Canada is quite different. In the broad cultural world we find a tremendous tension between regions in Canada. The small beach-heads established in Toronto and elsewhere among publishers, artists, writers, playwrights are in continual competition for the "too little, too late" handouts that some provincial governments and the federal State offers. And on the whole, cultural workers in Canada are so deeply colonized that they simply grumble a bit, and accept. In Québec, on the other hand, we had a period of tremendous social conflict during the early 1960s; when large sections of the student population were mobilized, a full blown terrorist campaign was underway, and militant minorities filled the streets with a variety of direct action. The climate in which the small minority of English Canadian middle-class professionals and the Québec cultural workers voiced themselves was dramatically different.

Teeple goes on to say, "Any profound challenge to the domination of capital, domestic and foreign, must begin, as it has in Québec, in the organised sector of the working class, because this sector has the means — at present poorly used — to organise and raise consciousness of the class which creates wealth but does not benefit from it." "That struggle, in the context of the "national" boundaries of Québec gave rise to a "common front" of unions and articulated class consciousness in the face of American capital and its administrators in Québec." This, needless to say, is facile substitutionalism. The forced interaction between the CNTU and QFL (Québec Federation of Labour) in Québec, not to mention the CEQ (Centrale de l'enseignement du Québec), plus the absence of a long-established social democratic party like the New Democrats converges into a particular set of factors underlining the origins of the Common Front. In Canada, the powerless strata of the wage-earning population cannot wait for some similar changes at the top of the trade union pyramid to say and do the things that its counter part is doing in Québec. We shall return to this later.

Nevertheless, the primacy placed by Teeple and Naylor on mass actions in the context as they analyse it, places the "social question" well ahead in importance to the national question in Canada. By the social question we mean that people's desire for social justice is much stronger than any national consciousness which concerns itself with mere symbolism or problems estranged from people's lives. Only when the solutions to social problems are impeded by the presence of imperialism, is it logical and necessary to add the national context. This happens to be the case with reference to almost all social problems in Canada today. But this approach to imperialist domination is far wiser and less likely to degenerate into jingoistic chauvinism or national liberationism which postpones the abolition of a class society and capitalist relations of production to the distant future.

One implication of this primary emphasis on people's social problems and the condition of their daily lives is that there can be no "first state" coalition with the few nationally conscious capitalists. This latter view is usually propounded by Marxists, and is supposed to encourage more individual capitalists to seek their fortunes with the nationalists, and at the same time show still other industrialists or businessmen an alternative to US domination. This is the "national liberation front" idea. It is a strategy used in "third world" colonies. Thus national liberationists here appeal to "all Canadians" and are convinced that once the dynamic of nationalism spreads we can begin the break of US control. It is then, contended that another "stage" emerges after victory when the working class settles its accounts with Canadian capitalists.

We are leery of abstract "stages" of development for coalition movements. If the analysis presented by Teeple/Naylor for instance is a correct one, namely that there is no independent Canadian *group* of capitalists that have fundamental differences with the American way of doing things, then the social struggle of ordinary people is the most important hope we have. This class of people must start its own liberation from the bottom of society (and in some instances has begun to do so), without formal alliances with privileged individuals and elites at the top of the power pyramid. The powerless class in Canada has no one to rely on but itself, and its weapons are creative social conflict, class struggle, and mass mobilisation, along the lines of an extra-parliamentary opposition. This is a clear rejection of the national front strategy, whose core idea is collaborationist no matter how "temporary," consisting of a coalition of various national interest groups and a multi-class approach that puts the growth of nationalism first, and "national independence" before social revolution.

What has been the background to popular struggle for social justice in Canada? Volumes can be written, but unfortunately, Canadian historiography is blinded by the recording of what various elite or amorphous social forces did and did not do, rather than accounting for popular struggles. *The People's History of Cape Breton* or Jack Scott's forthcoming *Class Struggles in Canada, 1789-1899* represent the kind of approach to history which is most meaningful. In another fine essay in *Capitalism and the National Question,* Roger Howard and Jack Scott in "International Unions and Ideology of Class Collaboration" add more evidence to the perspective of placing the social question first, and how from this position it relates to the national question. The authors deal with the fight for socialism, and the struggle between classes within the concrete setting of the all-pervasive influence of the reactionary American trade union organisation, the AFL-CIO's presence in Canada. The relationship between the form and the content of the social struggle has two aspects and is squarely stated. 1) There is a need to break organisationally from the American unions, and this must be done because a full social mobilisation of the working people of Canada must be based, and can only succeed, in the context of the historical experience and capacity of this class, set in the particular cultural topography in which it has developed and functions. 2) Howard and Scott, whose essay is superior to that of Lipton's in the same book, state,

> It is clear that a total break, organisationally *and* ideologically, with the internationals is a necessary first step towards the building of a movement that will serve the real interests of Canadian workers. If the organisational change is not accompanied, or preceded, by ideological change, there will be no possibility of permanent transformation; for it is in the field of ideology — the policy of class collaboration — that labour and especially its "left" section, suffers the greatest defeat... American unions fight furiously for control of Canadian locals and, in recent years, have spent millions to defeat efforts to establish an independent Canadian movement. John L. Lewis once claimed for instance that the United Mine Workers of America poured $1,124,000 into Nova Scotia up to 1920 to prevent the creation of a Canadian union.

With the rise of industrial unions

> ...the leaders of the AFL [American Federation of Labour], in fact, cooperated with the government and employers in destroying industrial organisations, such as the Knights of Labor, IWW [Inudstrial Workers of the World] and One Big Union. This situation was to continue until grassroots pressure led to the organisation of the Congress of Industrial Organisations.
>
> The AFL started out as an organisation based on principles of exclusion, and was bitterly opposed to industrial unionism, especially as it was represented by the Knights of Labour.
>
> Antagonism developed and the AFL appointed John Flett as their paid organiser in Canada, charging him with responsibility for quenching the flames of revolt. At the TLC (Trades Labour Council) convention of 1901, President Ralph Smith dealt with the growing crisis, saying: "I think it is of vast importance that this Congress should adopt some method of increasing its own usefulness. There ought to be a Canadian Federation, for, while I believe that unionism ought to be international in its methods to meet the necessity of combatting common fores, this use-

fulness is only assured by the strength of national unions. A federation of American unions represented by national unions, each working with the other in special cases, would be a great advantage over having local unions in Canada connected with the national unions of America."

The pro-internationals element was at a disadvantage at the 1901 convention. To avoid defeat on the issue, they adopted the tactic of tabling Smith's recommendations for an independent Canadian federation until the Berlin (Kitchener), Ontario, convention scheduled for 1902. This gave the AFL organiser Fleet and his colleagues another year to mobilise support.

Following his report on anti-AFL sentiment in Canada, P.M. Draper, general secretary of the TLC, appealed to the 1901 AFL convention for additional funds to be assigned to Flett, and warned that "a very strong feeling" in favour of national unions was growing in Canada. The convention delegates responded by voting $300 to finance Fleet's activities, and a convention committee commented, "It is to be regretted that…there seems to be a tendency toward severance among our Canadian brothers." Flett and others busily whipped delegates into line for the 1902 convention, while international executives put pressure on Canadian branches. J.H. Watson, BC vice-president of the Trades and Labor Congress, complained: "what do we find? Canadian organisers paid by the American Federation of Labor organising members of local unions and drawing their charter from a foreign country. But Flett's (and the AFL's) concerted and well-financed campaign proved unbeatable. Even Smith failed to get delegate nomination from the Nanaimo, BC, branch of the United Mine Workers, whose district he represented as a member of Parliament. Instead, he was delegated by a Vancouver local union.

A study of the 1902 convention proceedings suggests that the Canadian independent group realised that defeat awaited them. Only a token fight was offered; and after a one-day debate, the delegates passed a constitutional amendment which shaped the destiny of the Canadian Labour Congress from then until present. The amendment read: "in no case shall any body of workingmen belonging to any trade or calling at present having an international or national union be granted a charter. In the event of an international or national union of the trade or calling of the unions so charted being formed, it shall be the duty of the proper officer on the Congress to see that the said union becomes a member of said international or national union. Provided that no national union shall be recognised where an international union exist."

That "international" meant "American" was made very clear in 1912, when British-affiliated unions were expelled. The congress elected the AFL organiser, John Flett, as president, and he went begging to the American masters in a resolution: "Resolved that as the Trades and Labor Congress of Canada has placed itself squarely in accord with the principles of international unions, and as such action will reveal the loss of revenues…it is the opinion of the Congress…all federal labor unions and central trades and labor councils should be instructed to take immediate steps to make such arrangements with the American Federation of Labor."

The question of charters was referred to the Executive Council, which met with Flett and Draper in Toronto on 25 April 1903. Council minutes show how these two colonials represented Canadian interests: "President Flett and Secretary Draper said they were willing to concede the issuance of charters to the AFL." The request for the rights to issue charters was withdrawn without even a reference to the Congress which had passed the resolution. The line of capitulation was clearly drawn, and from this point on a long list of American-supported functionaries would attack independent unions as dual organisations.

The evidence points to a deliberate plan of conquest plotted by the American unionists, and the record of the AFL of Latin America tends to support this thesis...

Quoting at length from the Howard/Scott essay is justified because of the little known origins of the domination by American unionism in Canada. But we also want to quote at length to outline the resourcefulness and tremendous capacity of the working people of Canada. During the period when American unionism sought to control the labour movement here the One Big Union emerged. It is important to note that the OBU arose during a period of social conflict.

The most significant attempt to create an independent Canadian trade union movement was the organisation of the One Big Union. It was called into existence during the upsurge of labour radicalism by 1921-22. But during this short period of activity, the One Big Union raised some of the central issues involved in the development of an independent movement.

The impetus for the organisation of the OBU arose from the dissatisfaction of the more radical union leaders (almost entirely Westerners) with the prevailing policies of the international labour movement. These dissatisfactions centred around two interrelated themes: class collaboration and trade union organisation.

The issue of class collaboration came to a head when the conscription bill was introduced into the House of Commons on 1 June 1917, the day the US Congress adopted a draft conscription law. Prior to the war, the TLC had denounced the impending conflict as a struggle between the capitalist classes of various nations in which the working class had no stake. Even after the declaration of hostilities and the shock of the disintegration of international labour solidarity, the TLC opposed conscription either completely or within the context of the demand for "conscription of wealth" (i.e. nationalisation of industry) if conscription of manpower were legislated. But with the passage of the conscription bill and wholehearted support given to the war by the AFL, the leadership of the Canadian movement wavered.

At the TLC convention of 1917, the radicals proposed a national general strike to block conscription. But the TLC executive rejected this proposal on two grounds...

The first objection was because it would break the law, and the executive did not want to oppose the Federal government.

And the second objection was this:

It is just as well, at this time, that I should point out that the organised workers of Canada stand in a position that has no parallel in any other country of the world. This Congress can only exert its moral influence in the enforcement of decisions, and the economic power to support legislative demands is not vested in our movement, but is under the control of international officers of our representative unions. When the executive council of the American Federation of Labor reaches a decision, members of that council, being heads of powerful international trade unions, can use their influence effectively. The same applies to the parliamentary committee of the British Trade Union Congress, but in Canada we cannot use our economic power without the sanction of the heads of our international unions...In cases where our decisions are at variance with decisions taken by the American Federation of Labor regarding important national issues, it is difficult to secure that sympathy, that support in the exercise of our economic powers, as we otherwise would receive if the executive of the Congress were composed of powerful economic organisations. As a delegate put it: "President Gompers had committed the workers of the United States to conscription; therefore, a general strike was not feasible."

This issue, and the question of labour leaders participating in government bodies, plus that of industrial versus craft unionism, moved the radicals to organise the Western Labour Conference in Calgary during March 1919. One of the most important debates centred around political activity.

Although it did not go as far as the IWW stand of rejecting all political activity, the conference did reject the narrow parliamentarian view of politics. In the words of one delegate: "Power in politics is not found in Parliament but in the country prior to the election. Politics only exists where there are classes, and any action taken by a class in defense of its interest is political action. Hence you cannot define any particular action as political, but any action...used to control political power in order to use it for the benefit of that class — that is political action, and it matters not what method it takes." The founders of the OBU considered ongoing education in class consciousness to be more significant than occasional election campaigns and allocated one-third of its monthly dues to the general executive board for that purpose.

Howard and Scott then proceed to discuss the defeat of the Winnipeg General Strike by the combined forces of the Canadian ruling class and its government on the one hand, and the American Federation of Labour on the other. The authors also criticise the policies of the Moscow Communists in undermining the internal solidarity of the OBU by adopting the policy of the US Communist leader William A. Foster which was one of working within the AFL and not founding separate trade unions. These people still maintain this permeationist "boring from within" position today in Canada, as do the Trotskyists and the New Democratic party. We do not support this position. On the contrary, libertarian socialists have never shied away from the task of building new institutions or new organisations from the bottom up as the occasion determines, especially when bureaucratic degeneration has set into the established ones. There we join those who would urge the creation of new independent associations of producers in Canada. This is not simply a call for independent national or nationalist unions, but rather for new unions within a framework of revolutionary syndicalism.

We wish to use the same criteria consistently. To urge the creation of nationalist trade unions in and of itself is to urge a dangerous half measure.

It's the previously mentioned "first stage of development" approach again. The working people, both unionised and non-unionized, when they are prepared to move, will see through this "intermediate" objective. Again, as in all other questions, the social content of the conflict must come first, and not the form.

Howard and Scott sum up by saying:

> But necessary as it is as a preliminary step in the direction of more important developments, the switch from international to independent Canadian unions will not, of itself, result in any fundamental transformation of the unions from organs of class compromise to weapons of revolutionary class struggle.

They go on to add,

> The roots of the crisis in the unions are internal, not external, and are embedded in the class-collaborationist policy which is built securely into what has become the main activity and proud achievement of the labour movement — the union contract, the signing of which is a fundamental act of compromise with the class enemy.

Finally, the authors do well to warn us that,

> It would be a serious mistake to equate the union movement with the working class. The bulk of the working population is not in the organised union movement.

Ending the book, Teeple has an essay called "Liberals in a Hurry: Socialism and the CCF-NDP," and Naylor adds an appendix on the same question called, "The Ideological Foundations of Social Democracy and Social Credit." These essays contain many important insights, including some dealing with the origins of the CCF. When we hear certain nationalists in Canada rail against various "American ideological influences on the Left" while at the same time upholding the NDP as a genuine Canadian invention, they should be reminded, if they are at all aware of it, about the disastrous influence of British Fabianism on the CCF and later, the NDP.

Teeple ends his essay by challenging the stream of socialist orthodoxy on the question of State-ownership of the means of production. He rightly takes on this powerful myth, not only to demonstrate the vacuous nature of CCF/NDP socialism but also to bring in the more generous vision of Marx. We shall deal with this later.

With reference to the Waffle, Teeple again rightly suggests:

> The Waffle, however, is due some credit for helping to develop a consciousness of the colonial nature of Canadian society. Although this left wing has attempted to link the struggle for independence from the United States with socialism, these two struggles are linked only in name because the Waffle has not moved beyond democratic liberalism.

To summarise this collection of essays: Canada is not now and has never been an independent country; it does not have now and has never

had an independent ruling class; it has no independent trade union movement, and the few efforts attempted in this direction were crushed, with
the collusion of certain sections of the so-called Left. Finally, any independence movement has to be based on a radical analysis of the day-to-day
problems of the working people, namely, the primacy of the social question
is the only genuine basis for struggle against foreign domination, and for
collective self-determination. Further solutions to these social problems
must not be sought in vague abstractions, but within the cultural backdrop
out of which they arise, which entails an understanding of the specific
mould these problems in Canada assume. The impossibility of finding
solutions for some of our social (economic, political, cultural) problems in
a thoroughly colonised society under the domination of US imperialism
will make the relationship between the social and national question clear.
All this is implicit in *Capitalism and the National Question,* and a logical extension of its arguments.

Well and good. Much beyond this point, the book arouses all the disap-
pointments that most collections of essays generate. The book brings
together the work of some of Canada's outstanding independent Marxists,
a relatively rare event on the Canadian Left. For instance, there is a very
competent treatment of the class structure in Canada by Leo Johnson,
which is recommended although its relationship to the national question is
unclear.

Nevertheless, the book collectively demonstrates the limitations of
Marxism in Canada, and even more the abject poverty of the socialist
project. It is stunning to us for instance, that although the book is called
Capitalism and the National Question in Canada, there is in fact no thorough
discussion of contemporary capitalism. In other words, capitalism in
Canada is in no way situated in the general development of international
capitalism, and the array of contradictions in which its contemporary form
is immersed. There is no discussion of the nature of the productive process
in Canada, and the relations of production. There is no thorough discussion of the nature and present crisis in the meaning of socialism, or what a
socialist programme should include in Canada. There is no discussion of
the Canadian Left, outside of the NDP. And finally, there is no discussion of
a revolutionary strategy or alternative, namely, how and with what new
principles can we get from here to there.

Even a bare outline of some of the missing discussions is imperative for
our part if we are going to take seriously the present discussion of the social
revolutionary project. To begin with, we may be reminded that in an earlier
section of this critical review essay, we stated that it is incorrect to pay attention to Canada's ossified "federal" political superstructure. In effect, the
different principal regions of Canada, and in some cases the provinces, are
more genuine geo-political units than the federal one, and that any revolutionary movement must first and foremost be rooted in this regionalism.
This means that movement building will have the quality of regional
authenticity. Different regions having different urban/rural relationships
will mould the movement differently there than elsewhere. The political

economy of the regions and the level of its development will contribute in particular ways to the strengths or weaknesses of the movement.

This means that when we speak of putting social problems in their cultural cast, we mean placing them in their localist setting, taking into account the particularity and history of the popular struggles, popular aspirations, and quests for social justice of the region in question. What we are admitting here is reality: namely, that the west coast, the prairies, northern Ontario, southern Ontario, the Maritimes, and the North have much more of a cultural reality to them than the vague abstraction called Canada, held together by a powerful centralising State with its mystified but socially impotent political institutions. Indeed, there are probably cultural subregions within these larger land masses we just mentioned, such as Acadia, or Cape Breton in the Maritimes. Any movement solidly rooted in such organic areas becomes virtually impregnable against outside assault, especially if it is also based on a popular revolutionary consciousness which is itself interlaced with the daily lives of the people of the area. Any federation based on these genuine units, co-ordinated over the years from the bottom up, is more likely to be organic and meaningful.

But, in order for this rich diversity not to degenerate into balkanism or fragmentation, the decentralised and localised social struggle envisaged here must be of a libertarian nature. Not only would it otherwise be reactionary and bankrupt, it would also not work, and this would allow for the complete triumph of US imperialism. The kind of social struggle which is seen here as necessary is identical to a libertarian socialist revolution for, this is the only way it can survive and flourish. Such a mass movement based on small autonomous units blended into local and regional cultures, eco-systems in fact, will not only be self-reliant, but will implement large-scale co-ordination in a more egalitarian and effective way. Such a revolutionary movement would be more of a reflection of a future liberated society, than any vanguard political party ruled by "democratic centralism" and its consequent military discipline which inevitably leads to Stalinism. What, in effect, is foreseen here is the exact opposite of the traditional "revolutionary" group's view of social struggle.

The only realistic defence for areas north of the 49th parallel is by a people with a high consciousness of solidarity and mutual aid, capable of struggling city by city, community by community, street by street. The actual means of defence are several, and need not be discussed here. All potential enemies would know that any attempt at conquest would meet with total resistance.

But what are the conditions in our society which are laying the basis for the emergence of such a movement? More precisely, what is meant by the social question in the light of this perspective? At this point, we wish to offer a number of theses.

1) The changes undergone by capitalism during the last fifty years show themselves primarily in the increasing concentration of both capital and bureaucracy.

Monopolies, trusts, cartels, multinational corporations abound in countries of "private capitalism." During this same period of development the State has become the main economic factor and co-ordinator in these countries.

This process of concentration has led to certain changes in the economy. The failure to recognise these changes accounts for the shallowness of much that passes as "Marxist analysis" today.

The increase in the mass consumption of commodities has become an essential feature in the smooth functioning of capitalism. "Commodity fetishism" has become an irreversible aspect of this kind of society. The old forms of capitalism as characterised by economic depression, massive unemployment, and general stagnation must be put aside. Neo-capitalism generates expansion of both production and consumption for the sake of consumption, interrupted by minor fluctuations. This "ideology of growth" is obtained at the cost of an increased scope of exploitation and alienation of the producers in the course of their work. Labour discipline is bought especially in key industries, at the workplace in exchange for certain wage concessions. Increases in wages on the whole now approximate increases in productivity of labour. This means that the proportion of the total social product going to workers and to capitalists remains constant.

2) *The social structure has changed with the growth of bureaucracy*

The modernising of capitalism has meant the "rationalisation" of human activities. The bureaucratisation of all spheres of social life becomes a dominant feature of our type of society. In the process, inherited individual wealth is not the only criterion whereby influence can be gained either in the economy or the State.

The "traditional" ruling class based on the ownership of heavy industry, manufacturing, bank, insurance, is forced to share, on an increasing scale, the functions of administration and management both of the economy and of society at large, with a growing bureaucratic stratum. This has already happened in Canada during the last fifteen years and has brought individuals into the power structure whose ideology is part and parcel of Canadian liberalism grounded in the "Pearson Years." In Québec, the situation is somewhat different as this stratum developed much later on.

This stratum, in Canada or in other advanced capitalist societies, has become an indispensable part of the smooth functioning and "efficient" operation of the economy and shows deep, irreversible changes in its structure.

The bureaucracy has some of its roots in the workplace. The concentration of capital and the "rationalisation" of production from outside, create the necessity for a bureaucratic apparatus in the factory, office, or institution. The function of this apparatus is to "manage" the labour process and the labour force, and to co-ordinate the relations of the enterprise with the rest of the economy.

The bureaucracy also finds roots in the increasing number of individuals involved in the higher echelons of State activity such as public corporations and the State economic agencies. This is a result of the profound changes that have taken place in the economic role of the State.

The bureaucracy finally finds its roots in the political process of par-liamentarianism and in the trade union organisations. In order to channel people, and to better integrate them into the existing social order, a special political apparatus is necessary. This apparatus participates to an increas-ing degree in the day-to-day management of society, by muffling conflicts, and seeking modifications of this or that demand from below.

The growth of this bureaucratic and technocratic stratum has profoundly altered the internal structure of the ruling class. New elements have had to be incorporated into this minority, and privileges have had to be extended. In a word, hierarchical relationships have been realigned. This stratum is not a homogenous social formation in Canada. It has developed to varying degrees in various regions of the country. It is impor-tant to note that this managerial bureaucracy is not based on any fun-damental new mode of production or new pattern of the circulation of commodities. It is based rather on changes in the economic basis of capitalism's need for survival. Historically such developments usually ap-pear at the end of an era.

3) Capitalist society is based on class divisions.

The social relations at the workplace, in an economy of artificially en-forced scarcity based on a centralising technology, remains the basis of class society. In all societies these social relations are capitalist relations; that is, they are based on wage labour. Human beings are obliged to sell their labour like a commodity for money. This makes working persons into objects by selling their labour to someone else in order to survive. Their labour, bought and sold at will by a small minority, is the only thing valued by capital, because it alone can produce more capital. The rest of the in-dividual is incidental. Those who buy and sell labour power own most of the wealth that it produces and thus control, in one way or another, society as a whole. Those who are forced to sell their labour power to the highest bidder, are powerless as individuals.

Working people in a factory or office constitute less than half of the total exploited population of Canada. Nevertheless, should they stop working, the economy would grind to a halt. Therefore, the tension at the workplace, the point of production, dominates directly the whole or-ganisation of the economy and indirectly the whole of society. The or-ganisation of work is becoming more and more bureaucratised and is taking the form of an increasing division of labour, of time and motion studies, and a tendency to speed up the work process. The conditions of the workplace, which are not unlike a military operation, are subjected to the ruthless will of capital, personified in the bureaucratic managerial ap-paratus. As a consequence of new forms of both exploitation and domina-tion, this class of working people are becoming more de-humanised, de-personalised; they are being proletarianised in the sense of *1984* and *Brave New World.*[2]

The fate of this proletariat in political and social life has not changed over the years. It is as powerless vis-à-vis established power as ever; it has no substantial power to effect changes in the quality of its day-to-day life. The whole pattern of neo-capitalist society, of its economy, its State, its housing, or its education, of the objects it will consume and of the news it will receive, of the questions of war and peace themselves, remain decided by a self-perpetuating minority. The mass of the population has no control or power over this minority, be the society one of "private capitalism" and "liberal democracy" or "State capitalism" and a "dictatorship of the proletariat."

The development and bureaucratisation of capitalism today has not lessened its irrationality. Both at the level of the factory and office and at the level of society as a whole, the bureaucratic technocracy is a mixture of despotism and confusion which produces a major human and material wastage.

This then, we suggest, is what preoccupies working people far more than anything else. Unless we speak to these concerns we speak to nothing fundamental. These are the problems of neo-capitalism in Canada. This is the social question. But because Canada is a colony, the social question cannot be dealt with outside the fact that Canadian capitalism is an extension of American capitalism. And that, in the end, our economy and its social, political and cultural institutions serve the ideology and objective needs of the American empire. Thus, the social question must addressed on in relationship to US imperialism. In other words, people in this country can go just so far in their social liberation before they have to deal with the question of outside control. However, we cannot proceed with the question of outside control first (the national question) and work down to the social question, for this path, especially in, advanced industrialized, society like Canada, is dangerous as well as historically blocked.

4) *The degeneration of the Left in Canada.*

The roots of the impotent situation in which the Left in Canada finds itself is to be found in two intimately interrelated processes: the evolution of modern capitalism, partly outlined above, and the bureaucratisation of the traditional left groups and the trade union organisations.[3]

The degeneration of these organisations is not due to "bad leaders" who "betray." The problem is much deeper. It is due primarily to the overwhelming pressures of capitalist society which eventually transform these organisations into a mirror image of itself. Originally created to overthrow bourgeois society, these traditional organisations have increasingly adopted the objectives, methods, ideology and patterns of organisation of the very society they were striving to supersede. There has developed within their ranks, no matter what the theories, an increasing division between leaders and the led. Some of these organisations are caught up in this process consciously and indeed cultivate it, others deny its existence in a cloud of "radial rhetoric." This has culminated in the development all the same, of a bureaucracy and bureaucratic cast of mind which can be neither removed nor controlled from below. This structure pursues objectives of its own.

These organisations come forward with claims to "lead" the working class. In reality, they see the class as a mass to be manoeuvred, according to the preconceived ideas of those who dominate the particular political machinery. They all see the objective of liberation as an increased degree of participation in general "material prosperity."

The reformists like the NDP claim that this can be achieved by a better organisation of traditional capitalism. The Stalinists, Maoists, Trotskyists and Waffle claim that what is needed is a change in the formal ownership of the means of production along with State planning, which amounts to a kind of socialism from above. Their common ideology boils down to an increase in production and consumption guaranteed by the rule of an elite of managers, seated at the summit of a new hierarchy based on "ability," "experience," and "devotion to the cause." This objective is essentially no different from that of contemporary capitalism itself.

The degeneration is not due to the intrinsic evils of organisation. Nor is it due to the fact that reformists and Stalinists have "wrong ideas" and provide "bad leadership," as Trotskyists and Leninists still maintain. Still less is it due to the bad influence of particular individuals — David or Stephen Lewis, Khrushchev, or Stalin.

What it really reflects is the fact that even when struggling to overthrow capitalism, the working class remains a partial prisoner of the system, and this in a much more subtle way than is usually understood. It remains a prisoner because it continues to conceive of *its* liberation as a task to be entrusted to the leaders of certain organisations to whom the class can confidently delegate its historical role.

The bureaucratised, traditional Left organisations, parties and trade unions, have long ceased to express the historical long-term interests of the working people. The reformist bureaucracy aims at securing a place for itself in the management of the capitalist system as it is. The authoritarian socialist bureaucracy of one sect or another aims at instituting a regime of the Russian or Chinese type where it would itself become the dominant social group.

Despite their periodic conflicts with the ruling class, both reformists and authoritarians, whether in political parties or in the trade unions, have the effect of perpetuating present class society. They have become the vehicles through which capitalist ideas, attitudes and mentality seep into the powerless class. They seek to canalise and control all manifestations of revolt against the existing social order. They seek to limit the more extreme excesses of the system, the better to maintain exploitation within "tolerable" limits.

These political and trade union organisations are confronted with an insoluble dilemma. On the one hand they are, as institutions, tolerated by established society. On the other hand, they aim at maintaining within their framework a class, whose conditions of life and work drive it to destroy that very society.

The organisation which the majority of exploited and dominated people need must be based on a totally different philosophy and structure and use entirely different methods of struggle.

Apathy and depoliticisation result from bureaucratic degeneration. The working class organisations have become indistinguishable from bourgeois political institutions.

Apathy and depoliticisation result from changes undergone by neo-capitalism. Economic expansion, high employment, the gradual increase in wages, pathological consumerism mean that for a whole period (which has not yet come to an end), the illusion of progress still affects us. This illusion is deliberately and very skilfully fostered and manipulated by the system for its own ends.

The programme of reformists like the NDP has been realised in a whole variety of ways. Yet the more we have "changes" the more the basic features of our lives, like boredom, monotony, purposelessness, remains the same. The political path along which the NDP and the various "Communist" parties proceed proves its futility. After decades and decades of reforms and struggle, all that has been achieved in this land of incredible wealth and potential is that commodities can be spread more widely than before. The same social powerlessness exists, and the same economic insecurity prevails. What we have still amounts to charity, however bitterly we have fought for it.

Historical experience in Canada has shown that society will only be changed fundamentally through the autonomous and self-conscious activity of the proletarianised class. No stratum, category, party or other form of hierarchical organisation can achieve socialism "on behalf of" the proletariat and in its place. Socialism will only be built through social revolution. Socialism can only be built on the destruction of all bureaucracies. Social revolution does not only mean the abolition of all dominating and privileged strata in society. It therefore implies the abolition of any social group claiming to manage production or the State "on behalf of the people."

5) *The formulation of a revolutionary consciousness and of a social revolutionary movement in Canada will be meaningless (indeed impossible) unless it bases its ideas, its programme, its structure and its methods of action on the historical experience of the working class in this country and in other countries, particularly that of the last fifty years.*

This means that such developments as we describe as constituting the social question must draw the full lessons of the period of bureaucratisation and that it must break with all that is mere ritual or leftover from the past. Only in this way will we be able to provide answers to the real and often new problems which will be posed in the period to come. A radical analysis of the crisis of modern industrial society and of capitalism is imperative. The essence of the social question as outlined here is that the analysis or critique of the organisation of the economy and of work under capitalism must be at the centre of our reconstruction of the revolutionary movement. We must surrender the idea that capitalism creates rational factories and rational machines and that it organizes work "efficiently" although somewhat brutally, and for the wrong ends. Instead we must express what every person in every region of Canada sees very clearly: that work has become absurd, that it means the constant oppression and mutilation of workers and that the bureaucratic organisation of work means endless confusion and waste.

Where it exists, material poverty must be exposed. But the content of consumption under capitalism must also be exposed. It is not enough to criticize the smallness of the education budget; we must denounce the content of capitalist education. We must denounce work against the concept of the school as an activity apart from life and society. It is not enough to demand more public monies for housing; we must denounce and work against the prevailing ideas on housing and the way of life they entail.

It is not enough to denounce the present government as representing the interests of a privileged class. We must also denounce the whole form and content of contemporary politics as a business for "specialists," and the idea that parliamentarism is democracy. A revolutionary movement must break with electoralism, and on this there can be no compromise. It must show that revolutionary politics are not confined to talk of wages and government affairs, but that they deal with everything that concerns people and their social lives. *"Les vrais problèmes sont quotidiens,"* was the insightful slogan of the 1968 General Strike in France, and with reason.

The confusion about the socialist programme created by the authoritarian organisations of the Left must be exposed. The idea that socialism only means the nationalisation of the means of production and planning — and that its essential aim is an increase in production and consumption, albeit on a more egalitarian basis — must be denounced. The similarity of these views with the basic orientation of neo-capitalism itself, must be demonstrated.

Socialism is workers' control and management of production and of society and the localist power of workers' councils and community assemblies. The essential content of socialism is the restitution to people of the control over their own life, the transformation of labour from absurd means of breadwinning to the free and creative action of individuals and groups, the constitution of integrated human communities and the union of the culture and the life of people.

The libertarian essence of socialism should not be shamefully hidden as some kind of abstract speculation concerning an indeterminate future. The perspective with which we looked at the social question here should be presented for what it is: a prospective for the humanisation of work and of an entire society. Socialism is not a field of leisure attached to the industrial prison. It is not what commodities we can play with during the weekend, even though it might be a three or four day weekend. It is not transistors for the prisoners. It is the destruction of the industrial prison itself. *This means the defeat of American imperialism in content as well as in form.* This is the basis of our position. In an industrial society as developed as our own, we cannot separate this question of form from content, so the social question comes first and foremost. The limitations of its resolution by the presence of American domination of Canada are to be dealt with at that point. We are not third world voyeurs.

In all local struggles, the way in which the result is obtained is at least as important as what is obtained. Even from the point of view of efficiency, actions organized and led by the people themselves are superior to actions decided and led bureaucratically. They alone create the conditions of progress, for this approach alone teaches us to run our own affairs.

In Canada, as in other industrial societies, the mobilisation of youth is essential. Canadian society has lost its hold on the generations it produces. The rupture is particularly brutal in politics. Such a mobilisation will be impossible unless the broad outlines of a social alternative for the present and immediate future are clearly articulated. The social movement must help young people and contribute towards clarifying and generalizing their experience, the objective being the development of skills and a lasting social consciousness and ability to manage social affairs on their own.

Organising on the regional and local level must be based on the principles of direct democracy and be consciously anti-bureaucratic in manner. This implies a total rejection of "democratic centralism" and other forms of organisation that encourage bureaucracy. At the local level, and in any regional or large level co-ordination, the principles of autonomy, direct democracy rather than delegation of decision-making, and co-ordination where necessary, should be achieved through delegates elected and revocable at any time by their local groups.

The revolutionary movement should also seek to bring closer together the struggle at the workplace and the broader struggle of other sections of the population, equally deprived of any effective say in the management of the affairs that concern them most. But people, we must remind ourselves, cannot be expected to become participating citizens in their communities actively involved in important social issues, if at work, where they spend more than half their day, they are oppressed. Nevertheless, there are many people who are not part of the regular work force. A large part of educational work should be directed towards these other strata of our evolving society, as well as towards new strata of wage earners (various service workers, students, intellectuals).

We have written and spoken at some length on previous occasions about the importance of community work, no matter what importance is assigned to change in the workplace. People who are not part of the regular work force can be organized around issues like housing, transportation, pollution, health, and unemployment. All these issues should be raised within the perspective of community control. The generation of new forms of struggle and organisation is not only profoundly relevant to the socialist future, but also capable on a daily basis of undermining the legitimacy of corrupt contemporary institutions in the community. More than a challenge to legitimacy, these developing new social forms, whether they are co-operative housing, radical day-care centres, or community clinics, are, on the one hand, embryonic attempts at self-management, and, given a sense of economic reality, are also supportive in any community of the revolutionary movement. These networks of community groups can create a sense of cultural change which is indispensable to the growth of any new consciousness in a particular section of a city.

Today, no matter how active young women and men workers are at their place of work, support is essential at home and in the neighbourhood. This opens the whole question of cooperative living, new life-styles, communalism. The sterile privatism of traditional radical movements, where after one's daily work, a person goes home to the traditional bourgeois setting, does not go far enough. Revolutionary consciousness must be nourished in the entirety of daily life.

But in the final analysis, the similarity between the objects of these new social forms and actions, and those of the movement of workers' self-management at the workplace should be repeatedly pointed out, as should the only possible solution to both: the complete democratisation of society through social revolution.

The changes in modern capitalism have done nothing to lessen the contradictions of the system in the areas of production and work, which are reflected through the rest of society. These are contradictions focused in the alienation of the worker. In addition to these contradictions, in canada, by virtue of the domination of American capital, people are given conflicting signals of identity. On the one hand, they are told they are Canadians, and that is supposed to be different from being an American. On the other, they are surrounded daily by the values and images of imperial America. Nevertheless, this secondary contradiction can only be addressed by means of the first, that of the objective and subjective condition of working people. Only if people are determined to attain a different way of life, and have a positive alternative in mind, will the struggle be joined. It is simply not enough in Canada to tell working people that we do not want to be controlled by the Americans. Nationalists will use our hostility towards American domination, but towards what end? A new bureaucratic society, a State capitalist, or authoritarian socialist society directed by centralized State agencies in Ottawa? We must not let our desire to break American control distract us from the more fundamental project of breaking the existing social order. This project cannot come after, it must come at the same time, or it will never come.

Even in Québec, where there is a tremendous emotional investment in a distinct language, and a largely different culture, the cultural struggle touched a small minority of the proletariat. When this proletariat mobilised itself into the greatest General Strike in North American history on social issues, and realised that one of the limitations of the situation was foreign control, then that question became meaningful. It is becoming clearer in Québec everyday life that socialism comes first. But socialism will not be possible without self-determination, that is, the independence of Québec. It is now, when 30,000 people march on May Day in solidarity throughout Québec, that we see the momentum becoming massive.

The subjective undercurrents leaning towards nationalism do not exist in Canada. Nationalism's historical role was to bring the bourgeoisie to power. Where the bourgeoisie was only partly in power, and the country was dominated by imperialism, nationalism was used to change the balance of power. *Nowhere* have nationalists ushered in social revolution. To create a nationalist sentiment *ex nihilo* in an advanced industrial society is extremely dangerous.

The struggle for freedom, for social and cultural self-determination of Canada and Québec from external control is one and the same with the struggle against all hierarchy, and this, in turn, is the struggle against the hierarchy of ideas employed by the bourgeoisie to maintain its world.

The opposition between theory and ideology is no mere academic dispute — it is itself part of the struggle. Thus, we do not offer this perspective, the outlines of which we stated here, as mere "ideas," as just one more contemplative interpretation of our society. Ideas are, after all, alienated desire. We hope, with dialogue, to clarify theory and to practice this theory in our daily lives.

NOTES

1. *Capitalism and The National Question in Canada,* edited by Gary Teeple, University of Toronto Press, 1972.
2. See "Classes Sociales et idéologies nationalistes au Québec, 1760-1970," by Gilles Bourque and Nicole Laurin-Frenette, where they deal with the split between the "technocratic faction" and the "neo-capitalist faction."
3. For another analysis see "The Impoverishment of the Canadian Left," by Marjaleena Repo, *Transformation,* Vol. 1, No. 4.

Spring 1972

THE WAFFLE AND ELECTORALISM

The political tendency in question centred in or around the NDP is plagued by the myopia of pragmatism, which has been a set response to social and political questions in Anglo-Saxon cultures. Political pragmatism has always argued for the separation of ethical criteria used to assess tactics and strategy, means and ends. As in the USA and Britain, from where it is imported, it has contributed to the sterility of the "socialist debate" here. This country, which has been eroded away by neo-colonialism for decades, continues to be a wasteland with regard to philosophical creativity. It is no accident that although there has been an interest in socialism in Canada for many decades, "Canadian socialism" was and is divorced from the socialist debates happening in many other countries, especially those outside the English-language world. The diluted Marxism in Canada is a case in point.

This political pragmatism has origins dating back to the advent of American cultural domination. British Fabianism and American populism were both cornerstones of the CCF during its emerging years. British socialism has many characteristics of pragmatism, but unlike its Canadian off-spring, it has in the post-war period developed a growing minority of "international socialists" attuned to the constant search by European Marxism for more relevant definitions of social reality.

The day must arrive when the Canadian Left which is still open, opens itself even further to questions like, what is socialism? what is the nature of advanced or neo-? what is the nature of opposition in capitalist society? etc. The continuous and often tortuous process of redefinition is what is *new* in the New Left. It is a radical philosophical departure from the old left in many critical areas, so much so that the vision of what is a socialist society is different. After all, the problem of history is the problem of consciousness. The difference between the New Left and the Waffle (as reflected in its manifesto) is that the latter is more orthodox socialist than the present NDP leadership.

We have stated elsewhere that most of the classic contradictions in capitalist society are indeed still with us, but most of these have new forms. As capitalism has matured into neo-capitalism, an altogether new set of contradictions have also emerged, largely unrecognised by most socialists.

The reference that Reginald Whittaker makes to Marcuse is not intended for the Weathermen, or the FLQ as a matter of fact. It is, on the contrary, aimed at the permeationists; those like the Waffle who make the erroneous distinction between the position which maintains that "capitalism cannot be reformed as the NDP insists," but that the *political* structures and institutions of capitalism can be used to change the system fundamentally. What are, after all, the origins of these political institutions? Was not the franchise distributed at the height of the threat to 19th century capitalism, and did not this diffusion of "democracy" help stabilize the system? Have these representational institutions not been proven over the years to be a reflection of the basic nature of the political economy itself? Has not electoralism and liberal democracy been one of the main cosmetics of the capitalist system? It is Marcuse who has taught us, by the way, that in a modern technological society, any conventional opposition group inevitably assumes the values of the system it opposes and is eventually absorbed by it.

Whittaker maintains "...as a irrefutable thesis that a true socialist society can never be fully developed within a capitalist society through the liberal democratic process." Quite, but instead of going on to define what a "true socialist society" is, instead of going on to define what is done *outside* the liberal democratic process, like the social democrats from whom he chooses to disassociate himself, Whittaker proceeds to outline how we can use the system and get away with it. In other words, for some unclear reason Canada is going to be the historical exception. It is this pursuit, which is the consequence of the lack of a systematic analysis of the "political principle," which has made the Waffle a tendency in the narrowest sense. With all the allusions to extra-parliamentary activity, the activity has yet to take up a fraction of the energy that is put elsewhere. One cannot help noting the use of the word "activity" in contrast to other peoples' use of the word "opposition." The difference is important.

What the Waffle means by extra-parliamentary activity is the creation of a social movement, which in the end will not have its own direction but will be an extension of a transformed political party. Here we need to draw some insight from the history of the British Labour Party. It is supposed to have been a coalition between the parliamentary caucus of the party, the trade union movement and the co-operative movement. For years, the valiant Labour Left within the party has been trying to use the social forces outside of the parliamentary group to push the party to the Left. Its success has been marginal. You cannot be in and out of parliament and a national political party at the same time.

A close study of the history of the Labour Party Left and its fate is an almost prophetic look at the future of the Waffle. Just as the Labour Party has been a compromise between socialist objectives and the existing power structures at the national level, so the Labour Left has been a compromise between socialist objectives and the power structure within the political party. It has made important efforts to reform this party power structure, but the odds are against it. Alternatively, it has to choose between what are, in effect, electoral campaigns within the party, and political campaigns which can exist their own right.

Whittaker clearly understands the mechanics of co-option but these should not be confused with the limitations of the system itself. Once we delimit the boundaries of the system at any particular time and understand the new contradictions, then we have one choice, namely, to place both the means and ends outside these boundaries. The women's *action* that is used as an example was radical, but its initial demand was not. Consequently, the effect of the action was to have the demand absorbed, but the rest of the women's programme pushed into the background. The Waffle action is within the system, many of the demands are going to be modified, or the Waffle will have to work outside the system. One cannot be in and out at the same time while posing to be anti-system. This gives the political system the legitimacy which it so desperately seeks. Whittaker for his part, also gives our political institutions legitimacy by taking them seriously even at the "tactical" level. We are convinced that this is what liberal democracy wants more than anything else: stay inside, play the game within its rules.

The distinction Whittaker tries to make between the form of contestation and the simultaneous "pressing of the larger frame of radicalism" comes under a number of rubrics. André Gorz, for instance, advocated for many years such an approach under the clever title of "revolutionary reformism" (see his *Strategy for Labour*), and the European Communist Parties use a rather similar approach to rationalize their strategy. These approaches have not only not created qualitative social change, but have not mobilised the imagination and capacity for hard work of the masses. Gorz has now changed his mind after he witnessed the incredible potential of the May-June 1968 General Strike in France. He now seeks new forms of action, and new forms of social organisation. Thus, the tremendous importance of strategies directed at fundamental change as is occurring in Italy.

The Regina Manifesto was "radical" for its time. The CCF worked within the system, with a popular social movement behind it, pushing for radicalism, *through the existing political institutions.* Why was the "broader framework of radicalism" abandoned? Not as the account by David Lewis in the *Last Post* would have us believe because of the work of one man (however fascinating "journalistic" reading that makes). Such an approach is not a radical analysis. It is a distortion of history, and the kind of psychologism to which the commercial press reduces politics.

What Whittaker outlines as Waffle strategy is not in its programme. A small circle of "heavies" may utter this to themselves from time to time. When is this "broader framework of radicalism" to be pushed for, if not from the start?

Jim Laxer and the Waffle have made a whole range of gratuitous remarks to the effect that the New Left is a US import. Not only has recent history been falsified to prove this point, but the establishment has used this to beat off certain radical initiatives. The New Left is an *international* phenomenon. So is advanced capitalism. The New Left everywhere is open to the insights of their brother and sister revolutionaries in other countries. The New Left to be sure, is wrong when it imports uncritically the cultural forms of other cultures and tries to impose them here. We are the first to acknowledge our debt to the Waffle for helping us all grasp the outlines of the Canadian Project. But what indeed is Canadian about the NDP? Or its programme? Or its social democracy? Or the House of Commons? Is Women's Liberation Canadian? Why hasn't the Waffle attacked this movement as being imported?

For the record, all this is not to say that what the Waffle is doing is not without *historical* importance. I do not share the totalistic and millenarian critique offered by Jim Harding of the Waffle in the last issue of *Our Generation.* For one thing, the Waffle has helped all radicals to define themselves anew. It has helped make sharper the distinction between the radical farmers living in the pastoral tranquillity of rural Canada and those of us who are combatting the bitter realities oppressing people in urban areas at the local level. At no time can we deny the importance of radicalising the NDP constituency. But this cannot be confused with working within the NDP. The hundreds of thousands who vote NDP during elections have a very shallow commitment to the institution. How many popular campaigns has this party organised outside elections on one issue or another? The NDP as an institution is afraid of such mobilisations. The mobilisations might take their own course. It is interesting that nowhere does Whittaker discuss the dynamics of building a social movement. Nowhere do we see a discussion of how an extra-parliamentary opposition can be built.

What we face in defining social reality is not simply a question of the differences in party programmes but a crisis of *institutions.* In defining a socialist society we are attempting to understand a whole set of questions long since set aside by most socialists. These include the role and function of the political party, as well as a fundamental re-evaluation of this social form. It includes a critical assessment of parliamentary or representative democracy, and the role and function of the State. In other words, we need to question (by going to the roots of these institutions) the entire superstructure, and not simply the nature of the political economy. Marxist-Leninists after October 1917 changed many things, but continued to employ many of the political forms which they created in their struggle against capitalism, and continued to use the same theories of organisation. It was not long before many of the economic as well as the political forms and content of capitalism began to reappear in the societies ruled by the new bureaucracy.

The same logic that socialists apply to questions of the economy, must be taken to its consequence and applied to the dominant political institutions of the day.

Suffice to say that what we mean by *outside* the system is to undertake the task of social transformation in a *realistic* manner which is always the *most* difficult. It does not mean working in the fields growing potatoes in PEI or BC. It means working in an industrialised and technological society, in the factories, and offices, in the working-class residential districts, in the economy at its base. It means working outside the federal and provincial power structures, and creating new popular organisational forms at the local-municipal level, that is in the neighbourhoods, through urban communes, and in community assemblies developing the social skills individually and collectively of self-government and decentralisation.

To paraphrase a popular New Left saying, what we want is not the seizure of political power, but a situation in which it gets lost in the shuffle as people transform their society from the bottom up.

Summer 1981

QUÉBEC AND RADICAL SOCIAL CHANGE

After fifteen years of supporting the movement for Québec's becoming an independent and different society from the rest of North American, I have to admit along with others that the referendum campaign was not only an anti-climax to what preceded it, but had a contrived and hollow quality. The decisive turning point in Québec's history with regard to the national or the social question has yet to be reached.

The Left as a whole agrees that the PQ represents neither the vision nor the potential for either national or social liberation but the Left itself also lacks an alternative to the PQ. What the Left has offered thus far is a perspective which is the mirror-reflection of the PQ, a perspective which has not ignited the imagination of the people. The question has been posed, should we work for socialism first and then independence or independence first followed by socialism? Whichever way the question is posed the problem remains, namely, that both independence and socialism are defined by the Québec Left in traditional terms. Clearly, what has to be done is to look at these two concepts anew, drawing on historical experience to give a contemporary definition to the issue.

The Anarchist Tradition in Québec

During most of the socialism versus independence debate in Québec, the definition of these concepts left much to be desired. The debate was locked into the parameters set by events and debates in third world countries with regard to independence, and by events and debates in Europe as well as in the Third World regarding socialism. In fact, developments in the last twenty years in advanced capitalist societies, including Québec, have cultivated an entirely new terrain on which to base the revolutionary project.

Up until the 1950s, the left on a world-wide basis was dominated ideologically and politically by Marxism-Leninism on the one hand and social democracy on the other. We had the *hard* authoritarian socialism of the political parties that followed Moscow, and the *soft* authoritarian socialism of the social democratic parties of certain Western countries. This ideological hegemony of these two "socialisms" began to fragment in the 1960s.

Orthodox Marxism-Leninism was profoundly shaken by a series of events which included the critique of Stalinism presented at the 20th Congress of the Communist Party of the Soviet Union, the 1956 Hungarian Revolution, developments in Czechoslovakia with the subsequent Soviet invasion in 1968, and the series of revolts and strikes in Poland beginning in the 1970s and continuing today.

Social democracy on the other hand, was discredited with its exercise of State power in Britain, West Germany, Canada and elsewhere. Its inability to present an alternative to US imperialism during the Cold War, the rampant militarism of NATO, the Vietnam War, the international balance of power which exploits the Third World, and domestically the inability of its social programmes of reform to curb the injustice and ugliness of capitalism, all this and more, condemned the social democrats to merely helping to save the system from itself.

An important reaction to this process of dissolving ideological hegemony at an intellectual level was the emergence of the New Left. This movement, which at first set out to create an independent Marxism in some countries, in order to define its project more broadly, as in the USA, Canada, Australia and Japan, immediately challenged the old Left. A rich variety of periodicals and conferences expressed both a critique of the immediate past of the socialist movement and sought to formulate alternatives.

By the early 1960s, a new social movement had emerged among the young which advocated and practised an whole range of ideas that further challenged the form and content of the traditional socialism that typified the Marxist-Leninist and social democratic species. This broad movement stepped outside the domain of the old Left by helping to build poor peoples' organisations, tenants unions, and demands for radical democracy in schools, to name a few. It also spearheaded a large anti-war movement which played an important role in many countries. The New Left, suspicious of political parties and seeking to establish and practice participatory democracy, pioneered new social forms of organisation. Whether these social forms were called collectives, communes, or affinity groups, their basic practice was non-hierarchical and anti-authoritarian.[1]

The activists of this New Left social movement were in fact unconsciously discovering another long-established socialist tradition, a movement of great importance until the end of the First World War, and which in some countries continued to play an important role until the beginning of the Second World War. It was a movement that was attacked by the mythology surrounding October 1917, while the efforts of the Marxist-Leninists through their Third International tried to destroy and bury it, as the social democrats tried to do through the Second International. In broad terms, the movement and tradition we are referring to embraced Anton Pannekoek, Herman Gorter, Karl Korsch, (who were Council Communists proposing forms of organisation other than a Bolshevik party, but who remained Marxists) and the anarchists. This anti-authoritarian socialist tradition is also referred to as *socialisme libertaire ou socialisme autogestionnaire* of which anarchism can be said to be the cutting edge.

The old Left in Québec, both in its Marxist and social democratic forms, also suffered from the disorienting effects of the international crisis in ideological hegemony. By the 1960s, with the rise of the new nationalist movement we began to witness a parade of third-worldism, followed by all the refinements of Marxism, succeeded by all of the vulgar forms of neo-Marxism-Leninism.

Throughout the 1960s, the new social movement in Québec laid the basis for a new praxis dealing with the realities of everyday life under neo-capitalism. At the workplace the trade unions were undergoing rapid radicalisation through a series of important strikes and political events, and in the neighbourhoods a series of important urban struggles began which attempted to organise the poor, tenants, and users of various municipal and social services. The social movement often cross-fertilized with the nationalist movement, while certain sections of both continuously overlapped.

This libertarian current underlies the history of Québec as far aback as the late nineteenth century. The anarchist ideas of Pierre-Joseph Proudhon had some currency in Montréal. We have accounts of May Day demonstrations before the First World War in which French-Canadian workers carried the black flags of anarchism. These and other similar indications however marginal, as in other countries had an echo among a people who sought freedom. Between the two World Wars, non-French-Canadian minorities became interested in the free forms of socialism as they attended the meetings of such anarchist celebrities as Emma Goldman and Rudolf

Rocker in Montréal. Albert St. Martin, a pioneering Québec socialist, had close ties with these circles and was much influenced by various libertarian socialist ideas.

In Québec cultural circles from the end of the Second World War to the present, libertarian and anarchist ideas were very much present when one thinks of artists like Paul-Émile Borduas, Claude Gauvreau. Henri Mosseau, Armand Vaillancourt, Janou St. Denis, Denise Boucher, and others who during the 1950s frequented the cafés on rue Clark.

Throughout the 1960s and into the 1970s it is important to note that anti-authoritarian ideas were not self-consciously held by the New Left movements involved in the urban and community struggles or in the labour movement. These intuitive and instinctive tendencies arose from common sense reactions to the bankruptcy or dogmatism of the old Left and from the useful experience of the new activists. This new generation was generally unaware of the origin or history of these ideas, either in Québec or in other cultures. Throughout the immediate past there were very few who referred to themselves as anarchists, and there were certainly very few anarchist circles. It was more a response to everyday life with a set of social reactions, rather than a comprehensive social philosophy. Thus, many of these anti-authoritarian actions and ideas lacked clarity, and lacked the force which they could have had. Nevertheless, the libertarian idea in one incomplete form or another continued to be presented. In many instances ideas like *autogestion* (workers' self-management) which are one and the same as anarchism were co-opted by social democrats and Marxists because of the appeal to freedom, but were inevitably deformed by these advocates.

> *Sans tomber dans le messianisme...notre seul chance de survie au point de vue économique et culturel est de parier pour une utopie socialiste dans le sens d'un projet global qui orienterait notre action vers une image idéale du futur. Société industrielle avancée, le Québec pourrait plus qui bien d'autre pays se rapprocher de ce rêve permanent des travailleurs qu'est le contrôle non seulement de l'État mais encore de la région, de la municipalité de ceux qui y habitent ou y travaillent et non par une minorité de possesseurs de capitaux.* (Gabriel Gagnon. "Les voies de làutogestion" *Partis Pris*, Vol.4, No. 7/8, Mars—Avril 1967.)

During the 1970s, the anti-authoritarian movement acquired additional dimensions through the radical women's movement, the ecology movement and the gay liberation movement. Once again not only was exploitation in its various forms condemned but *domination* as well. Throughout these two decades, especially the last four years under the PQ, the State came under harsh criticism. The State was found unable to solve the social crisis and instead was growing in size and its centralised bureaucracy becoming more impotent.

The 1970s also witnessed the emergence of a counter-culture in Québec which not only questioned our society but in doing so further undermined existing authority, deeply affecting the social perspective of the new generation.[2] From *Mainmise* to *Les Temps Fou*, from the Rhinoceros party to a wide range of community newspapers, community radio stations, video networks and periodicals, to new experiments in living communally in the city or countryside, with new music and art-forms (from poetry to pottery), once again the bourgeois order of things as well as the old Left was being critiqued in practice. Sonia "Chatouille" Coté, candidate for the Rhinoceros Party summed up this social perspective well when she stated: *"je ne veux pas de pouvoir, pas de leader, je veux du plaisir, je veux que les gens sortent, d'eux-même, qu'ils laissent tomber les carcans de la société, je suis pour la marginalité, mais une marginalité élargie qui finalement s'infiltre dans toute société."*[3]

The crises of the old orthodoxies were now almost complete. On the Left, the checkered history of the NDP and the mild reformism of the PQ demonstrated the hollowness of social democracy. The Marxist-Leninist sects, thoroughly discredited by their opportunism, by the changes in China, Eastern Europe, the invasion by Vietnam, find their influence waning in the social movement and the labour movement.

We nevertheless still have in Québec those in the old socialist programmes who persist in pursuing their own power ambitions through national State power built through the old route of parliamentary electoralism. The dismal record of the NDP in Saskatchewan, Manitoba, and British Columbia is not enough for this Club of 100 left-wing notables. Such efforts are doomed to failure in North American, as are the even more fanciful efforts of taking a Eurocommunist or Eurosocialist route to social change by imposing reforms from above via the State. The drama of socialism from above as opposed to socialism from below will continue in Québec, with the important difference that the struggle is open and recognisable.

By the mid-1970s, new social values intervened in the national debate in Québec. After the PQ came to power the consensus in the nationalist movement began to rapidly break down. Pioneering work on the national question by Jean-Yves Soucy, Jacques Mascotto, and Louis Leborgne set the pace. Their critical examination of the inadequacies of Marxism-Leninism in comprehending the national question dispelled many important myths. The rigorous course that Soucy and Mascotto followed led them, like many other intellectuals, to abandon Marxism. Another pioneer investigator of the national question in Québec, Nicole Laurin-Frenette raised a substantial thesis in her new work, namely, that the national liberation project in Québec was seriously distorted by a dangerous reliance on the State. This fixation on the State, she wrote, crippled the aspirations of a whole generation that hoped and worked for an independent society. The hold of Marxism on the minds of academic intellectuals as the sole revolutionary tradition began to break.

The recent referendum witnessed another unprecedented schism among those who desire an independent Québec. The many "mais oui's," "abstentionists," "ballot spoilers" indicate that an important minority in Québec is having for the first time second thoughts about achieving national liberation from above.

Anarchism and the National Question

Anarchists believe in cultural diversity as opposed to cultural homogeneity and therefore the anarchist movement has always championed cultural and national autonomy and self-determination. Since cultural regions and nations should choose to federate freely, according to the anarchists, then these same units have the freedom to leave any union at will. But in their struggle to advance the cause of the oppressed, the anarchists made not only the same distinction as did other socialists between the capitalist minority and the urban and rural working people, but also distinguished between the State and the people or nation.

Michel Bakunin, one of the leading figures of anarchism, in 1848 hailed the national movements as a great liberating force. He observed: "The social question on the one hand, and the question of independence of all nations, the emancipation of peoples on the other hand, signifies emancipation within and without...Everybody had come to the realisation that liberty was merely a lie where the great majority of the population is reduced to a miserable existence, where, deprived of education, of leisure, and of bread, it is fated to serve as an underprop for the powerful and the rich...It has likewise been felt that, so long as there may be a single persecuted nation...the decisive and complete triumph of democracy will not be possible anywhere. The oppression of one is the oppression of all,and we cannot violate the liberty of one without violating the freedom of all of us."[4]

Nationality, however, had to be seen, according to Bakunin, in the context of the supreme principle of liberty; it could not in itself be elevated above liberty because it would separate people and could be thus associated with a threat to liberty. With this perspective in mind he criticized Mazzini and the movement for Italian unification. He maintained that in Italy there had been a spontaneous and free spirit of the Italian people that had overthrown and driven out the foreign oppressor — and this was a "natural necessity, identical with the concept of liberty": It had overthrown the despotic governments which, independent of each other but dependent on the foreign domination of Austria, had arbitrarily divided the Italian nation — and that had to be done to restore the free and living unity of Italy. But the leadership of the Italian movement was Statist, and in the very process of liberation the real liberty of Italy had been destroyed by the creation of one new State to replace the old ones.[5]

> Mazzini had not understood that the spontaneous and free union of the living forces of a nation had nothing in common with their artificial concentration at once mechanistic and forced in the political centralisation of the unitary state; and because he confused and identified these two very opposing things he has not only been the promoter of the independence of his country he has become at the same time, very much in spite of himself without doubt, the promoter of its present slavery...[6]

According to Bakunin, the popular spirit of national unity instead of being encouraged to develop through the free federation of communal regions of Italy was being crushed by the unitary State, which imposed an oppressive unity from above. Bakunin did not believe that the replacement of the monarchy by a republic, as Mazzini advocated, would materially alter this situation. Unresponsive to the real needs of the people, the State, whether monarchical or republican, perpetuated the economic system which generated social injustice, thus depriving the people of real liberation and choking the unifying popular spirit. Statist patriotism is first and foremost the passion of the ruling class, which becomes love of authoritarianism embodied in the State and hostile to the very nation itself.

Peter Kropotkin, another anarchist theorist, made a sharp distinction between the nation and the State. In his view the nation comprised all the people associated with a particular geographic environment,and he envisaged it organising itself without the State. On the other hand, he always maintained that the State, whatever the type of government, tended towards centralisation and was the machinery whereby *one section* of the people oppressed the majority in their own interests.

Kropotkin maintained that "no serious economic progress can be won nor is any progressive development possible until the awakened aspirations for autonomy have been satisfied." Every nation must be fully free, these and other anarchists insist, and every union, federation or confederation between nations must be joined freely, as must every separation of one nation or another from any association be done as a matter of course.[7]

If we are to define a nation as a society with a prevailing culture with extensive similarities, the contrast between nation and State can best be illustrated by looking at North and South America as an example of the anarchist thesis. The Nation-State historically has not evolved organically, creating itself, as is often asserted, but has been rather the artificial creation of the State from above, mechanically imposed on various groups. In North America, the USA succeeded in combining all the land between the Atlantic and Pacific oceans into a powerful Nation-State, a process greatly furthered by favourable circumstances of various kinds. This happened in spite of the fact that the USA contained a wide mixture of people assembled from Europe, Africa and other continents.

South and Central America, however, are separated into some sixteen different Nation-States, although the ethnic relation between these peoples is incomparably closer than it is in the USA, and the same language — with the exception of Portuguese in Brazil and various native Indian languages — prevails in all. But the political evolution of Latin America was of a different order. Although Simon Bolivar, the "liberator" of South America from the Spanish yoke, sought to create a single State for all South American countries, his plan did not succeed for ambitious dictators and militarists, like Pietro in Chile, Gamarra in Peru, Flores in Ecuador, Roses in Argentina, opposed this project by all possible means.

The result of the lust for power of small minorities and authoritarian individuals has been the creation of numerous Nation-States, which in the name of national interest and national honour, wage hostilities against one another on an ongoing basis. If political events in the USA had developed as they did in South and Central America, then there would be today a variety of Nation-States consisting of Californian, Michigan, Kentucky, etc. Here is no better demonstration that a Nation-State's existence is founded purely on power politics.

Culture and the Nation-State

Culture rests neither on brute force nor on blind faith in authority; its effectiveness is based on the culmination of efforts for spiritual and material welfare freely accepted. The decisive matter here is natural need, not an edict from above issued by a cultural bureaucracy. For this reason, in all historical periods, culture has gone hand in hand with voluntary association; in fact, these two factors are mutually dependent. Only voluntary determination, which in most cases arises unself-consciously, unites people of different cultures, and in this way produces new forms of cultural expression.

The situation is not unlike what happens to an individual. One reads the work of an intellectually stimulating and compelling foreign author completely voluntarily. The reader is interested completely voluntarily. The reader is stimulated and influenced by the force of the ideas. In this way, cultural and intellectual forces cross-fertilize and influence each other.

This natural, unforced assimilation goes on without an overseer because it grows out of the personal requirements of individuals and corresponds to their experiences. The cultural process goes on within cultural regions or nations, and between these same units peacefully and without friction, the less State politics are involved.

In his monumental work, *Nationalism and Culture,* the well-known anarchist, Rudolph Rocker, gave a brilliant analysis of how the strongest cultures in history were local and regional ones, citing many examples which show that their greatness evolved from below with the least amount of State presence. In describing the culture of ancient Greece, he wrote: "Every city had its singers and poets, and there is scarcely another period in history in which, in so small a country and in such a comparatively short time, such an astonishing number of poets and thinkers made their appearance as in the little communities of Greece." Art, he noted, was not a private matter for the Greeks, for they developed a living art, through which every phase of personal and social life was intimately connected. A high level of national or political unity, thought to be indispensable to the development of any kind of culture, was lacking among the Greeks. Ancient Greece never knew what national unity and the Nation-State meant, and when towards the end of its history national-political unity was forcibly imposed during Alexander's time, the culture stagnated.

What united the Greeks was their common culture, manifested in thousands upon thousands of different ways, not an artificial bond to the Nation-State, in which no one in Greece felt any interest and the essence of which was always alien. Such a civilisation was the result of political decentralisation, an internal division of Greece into hundreds of communities, which stimulated new aspects of culture and diversity.

Ancient Greece is an example of the social conditions under which cultural expression flourished. The evidence shows that the less the State is developed, the richer are the forms of cultural life; the more dependence on authority dominates, the more impoverished the level of intellectual and social culture of a society becomes, and the more completely natural creative impulses die.

Québec is a geographically vast area, with strong regional cultures, to be sure, linked by common historical and other experiences. What we have said about culture, we can say about language or speech. Speech is an expression of social unity, which responds to intellectual and social change, and is, in turn, dependent on change. Thus, Québec has a rich and varied language filled with local experiences and insights. Although speech expresses individual thought, it is not a purely personal affair, as is often assumed. Rather, it is continually animated and influenced by the social environment. The French language has been enriched not only by local cultural developments, but by the new social movements, such as the feminist and ecology movements as well. People's thoughts mirror both the environment and all social relations. The *social* character of thought and language are undeniable because these are functional.

State education, however, has attempted to make language uniform and sterile. The language of Rabelais was hardly understood in France a hundred years after his death, and is understood today only by using a special dictionary. The establishment of the French Academy in 1629 gave the French language a strict guardian that endeavoured with all its power to eliminate from it, popular expressions. Called "refining the language" in fact, it deprived it of originality and bent it under the yoke of an aristocratic despotism from which it was later forcibly freed. Fénélon, Racine and Diderot cried out. But the defenders of the national-Statist ideology continued to maintain that nationality represents a natural inner unity, something permanent, and unchangeable in its deepest essence. Although they could not deny that intellectual and social life was subject to change, they tried to save themselves with the assertion that these changes affected only the outer conditions, not the real nature of nationality. The profound changes which occurred in the French language with the French Revolution show how wrong this view is. A complete about-face in language burst the controls which the aristocracy and the literati of the salons had on language. In fact, only the Revolution curbed its decline. Paul Lafrague says, "New words and expressions assailed the language in such number that newspapers and periodicals of that time could have been understood by the courtiers of Louis XIV only by means of a translation."

Likewise in Québec various regional cultures have been deeply influenced by local history and experiences. In certain regions, the presence of native Indian culture has also contributed to cultural enrichment, as have the many immigrant cultures in Montréal and other cities. Therefore, what our choice adds up to is one in which, either Québec becomes a federation of free regional cultures blending together organically on the basis of social community and cultural interests, or takes a plunge into an era of mechanically created "national" culture which is State-sponsored and serves the development of State capitalism and a "repressive tolerance" (to quote Marcuse).

The world order dominating our planet (to refer to the concept of Immanuel Wallerstein and the new economic historians) is a world capitalist system. It transforms daily and uniformly, language, economic organisation, State cultures, manufacturing a common ideology of domination through established political and economic structures. Flags and anthems remain different, but the process of cultural homogenisation grows uninterrupted. The State and the economic corporations are two primary grids through which the world system perpetuates itself. Where this system is weakest is at the local and regional level, and because of this we must rethink our goals of social and cultural liberation. Québec can survive culturally as a nation only if a liberation process freely brings together various regional cultural forces from the bottom up.

Art and culture stand above the Nation-State. A creative person, seeking to express an enduring quality in the life of an individual, community or environment, invariably alludes insights that are true for another people in another place. The colour or form of this expression might be different, but the content or basic idea will often be similar. The role of art and culture to show the diversity and variety of *basic* human expressions. The forms of these cultural expressions are often profoundly influenced locally and regionally on the one hand, or from afar away lands on the other. The various regions that constitute contemporary Nation-States often have *less in common* with each other than with neighbouring cultural regions across borders. Nevertheless, what is perceived as culturally common within a nation has to do more with social solidarity and the sharing of a similar history and language than it has to do with the creation of a State. Believing otherwise is clearly the result of a decades-old educational system promoting the supremacy of a single authority, be it Church or State.

The primary objective of the modern State and its economy has been to weaken or do away with local institutions, traditions and liberties as well as intercommunal or regional ties which have spring up from the very life of the nation. All are taught to look to the capital, as forceful interference or centralisation gradually monopolizes all political authority. Government does not mean self-government directly by the people. Government means being governed by a caste apart from the people, albeit with some symbolic accountability. The State means the government of people, through social control, and not, as the early socialists hoped for, an administration of things.

Revolutionary Federalism

The organisational origins of the revolutionary trade unions were federalist, thought to be the most egalitarian and democratic form of worker's organisation. The reformist trade unions of today still use a distorted kind of federation or confederation as their basic structure. Our trade unions in Québec also have federalist forms of organisation of one kind or another. In countries where circumstances permitted the growth of radical trade unions, the labour movement was always built from the bottom up on a federated basis freely agreed to. Wherever the working class itself was engaged in constructing its own organisations, these invariably were federations.

Fourier, Proudhon, Pi y Margall, Bakunin, Kropotkin, and others proposed a form of revolutionary federalism which would restructure society from the bottom up, creating federations of municipalities and regions leading to the dissolution of the State. Such combinations were seen as naturally protective of cultures and local/national diversity. State centralisation has assumed in the interim an even greater scope than in the nineteenth century when these individuals were living. A federative social organisation, supported by the common interest of all and based on the free agreement of all human groups, is the only way we can liberate ourselves from the bureaucratic State. The history and organisational principles of some of Québec's trade unions, movements that have arisen from below, are an application of radical federalism.

To the extent, however, that our trade unions mirror the political organisation of the State, they become demobilised no matter how flamboyant their anti-capitalist rhetoric. The more a trade union melds anti-authoritarian socialism with an anti-authoritarian federative social organisation clearly controlled locally, the more workers have a militant movement stepping outside the norms of conventional society and opening new vistas of what is possible.

So revolutionary federalism, which is the form of social and political organisation that libertarian socialists and anarchists put forward, is an *organic* collaboration of all social forces in a larger society oriented towards a common goal based on covenants freely arrived at. Such a federalism is not a disintegration of creative activity, not a chaotic running here and there; it is the united work and effort of all members for the freedom and welfare of all. It is unity of action, sprung from inner conviction, not external compulsion, which finds expression in the solidarity of all. The voluntary spirit, working from within outward, does not exhaust itself in the mindless imitation of prescribed patterns permitting no personal initiative. Monopoly of power must disappear, together with monopoly of property. Instead, we will have liberation from capitalism; in order to produce materials for human need; liberation from the State in order that society and culture can meld on a basis of freedom.

Self-determination is rooted in the self-determining individual, community, region, and federation of regions. The present situation simply perpetuates dependence on a higher power, that source of all religious, ideological and political bondage which chains people to the past and condemns us to cultural atrophy.

While an anti-capitalist consciousness has been growing in Québec in the last twenty years, a parallel anti-authoritarian consciousness has also spread in the popular neighbourhoods of our large cities, among the unionised working class, and especially among the young in general. It is only since the PQ has come to power, however, that we have witnessed an explicitly anti-Statist consciousness.

During this twenty year period, the imposing authority of the Church has been undermined, the school system has been undermined, the school system has been seriously questioned as an educational experience, and a new generation has distanced itself from many bourgeois values which include the nuclear family and marriage. During the PQ years, the growing criticism of what the "good guys of the PQ" have done has put into question the legitimacy of the State. Experiencing the reality of centralised power and bureaucracy, many people have concluded that the exploitation of capitalism and the dominant authority of the State are linked and inseparable.

An important manifestation of this anti-authoritarianism has been people's questioning of political parties as vehicles of change. The Marxist-Leninist parties, all of whom are struggling among themselves to lead the working class towards a new dictatorship, have been blocked by a popular libertarian response.

The anti-authoritarian movement includes more than the anarchists. It includes militants in the women's movement who not only condemn patriarchy, but all authority; it includes ecologists who not only denounce the pillage of capital against nature, but the State's role as well, as it develops more legislation and more government inspectors while collaborating in other ways with ecological crimes; it includes workers in trade unions who oppose the formation of a single trade union in Québec and the founding of a labour or socialist party as realistic solutions to working-class exploitation; it includes citizen's groups in neighbourhoods who persist in their self-help and self-reliance projects in the areas of housing, tenant rights, traffic control, green spaces, day-care centres and community services.

This anti-authoritarian and libertarian consciousness arising from people's experiences leads to a self-consciousness which itself, moves towards an organised movement. Conditions in our society, along with the experiences of the last two decades, are the pressures moving this potential into a self-conscious social force.

Authors Désy, Ferland, Lévesque and Vaillancourt are correct in their *La Conjoncture au Québec au Début des Années 80: les enjeux pour le mouvement ouvrier et populaire* that the labour movement shows three important tendencies: Marxism-Leninism, social democracy and anarcho-syndicalism. They are, however, very limited in their understanding of the history or theory of anarcho-syndicalism which they view as a defensive position.

Trade unions were among the few organisations authentically created by the working class itself. These organisations, anarcho-syndicalists believe, can undertake economic, as well as political struggles, and that they can have social, as well as cultural aims. Since the determining historical factor in any society is "who controls the economy," that, to the anarcho-syndicalists, is the priority for social struggle. When the working class takes control of the economy and disarms the State, power is dissolved; in this sense, they are anti-political (power). Anarchy-syndicalist unions are quite capable, more so than is a socialist State, of directing a productive economy by socialising all property directly in the hands of the working population (and not nationalising the economy under the control of some "benevolent" State bureaucracy), and thus setting up co-ordinated economic bodies which would, along with communal organisations, administer the economy based on workers' control. It is, after all, the workers who know how to run the industries, in the areas of resource extraction, manufacturing and services. In such a scenario of what use are political parties or the State?

These ideas and actions, put into practice at various times in history, were aborted, not because they did not work, but because they were destroyed by force by the Right and the authoritarian Left, often together. And, because of the ideological hegemony of Marxism and social democracy, the literature on these short-lived experiences has been buried. Today, people are discovering the libertarian socialist and anarchist traditions. Wherever people become interested in self-management, they seek out its history. Wherever this history is not falsified, they discover that it goes back to the Parisian sections during the French Revolution, to the Paris Commune, to the movement for workers' control and the Soviets during and immediately after the Russian Revolution (destroyed by the Bolshevik dictatorship), to the vast communalisation of the Ukraine with the anarchists of Mahkno (destroyed by the Red Army), to the social revolution during the civil war in Spain (1936-1939), where thousands of factories and farms were taken over by workers (only to be destroyed by the Stalinists on the one hand and the Fascists on the other), to the Hungarian revolution of 1956, to the massive general strike in France involving 10 million people in 1968, to Portugal in 1975, to mention a few examples. These, and similar attempts by the working class to take direct control of all economic and political power by completely reorganising it and pushing for complete decentralisation, thereby destroying all forms of minority control.

Some of the organisational principles of anarcho-syndicalist ideas and their application in unions are as follows:

- all decisions are made by the rank-in-file membership. In the case of a general strike, previously decided battle plans are implemented;
- no worker is forced to belong to a union: one belongs because ones to be a militant, and pays dues by choice;

- all relations between different trade unions are based on federalism, which means local, regional, and national federations founded on voluntary association;
- all elected persons fulfilling administrative posts are revocable at all times by the base and are volunteers *without pay.* There are *no paid functionaries* in anarcho-syndicalist unions. All important tasks are carried out after the working day by the militants. Even the national co-ordinating and administration committee does union business only after work. Jacques Godbout (*Le Devoir,* 26 August, 1980) in trying to sort out the reasons for the conflict between the elected officials of the Confédération des syndicats nationaux (CSN) and the permanent staff, would have been well-served to have studied the anarcho-syndicalist tradition. How is it that today, in Spain for example, the third largest trade union, the anarcho-syndicalist CNT (Confederacion Nacional del Trabajo) with a membership of 250,000, functions militantly without a single paid official? This same CNT was the largest union with 2 million members in Spain in 1939, before Franco won the civil war, functional the same way;
- direct action is proposed and used by anarcho-syndicalist unions as a means of gaining economic concessions and no collective agreement is signed and sanctioned by law. Agreements gained from strike actions tend to be verbal, and the workplace is subject to strike action at any time. When circumstances require or permit, direct action leads to a general strike through which workers contest the established monopoly of economic and political power. A general strike could lead to workers' control of the economy and the replacement of the State with a confederation of trade unions and communal unions;
- the unemployed can remain active members of an anarcho-syndicalist union;
- all elected delegates or delegations to confederal meetings are not only revocable at all times by the base, but are strictly mandated on all subjects on the agenda through the decisions of the general assembly of workers. The delegates do not represent themselves but the decisions of their base. Thus, anarcho-syndicalist practice is one of direct democracy, as opposed to representative or liberal democracy and long-term mandates,
- anarcho-syndicalism is not only opposed to all political parties, but has nothing to do with parliamentary elections and refuses to deal with the State or otherwise seek its intervention.

With these organisational principles, anarcho-syndicalism attempts to live self-management within the trade unions, building the experience of the working class today for a self-managed society tomorrow. The anarchism of this revolutionary syndicalism attempts to fight both exploitation *and* domination in all forms. Anarcho-syndicalist principles assume that the working class is quite able to meet its own needs and aspirations, without vanguard political parties or social democratic parties. Anarcho-syndicalism, like anarchism in general, once thought to be dead by Marxists and social democrats, as well as by the ruling class, has not only re-emerged in Spain, but also in Italy, France, Portugal, Greece, Germany and Sweden. It grows wherever people strive for both political and economic democracy and therefore, an end to both capital and the State.

The Second Front of Reproduction

The authors of *La conjoncture au Québec...* also note an anti-authoritarianism in the social and popular movement which they refer to as populism, a tendency recently supplemented more and more by libertarian principles. This trend, with its clear perspective on community organisation, encouraging localised struggles, in addition to broadening its organised base in a neighbourhood to reach out to larger urban struggles (this is especially the case in Montréal), is an indication of maturation. The debate on community organisation through street committees or bloc associations federated into self-governing neighbourhood councils, which themselves federate on a municipal basis, has the potential to move much beyond populism. Here again, community activists, on the basis of their own experience, are looking to the history of libertarian socialism. The libertarians in popular movements such as the anarcho-syndicalists in trade-unions, stress the need for an overall extra-parliamentary social struggle.

The growth of the anti-authoritarian and libertarian, if not anarchist consciousness, in the cultural, feminist and ecology movements, is laying the basis for a movement for socialist self-management. Such a movement, unlike a political party, will not consume or dominate the various dimensions of the revolutionary project. On the contrary, the organisational principle will be *federated with autonomous* movements as its basis. The contribution of the anarchists in such a movement will be the same as that in the labour movement, namely, to help ward off the hard and soft left-wing authoritarians and encourage the development of a theory and practice of self-management.

Such a convergence of an anarcho-syndicalism in the workplace, with its emphasis on workers' control and a libertarian socialist movement stressing community control through individual and collective self-determination, can contribute to the realisation of socialism from below. Together, it forms a new perspective on the national and social question. It represents a social struggle of people attempting to take control of society and its institutions directly, without the intermediation of any elites.

The beginning of a significant social struggle in Québec will become clear to all when this radical movement of the Left confronts established political power at the bottom of our society as a priority and takes popular control across Québec in the school commissions, in the administrative bodies of the hospitals and the CLSCs (Local Community Service Centre), in the city halls of the municipalities and pushing these institutions into examples of intermediate self-management. Such a thrust towards a broad

and co-ordinated basis will be the immediate face of socialist self-management.

What then, do we do next? For us, it means whatever increases the con-
fidence, the autonomy, the initiative, the participation,the solidarity, the
egalitarian and mutual aid tendencies and self-activity of the people.
Sterile and harmful action is whatever reinforces the passivity of the
people, their apathy, their cynicism, their differentiation through hierarchy, their alienation, their reliance on others to do things for them and the
degree to which they can therefore be manipulated by others — even by
those allegedly acting on their behalf.

All this because socialism is not just the common ownership and control of the means of production and distribution. It means freedom,
equality, reciprocal recognition and a radical transformation of all human
relations. It is positive self-consciousness. It is people's understanding of
their environment and of themselves in relation to it; it means further, a
control over their work and over such social institutions as they may need
to create. These are not secondary aspects which will automatically follow
the expropriation of the old ruling class. On the contrary, they are essential
parts of the whole process of social transformation, for without them, no
genuine social transformation will take place.

NOTES

1. See "Root and Branch: the New Left in the 1960s," in chapter 1 of this volume.
2. *La contre-culture au Québec*, by Paul Chamberland. Dossier — Québec (Livre — dossier Stock No. 3, 1979).
3. *Le Devoir*, 26 mai, 1979, interview by Natalie Petrowski.
4. "Appeal to the Slavs 1848," in *Bakunin on Anarchism*, edited by Sam Dolgoff, Black Rose Books, Montréal, 1980.
5. *Michel Bakounine et l'Italie, 1871-72* (Archives Bakounine, Editions Champ Livre) partie I, p. xxi-xxii.
6. "Bakunin, Kropotkin, the Anarchist Movement," by Jean Caroline Cahm in *Socialism and Nationalism*, Spokesmen, 1978.
7. Ibid.

This essay first appeared in early 1981 in *L'Impasse: enjeux et perspectives de l'après-référendum* (Éditions Nouvelle Optique, Montréal) a collection of essays edited by two well-known radical Québec academics, Nicole Laurin-Frenette and Jean François Léonard. The book consists of essays from people in the trade unions, ecology, women's movement, citizens' groups and the left-nationalist tendency.

McCARTHYISM IN CANADA: OUR RESPONSE

As we were going to press, the news story broke exposing the federal government as having encouraged police surveillance of political activities, violating the civil liberties of individuals and groups. Jean-Pierre Goyer, the solicitor-general at the time, submitted a letter to members of the cabinet describing a revolutionary "conspiracy", and attached a list of twenty-one names of people who were allegedly involved. In Goyer's letter of June 15, 1971, he makes reference to an article, a journal, editors and concepts which he implies were the ideological source for this revolutionary movement. Before the mass media named this journal, regular readers of *Our Generation* must have guessed that the references in Goyer's letter were to this journal.

As the exposé becomes broader, we hope that the larger questions are discussed more widely than ever before. For example, what is wrong with our political institutions, and why do they have to be protected by this kind of secret police activity? What is, in fact, an Extra-Parliamentary Opposition (EPO)? What do we mean by radical social change? And what are the strategies we have been advocating during the last sixteen years through this journal and our actions? Because to say that Goyer and his police agency have got things garbled is a gross understatement.

The State, under the dominance of the Liberal Party, contrary to all its stated values of belief in civil liberties, has created a parapolice secret intelligence agency with the power to use RCMP intelligence, to carry out the surveillance of persons and groups who advocate fundamental changes. In Québec, the State created a similar secret apparatus, and compiled a list of 30,000 names, complete with dossiers. This was recently revealed when the PQ took over. So much for the government's rhetoric of believing in civil liberties, freedom of speech and press, and the right to be free from discrimination because of one's political beliefs.

What's so secret about this "secret" list? When this list finally becomes known (we know some of the names at this time), we are sure that most thinking, active political people in Canada will recognize some of their names. Why? Because they are people who have been honestly stating their philosophy and acting on it for most of their adult lives. Speaking for ourselves, we have not only stated what we believe in, but have circulated our analysis as widely as possible. There have never been any secrets as far as we are concerned. The secret is not the people on the list nor what they have advocated, the secret is the State's: the fact that is has illegally and in the face of everything it supposedly stands for, kept watch on the public and private lives of people because of their political views. In the end, what the secret police have found, speaking for *Our Generation*, was simply what we have been writing about all along. This being the case, they have been reduced to distortions, painting a picture of lies about a conspiracy.

The State, through Goyer, has implied that the EPO was an organized conspiracy, the purpose of which was, among others, to infiltrate various government agencies. The mass media has gone on to extrapolate that there was a leader of the EPO. The idea of an EPO was first discussed in Canada in an editorial in *Our Generation*, vol. 6 number 4, Fall 1969. The idea was further discussed at a three-day public conference in Ottawa soon after, attended by some two hundred people, some of them you, our readers.

A few brief quotes from the editorial gives some idea of what we said at the time. "The fundamental pivot of our position is that all social and political questions...are deeply connected; that what we oppose, is, in fact, a system...We wish to create a political movement of people with the capacity to determine their own lives...The idea of EPO is that a coalition of individuals and groups with a common critique of liberal democracy and a minimum programme choose to act together and separately within such a framework."

Needless to say, the very idea of an EPO contradicts, not only the notion of a conspiracy, but equally the idea of a formal structured organisation. None ever existed, and certainly not headed by one person. The concept of the EPO, however, did have influence across the country, and continues to be discussed in one form or another. It was, of course, attacked by liberal democrats and the old Left.

The one direct quote in the Goyer letter was from an article called "The New Radicals and the Multiversity" by Carl Davidson, from vol. 5, number 3 (Nov.-Dec. 1967), two years before the idea of an EPO was mentioned. The quotation is used out of context to link the whole matter together.

The Goyer letter implies that the twenty-one "subversives" are a tightly knit group, with *Our Generation* as their vehicle of printed expression. At this point, we are not privy to all the names. Of the few we do know, however, some of them are present or former editors with whom we have worked; others are not even acquaintances.

If these then are some of the distortions, what are some of the facts? Here we can, obviously, speak only for *Our Generation*, the words we have published and the political actions we have taken as individuals. It's extremely important to make clear here, again, that we cannot possibly speak for the 21 people on the "subversives" list.

Our Generation was founded in 1961 as a peace research journal; later when it deepened its analysis of our society and developed its focus, it always spoke for radical social change — how could we come to any other conclusion, given our understanding of the way things are? How can a world based on ruthless competition and American neo-capitalism, based on the monopolistic control of natural resources and the tremendous wealth that this control brings to a small elite, allow cultural entities to opt out of that system? How can a social system based on entrenched hierarchy of decision-making allow people at the bottom any meaningful control?

These are a few of the basic questions that we have asked and discussed at length in *Our Generation*. That they have frightened the State to the extent they have, shows that these ideas are fertile and have struck a nerve.

The evolving analysis we have presented has been a radical one, that is it has attempted to go to the root of the problems facing our society. The solutions offered have more often times than not been revolutionary, that is basic, or fundamental. The word "revolutionary" is fraught with history, images and connotations. Nevertheless, every historical period, and every society defines the word for itself. Because we live in an advanced technological/industrial society, we obviously do not imply a simplistic notion of revolution à la Petrograd, 1917, or Shanghai, 1927, or even Barcelona, 1936. The contemporary meaning of this concept has been, and will continue to be the subject of debate in *Our Generation*.

Human beings tend to see themselves reflected in the world they live in. The State is anchored on its monopoly of violence. The police apparatus which operates with violence, secrecy, hierarchy, and intrigue tends to look for these qualities in society. This is what they saw in the New Left. They were and are wrong. This society is in a profound crisis, spiritual and cultural, political and economic. Intrigue and intimidation don't offer solutions. Fortunately, they have again exposed themselves for more people to see, and in doing so, have given us another opportunity to continue the debate on basic issues thereby nourishing the dialectic between theory and practice.

Summer 1977

ADDENDUM

Since our comment on the State's blacklist in our last issue, we have learned more on the nature of police practice in Canada. In bits and pieces, the Canadian people have become more aware of the fact that the RCMP does not feel answerable to government authorities and that police departments across the country are amassing sophisticated surveillance technology. Specifically we have learned from the press that the police use cryptic sources to obtain information illegally and which the police feel quite comfortable in protecting from any public knowledge or scrutiny.

The *Praxis Institute* break-in on December 18, 1970 illustrates this well. This institute was founded and administered by our friends, two of them former editors of this journal. Before the break-in they suspected that they were being watched. Information about them was published on November 26, and 27, 1970 in the *Toronto Telegram* under the editorship of the professional anti-communist, Peter Worthington. This person did not reveal his sources for the articles, but the nature of the material published could only have come from police files. Soon after these articles appeared, the two Praxis directors were harassed by threatening phone calls both at home and work. Three weeks after the articles appeared, the break-in occurred. Two weeks after the break-in, Worthington claims two men in trench-coats with Eastern European accents handed him the stolen files from Praxis which he handed over to the RCMP. He claimed he did not know what exactly happened, the RCMP admitted that the stolen files were given to them from another source and which they could not reveal, because the sources have relatives in Eastern Europe.

We review this information in order to draw some parallels with our own Montréal situation. Since 1973, one of the editors of the journal has been harassed and spied on by a local right-wing vigilante group complete with East European accents. The editorial offices of the journal and Black Rose Books have also been harassed. The harassment takes familiar forms. The editor is telephoned regularly and threatened or insulted. His whereabouts are known, including trips abroad. The editorial offices have been broken into, the famous police technique of collecting and sifting through a group's garbage has been used, and some large advertising signs on the exterior of our offices have been torn down. On one occasion a man visited the offices pretending to work in the printing trade, and took an unusual interest in the material we published, leaving behind a phoney business card. Each time a major incident takes place the Montréal police are notified but no apparent follow-up is made.

Because of recent revelations that the RCMP used their own unofficial agents for information on the *Praxis Institute*, it is hard not to conclude that the present harassment and information gathering directed us may be RCMP-linked.

The astonishing thing is that this right-wing group in Montréal could not be possibly passing anything of informational value to the police, since a journal by its very nature is an open activity, and our practice as political activists is also public. In spite of continuous harassment we have not, needless to say, changed our well-known telephone numbers, to these agents' disappointment.

As we pointed out before, the nature of the secret police is that it expects others to behave as it does: furtively and with cloak and dagger. The fact that our concepts of social change can only work if they are open and widely discussed, must seem inconceivable to both the secret police and its outside agents. We want to simply put on record, especially to you, our readers, some of the problems we must deal with as a group of outspoken and uncompromising critics of our liberal democracy.

Chapter 3

THE SOCIAL QUESTION: THE NEW LEFT

Fall 1967

THE STATE OF THE MOVEMENT

For the first time since the 1930s, we hear the open use in North America of the words, "rebellion," "revolt" and "revolution." The long, hot summers in the USA do not only affect the life and work styles of the people in the black ghettos. They affect the styles of many other minorities struggling for peace and freedom. This includes the people in the peace and anti-Vietnam war movement, Spanish-Americans, Puerto-Ricans, Native Americans, French-Canadians, the anti-poverty movement, the industrial workers and the students. Finally, it affects the North American power elite which is beginning to suffer from a kind of Parkinson's disease.

The evidence is clear. The black power movement will have within it an important trend towards urban guerrilla warfare which will express itself beyond the long, hot summers into the long, bleak winters. Given the continued turbulence in Québec, the Québec Liberation Front (FLQ) type activity will re-emerge again soon, amongst other forms of agitation. Also for the first time, the student power movement will swing into sabotage against physical property on campus as a new phase in shaking up bureaucracies and declaring solidarity with the ghettos. Alongside this thrust, non-violent direct action will re-assert itself, Minneapolis being but one example.

But somehow, more people must find the sources of courage and fearlessness in order to act. This question is essentially existential. It is a question which, in a society that by all appearances continues to be stable, confounds us.

Our friend, Thomas Hayden, puts it thus: "It is not enough to take 'positions' on vital issues; not enough to join, or withdraw, from a radical party; not enough to pass resolutions, form committees, and publish magazines; not enough to take 'the correct attitude' on the role of the Left. Needed also is the quality of existential struggle with the real problems of making change while maintaining integrity. How do you change a relatively stable society?…" We must state clearly again and again, that the more we carry out our work, the more we realise that out goals in many instances are quite different from previous radical movements. The original utopias can stand overhauling, for we have to find ways whereby the majority of people can participate in fundamentally changing our society. This is a necessity in our advanced industrial/technological society, for the negative implications of not doing so go beyond "1984."

The first phase of the movement was sporadic, nihilistic, and populist, and we use these terms in the literal sense and not pejoratively. We now find that more of the intellectual energy of the movement is focused on what the new society should look like, as well as how to get there. Two questions that cannot, and must not be separated.

Spring 1968

STRUGGLE IS FREEDOM, IT'S JUST BEGINNING

Our Generation and its editors have over the years analysed, reported and theorised about the nature of the moulded industrial/technological societies of the Nation-State and, in particular, the inability of this collection of anachronisms to solve their basic international problems. We have determined this because this kind of society is *structurally* incapable of proceeding with disarmament, decolonisation and development (which are all interrelated). Massive internal upheavals will occur because of the inability of these countries to set human priorities abroad, this same lack also reflected internally, thereby creating a contradiction incapable of resolution at the present level of our situation.

Furthermore, since many of these societies in the East, as in the West, have their own internal pulse, the form and substance of the revolutionary syndrome is different even though the fundamental nature of the sickness is the same. Playwright Arthur Miller, recently put it thus:

> From Moscow to Warsaw to Prague to Paris to Rio to Berkeley and New York, there is a deep and boiling rebellion against institutions and institutionalised feeling. Be it a government, a university, a moral code or a way of life, the institution as king is naked now. The mere fact that it exists is no longer proof of its value. In the past four years the war in Vietnam has become an institution, an institution with high private, sacred ceremonies of death and sacrifice, and all the sanctification of a holy crusade...

Our Generation and its editors have, since our inception, analysed, reported and theorised about the movements in opposition to the status quo (those independent of the "ideological" blocs of the East or West) and their alternatives. We have dealt with the political sociology of these movements, their means and ends. We have opened our pages to their leading thinkers and activists. In particular, during the more intense and visible period of the nuclear arms race we focused on the peace movement. Indeed, at a critical point during this period we urged the creation of an international, non-aligned peace movement. It was not long after, and with the efforts of many other people in other countries, that the International Confederation for Disarmament and Peace (ICDP) was born.

We always maintained on the basis of sociological studies that the peace movement had more of a revolutionary potential than its initial nuclear disarmament phase, and this we attempted to demonstrate editorially, and by turning readers' attention to the writings of A.J. Muste. It was also apparent to us, again substantiated by sociological studies, that the vast majority of the participants in the peace movement were young. When this is stressed, observers noted that this is usual for such movements; however, we noted that this modern manifestation had unique political dimensions.

This youth phenomenon was a feature common to all nations that had massive peace movements, which in turn proved a commonality amongst countries permeated by a war psychosis and extensive armament programmes. This is not to suggest that the common phenomenon of rebellious youth had no additional, and sometimes equally important cause, such as the civil rights struggle in the USA. But in almost all other countries with developed radical youth movements, the question of world destruction and its ugly contemporary expression, the war in Vietnam, was central. In the USA, the contradiction was more acute, the consciousness and action more developed because the international question was linked most visibly with that society's inability to grant human rights to its African-American citizenry.

Because what will happen to the USA as a politico-economic supermarket and socio-cultural air-conditioned nightmare will also determine the nature of industrialism and technology in all other countries, *Our Generation* is primarily concerned with studying and analysing North America.

In drawing tighter the analysis of our social crisis, especially its sociocultural and political aspects, in contrast to the strictly economic, we naturally began posing the larger theoretical question of how does a technological society *fundamentally change* (we have never doubted this possibility, unlike most in the old Left); what are the constituencies crucial to that change, and who are its central agencies?

We have maintained throughout that there is something profoundly revolutionary about the state of youth. Not only has the development of movements of contestation fortified this notion, but recent society-shaking events have corroborated this. In France, for example, it was youth, students, young workers and young professionals, who were the centre of the revolutionary upheaval. It was this section of society which contested not only the violence of the State, but also challenged the intellectually rheumatized leadership of the centre, old Left opposition (Communist and Socialist), and trade unions. It was this radical constituency that *refused* to separate the socio-cultural and political questions and demands (incorporating the economic) from the strictly economic and material issues of the revolution. The fact of the matter is that "In the mind of the student revolutionaries, Government and Opposition, are lumped together in one dreary, fossilized, discredited bunch." (*The Observer*, London, May 19, 1968.)

The most recent revolutionary outbreak was in France — not a revolution in the traditional sense of armed uprising but nonetheless, in a developing creative political style of the second half of the twentieth century, an authentic revolution. There were many mistakes made and although this editorial is not the place to discuss them, it is our contention that *one* of the principal reasons for the defeat was that some of the "means" used in the contestation were not creative enough. The reported police agents and provocateurs in their midst notwithstanding, the revolutionaries slipped simply into the standard self-defeating responses of classical insurrection. These "means" are vulgar incongruities, ahistorical and staid in our type of society. "Revolutionary violence," is *no* substitute for militancy. Such a strategy cannot be the *main* thrust of revolution in technological societies. There is no "revolutionary violence," there is only reactionary violence, since violence is in the final analysis the main pillar upon which the power elite rests. In a revolution, contestation, confrontation, militancy are not equitable to violent offense. In saying this, we in no sense wish to associate ourselves with the reformism of the discredited opposition. In discussing this question we must also answer, how was it that the supportive mood of France turned about in the time span of a few weeks; how could it have been maintained as the concrete basis for a democratic non-violent revolution?

Most of the underlying causes of the French revolution — growing rigidity of conventional techniques of organisations including government and the inchoate, unsatisfied aspirations of the international underground known as "youth," "the new generation," "our generation" — are present in every industrial nation. What has happened in Paris is, after all, simply a development of events which have already occurred in Berlin and New York.

> This is revolution. What is happening in the Sorbonne and the Free University of Berlin, in France, West Germany, Italy and (embryonically) in Britain, is not a mere generation conflict. Nor is it just a fight for university reform — not any more. It is a total onslaught on modern society. This particular rising will probably fail. Its roots are too shallow: the State, its enemy, too massive. But it has already stormed places thought impregnable...
> The enemy is the "bureaucratic State" — east and west. It is the society organised for efficiency at the expense of liberty, the system which "offers the people consumer goods and calls them freedom." It is the system which adapts education — so it seems — to the mass production of docile technocrats. It is the party system posing as true democracy, repression masked as tolerance. (*The Observer*, May 19, 1968.)

It is indicative that the International Confederation for Disarmament and Peace which we helped create, along with the German SDS (Students for a Democratic Society), have called and organised the *first* international student and youth conference of the New Left. This conference, to be held in Europe during August, will bring together the leading spokesmen and organisations of the new radicals laying the basis of the *new internationalism. Our Generation* has been invited, and three of our editors will be attending this conference. In our next issue, readers will have an opportunity to examine our reports.

Our Generation and its editors have raised the questions touched on in this editorial over the last six years. In all modesty we feel, along with many others, vindicated by events. We conclude with the prophetic words of C. Wright Mills, written in 1960, his absence felt more than ever.

But take heart American: you won't have time to get really bored with your friends abroad: they won't be your friends much longer. You don't need them; it will all go away; don't let them confuse you.' Add to that: In the Soviet bloc, who is it that has been breaking out of apathy? It has been students and young professors and writers; it has been the young intelligentsia of Poland and Hungary, and of Russia too. Never mind that they've not won; never mind that there are other social and moral types among them. First of all, it has been these types. But the point is clear — isn't it?

"But it's just some kind of moral upsurge, isn't it?" Correct. But under it: no apathy. Much of it is direct non-violent action, and it seems to be working, here and there. Now we must learn from their practice and work out with them new forms of action.

"But its all so ambiguous. Turkey, for instance. Cuba, for instance." Of course it is; history-making is always ambiguous; wait a bit; in the meantime, help them focus their moral upsurge in less ambiguous political ways; work out with them the ideologies, the strategies, the theories that will help them consolidate their efforts; new theories of structural changes of and by human societies in our epoch.

"But its utopian, after all, isn't it?" No — not in the sense you mean. Whatever else it may be, its not that: tell it to the students of Japan.

Isn't all this, isn't it something of what we are trying to mean by the phrase, "The New Left?" Let the old men ask sourly, "Out of Apathy — into what?" The Age of Complacency is ending. Let the old women complain wisely about "the end of the ideology." We are beginning to move again. (*New Left Review*, 1960.)

THE CYC: THE BIRD THAT CANNOT EVEN FLY...

> In the interplay of theory and practice, true and false solutions become distinguishable — ever with the evidence of necessity, never as the positive, only with the certainty of a reasoned and reasonable chance, and with the persuasive force of the negative. For the true positive is the society of the future and therefore beyond definition and determination, while the existing positive is that which must be surmounted. But the experience and understanding of the existent society may well be capable of identifying what is NOT conducive to a free and rational society, what impedes and distorts the possibilities of its creation. (Herbert Marcuse, *Repressive Tolerance.*)

In a society of repressive tolerance and one-dimensionality, to use the terminology of Herbert Marcuse, institutions are created which absorb dissent and opposition, making these qualities harmless. Because it is also a society of abundant goodies, social activists are co-opted and socialised into believing that an employed liberatory rhetoric implies opportunities for radical change.

When the Company of Young Canadians (CYC) (their organisation was similar to the U.S. Peace Corps/Vista) was conceived by the Federal Government, there was, in this country, a movement of youth which was *feeling* its way towards an effective opposition. Even with all its weaknesses, the Canadian New Left was closer than any post-war group to reaching out and influencing new constituencies. It had broken out of the old Left shell of preaching to the converted while within the young organism a new radical consciousness was being generated amongst an important minority.

Herbert Marcuse has taught us that in a modern technological society any conventional opposition group inevitably assumes the values of the system it opposes and is eventually absorbed by it. This tendency, plus the political myopia of the new radicals regarding the CYC, created an aborted New Left. The repressive tolerance of Canadian liberalism with its central ingredient of cynicism successively added to the havoc surrounding the still-birth. There was in this drama the sound folk-wisdom of the young, instinctively suspicious of the top-down "initiatives" of governing bureaucracies, coupled with the experience of seasoned radicals and the "grand strategies" of a group of intellectual eunuchs who merely verified the nature of their political sexuality by joining the harem on Chapel Street. The tension between these two groups in a situation where the curse of Sisyphus still prevailed, turned a tender daydream into a nightmare. But who benefited from the organisational collapse of the New Left in Canada?

Goodies from a Porkbarrel

An unemployed student wrote us recently, "...it seems that the directors of 'wars on poverty' are the first to solve their poverty." *Item:* CYC Executive Director — *annual* salary $20,000, transportation and communications budget — $55,646. Two Associate Directors — *annual* salary $17,000, transporation and communications budget — $52,720.

Item: "One worker, on contract received $75 a day along with an all-expenses paid trip to New Orleans and California." "Here was a Company that went out one day, without any policy being set, and spent $33,000 in Montreal on deluxe model cars for its staff, that has run up a long distance telephone bill of $40,000," "that has two paid workers for every volunteer, and spent on average a sum of $12,000 annually (the company said $10,000) for each volunteer in the field..." (Joan Cohen, the *Ottawa Citizen.*) And there is *much* more information of this sort available.

The CYC tried hard not to rock the political boat during its twenty-month history, and largely succeeded, except for a few headlines over some tinkering.

Thus, the first episode in this soap-opera concludes with the successful co-option of some former activist, corruption, no significant social action, a chorus of "we told you so," and the temporary obstruction of the growth of a radical youth movement in Canada.

Besides entertaining the opponents of social and political change in Canada, the ghosts of the "National Defense" department (former occupants of the Chapel St. HQ of the CYC) must have gotten a real charge out of this story. The moral is more activists should take horror films seriously.

Spring 1968

WHAT IS THE NEW RADICALISM?

The purpose of this article is two-fold: to clarify to readers the general contours of the new radicalism, and to sketch some of the present ambiguities we have in the new movement. This purpose is particularly difficult in that the form of the subject-matter is shapeless when compared to orthodoxy, and yet so dynamic. Its effect is widespread and profound, yet scattered and difficult to focus. It is part of a society in chaos and disintegration, yet highly structured vertically, maintaining a firm political grip. In the history of ideologies and social movements, we are in the same situation as the utopian socialists and anarchists of the early nineteenth century, yet, in the history of human society, we are bordering on a crisis that can atomize the planet and bring it to a halt, or at a minimum, choke off some vital arteries of human existence. It is out of this terrifying dialectic between a hope for something new and impending disaster that new possibilities are affecting the existing facets of life. Justified or not, this tension is felt more acutely by this generation than any previous one.

The new movement of students and youth has recently received an additional push into historical relevance and political reality. The disaffection from existing society and its mainstream institutions has now become an international phenomenon as never before. Whereas, previously, those involved in traditional politics believed that industrial/technological societies in the northern hemisphere were both incapable of producing new forms of radicalism and fundamentally changing their social structures, recent developments challenge this notion. The idea that the best these societies could hope for in the area of social change is one or another form of meliorism is no longer valid.

In the early 1960s there was a great deal of student political activism. In Japan, Korea, Hungary, Latin America, Britain, masses of students were involved in a variety of issues. The youth movement in the US was still beginning, based around civil rights in the South by means of Freedom rides and direct action, and through pressure group actions including demonstrations in the peace movement. Now, however, young people no longer strike out against separate issues, but rather move on the whole along a broad front of activity interrelating social and international questions. In addition, the impressive youth opposition within the US gives a new political relevance to similar activities elsewhere. The power of example cannot be overestimated in the youth movement. The stark similarity in critiques and demands of young people in the US, Canada, Britain, France, Italy, West Germany, Czechoslovakia, and Poland are laying the basis for a radical and genuine internationalism, thus superseding the limitations of the earlier actions of the 1960s, as well as those of the socialist movements in the first quarter of this century. The Toronto *Globe and Mail* in a series of superficial articles called "The Angry Young World" symbolised the worried establishment, yet understood the threat of the new internationalism. In patronizing prose, the series of articles were labelled: "In France: Students want the tight rein relaxed;" "In the US: A new force in the political system." "In Britain: Rioting is fun until the blood flows;" "In Germany: Students are anti-power;" "In Italy: The constant war cry is reform or bust;" "Poles and Czechs demand democracy."

This is a *transitional* movement whose purpose it is to change society, but also to change itself. Theory and practice are mutually interdependent and this socio-political movement has set for itself as a goal, the elaboration of a new theory through the process of testing existing hypotheses and insights in actual political practice. It further means that the movement values *diversity* over unity, *experimentation* over orthodoxy, *local initiatives* over national direction. It is true that the movement is as yet without a historical perspective, although now that the European movements are born, and with increasing direct contact, the militants in North America will overcome this shortcoming. The movement is, in a healthy way, against intellectualism although it is not anti-intellectual. It is anti-dogmatic, and anti-sectarian but progressively ideological, understanding the tremendous importance of first creating an existentially committed constituency.

No one can begin to think, feel or act now except from the starting-point of his or her own alienation....We do not need theories so much as the experience that is the source of theory. (R.D. Laing, *The Politics of Experience*.)

The Two Wings of the Movement

The movement has two basic sections — the *New Left* and the *psychedelic Left*. Like all revolutionary avant-garde movements, the new radicals come from the ranks of the privileged or semi-privileged. In the case of our society, they come from the middle-classes whose interests are locked into the status quo and who thus help maintain the style of oppression peculiar to our type of society. Suffering from "alienation," these youth have chosen voluntarily to struggle against various forms of oppression — war, poverty, the multiversity, middle-class life styles and conformity.

There are basically two forms of "alienation": *social alienation* which is an *estrangement* from mainstream society, the surrounding purposelessness, hypocrisy, selfishness, moral sterility and inaction, and *personal alienation* which is a separation from meaningful or creative work, education or leisure, to the point where one doubts the whole purpose of one's existence. The individual becomes isolated from his or her environment, loyalties disintegrate, and most associations are shattered. The majority of young people today are alienated in one form or another, and many of them in both ways.

Those who are principally alienated in personal terms form the core of the psychedelic Left. They seek personalist solutions in the form of withdrawals from society into intentional "utopian" communities, drugs of various kinds, or psychotherapy. During the 1950s the "beatniks" or "beats" symbolised this form of personalism; recently the "hippies" do so with more explicit and articulate values and with more creative methods of self-expression. They have become numerically a very wide phenomenon. More recently still, the "yippies" (politically-oriented "hippies") have come to the fore and have created the Youth International Party. Each successive wave of youth tends to increase numerically, and tends to branch off into new trends. The "hippies" have been influenced by the New Left and the provos on the one hand, and by their own success on the other. The psychedelic movement has influenced almost all of the arts profoundly, has established a separate and effective counter-communications network of over 200 newspapers throughout the continent (most of them co-operating with an underground press syndicate called the Liberation News Service), reaching an estimated audience of close to 500,000. This does not include the publications of the left-of-centre to the Left, nor does it include RAMPARTS. The psychedelic Left has managed to create its own *youth culture* which has given the whole youth movement a *social* and *cultural reality*. Needless to say, the Establishment desperately and ruthlessly tries to sponge off and manipulate this cultural revolution.

What is special about the present case is the scale on which the cultural revision is taking place and the depth to which it is reaching. I have referred to the "culture" of the young, but would it be an exaggeration to call what is arising among them a "counter-culture?" That is, a culture which so radically rejects the mainstream assumptions of Western society that it is scarcely recognisable to many as a culture at all, but looks, instead, like a barbaric intrusion. (Theodore Roszak, "The Counter Culture: Youth and the Great Refusal," *The Nation*, March/April, 1968.)

Although the psychedelic Left is not considered "political" by the New Left in that as a movement it does not have an analysis of power and does not organise for its redistribution, the fact remains that as a movement it is having a *political effect* both on society as a whole and, more importantly, on other youth by its attractive example. The malaise and vague discontent felt by the new generation expressed in J.D. Salinger's novel of the 1950s, *Catcher in the Rye* finds an outlet short of political expression with the psychedelic Left.

The underlying unity of youthful dissent consists, then, in the effort of beat-hip bohemianism to work out the personality structure, the total life style that follows from New Left social criticism. At their best, the beats and hips are the utopian experimenters of the social system that lies beyond the intellectual rejection of the Great Society. The counter culture is the embryonic cultural base of New Left politics, the effort to discover new types of community, new family patterns, new sexual mores, new kinds of livelihood, new aesthetic forms, new personal identities on the far side of power politics, the bourgeois home, and the Protestant work ethic. If the experiments are new and often abortive, it must be remembered that the experimenters have been on the scene only for a dozen years and are picking their way though customs and institutions that had more than a few centuries to entrench themselves. To criticise the experiments is legitimate and necessary; to despair of what are no more than beginnings is premature. (Theodore Roszak, op. cit.)

Those who are principally alienated in social terms from the core of the New Left: this form of radicalism begins with rebellion against existing institutions and later develops by actual commitment to a particular student or youth organisation that seeks to change society. The New Left was born in various Western countries under largely similar circumstances. Emerging from the silence of the 1950s into the chilling horror of the nuclear arms race, the peace movement gave contemporary youth its first opportunity for self-expression. Whenever the peace symbol was carried or worn, the majority of participants involved in the picketing, mass demonstrations or direct actions, were young people.

Roughly since 1960 there has been a social movement, composed mainly of students, which has threatened the equilibrium of American society. This threat was not, at first, unambiguously radical: it was liberal in the nature of its surface demands (such as racial integration, an end to nuclear testing, and free speech) but radical in its distrust of compromise and in its proclivity for direct action. Over a period of years form and content merged, and the result was something that could legitimately be called a New Left. The concept of participatory democracy, as evolved by SDS and SNCC, offered both a mode of operation and a critique of welfare-state liberalism. Moreover, it furnished the basis for a revolt against the university environment in which most New Leftists found themselves. The idea that the "normal channels" are instruments of manipulation, and that people must be motivated to make decisions for themselves, was clearly applicable to the university as well as to other areas of society; this is what made student radicals realise that they no longer had simply to fight other people's battles.

Since 1965, the New Left had undergone a number of changes, both in its conception of society and in its strategic thinking. Draft resistance, underground newspapers, guerrilla theatre, above all black power, are terms that would have evoked few signs of recognition three short years ago. But none of them should be surprising in the light of what the New Left had become by 1965. For they are all variations on a theme: the recognition that...liberalism was not enough, that the good society was one in which people shaped their own institutions to meet their own needs. (James P. O'Brien, "The Early Days of the New Left," *Radical America*, May/June, 1968.)

The Ideological Formation of the New Left

Leszek Kolakowski once stated, "To construct a utopia is always an act of negation toward an existing reality, a wish to change it. But negation is not the opposite of construction — it is only the opposite of affirming existing conditions." The issues around which the New Left built its existential base, and slowly generated an analysis of power in society, thereby funnelling together the elements of an ideology included: foreign and defense policy (its present focus being the war in Vietnam), the educational system (as the key set of institutions which socialise and condition the acceptance of established values), organising the underclass in its social and economic manifestations (reflecting ethnic and racial discrimination in this society as well as exposing the myth of equal opportunity), decolonisation of the Third World, and human rights.

The evolution towards its ideology was one which moved away from liberalism and the single-issue approach to social questions premised on the notion of a pluralistic society. The cutting edge of this evolution was the concern with world peace and human rights in a dynamic context of social justice.

The single-issue campaign or organisation stands for a refusal to work out an explicitly political philosophy and analysis. Without a radical analysis it becomes impossible to develop organisational tactics and movement strategy that propel us towards a community fundamentally different from present-day society. The Columbia University insurrection demonstrates how with the New Left, *action* is the final unifier of theory and practice. In this particular action, the question of the human rights of African-Americans, the undemocratic structure of the multiversity and its nature in society, and the relationship of this institution to the American war machine were married.

There is now the realisation that change cannot come about without a commitment to a sustained struggle for reconstruction, that indeed it is an unending, lifelong struggle. Those who have given so much time and energy to single-issue campaigns have learnt how to make the connections between different issues and the reality of power. This approach is no longer glossed over. The new politics must necessarily be a direct response to a situation which can be characterised as one of crisis in which there is no certainty of the outcome. The New Left is now a movement within which there are various levels of sophistication and consciousness. The new radicalism is still organic enough to allow people to enter its various stages of politics and permits free graduation. It is thus a self-sustaining set of currents constantly replenishing itself. It confronts a crisis which involves our very condition, the nature of society, and the role human beings play in the world.

The components of the embryonic ideology are the search for *a new theory of history*, human society, human nature, social change and the historical agencies of social change. It's a large task but the problem of history is the problem of consciousness. It was Hegel who first pointed this out, followed by the neo-Hegelians and all those who have since sought a global understanding of life on earth.

For the New Left, the idea of the new radicalism is to be treated in an open fashion, as part of the quest for the good life based on justice and equity. It is not surprising, therefore, that the attack on the dogmatism, the sectaries and the "mindless militancy" of the Left have raised so much anger and criticism of the New Left from traditional socialists. The New Left is constantly under attack from both the ideological East and West.

Nonetheless, through the vigour of its analysis and by capturing the mood and the tone of those who are becoming increasingly discontented with the new welfare capitalism, the New Left has successfully breached the apathy maintained by the fantasies of cold warriors and by the consumption spectacles of our technobureaucratised affluence, giving a generation its first taste of democratic politics.

The cleavage between the old and New Left is profound and in certain important areas unreconcilable. The major portion of the blame for society's contemporary crisis is assigned to the historic failure of Western socialism to evolve a theory and practice of democratic socialism. This is held to be so even though one does not proportion out an equal amount of blame to such disparate vintages of politicos as the socialists, communists, eight varieties of Stalinists, revolutionary socialists and leftwingers. The mechanistic socialism of the Communist parties which modeled themselves after Russian and, more recently, Chinese examples, are partially responsible for the failure. But the "democratic socialists" whose capitulation before the centralising concepts and Statist ideology of corporate liberalism, its mesh of technocratic manipulation and concomitant ravishing imperialism/colonialism, are also responsible.

I think the movement wants to build a society both communal and libertarian, both fraternal and free. The inarticulate major premise of Cold
War ideology is that you have to choose between brotherhood and
freedom. If you want brotherhood, Gemeinschaft, a sense of common
purpose, then you must take totalitarianism with it; if you want to be
free then you must put up with its necessary institutional basis, private
property, and with its inevitable accompanying atmosphere, competition. We deny that this choice is necessary. We affirm that it is not beyond
the wit of man to make a society characterised by both love and liberty.
(Staughton Lyne, "A Good Society," *Guardian*, March 16, 1968.)

The idea of the good community has led the New Left to stomach many
different tendencies, including basically reformist and revolutionary sections. There is a continuous tension between both, and each struggle resol-
ves itself on the level of debate and action, only to be mounted again on
another. It is a dialectical process that cannot be resolved, except by sup-
pression, which would only have a temporary effect of resolution. Hopefully, the New Left will have gained enough historical hindsight to
understand the nature of this dialectic and learn the basis of its motion as a
means of enriching its radicalism.

The central core of the working ideology of the typical radical activist is
not defined by any one issue, but consists of a choice between two alternative modes of operation: *permeation* or *Left opposition*. The former
seeks to adapt to the ruling powers and infiltrate their centres of influence with the aim of (someday) getting to the very levers of decision-
making — becoming a part of the Establishment in order to manipulate
the reins to the Left. The latter wish is to stand outside the Establishment
as an open opposition, achieving even short-term changes by the pressure of a bold alternative, while seeking roads to fundamental transformations. (Hal Draper, *Berkeley: The New Student Revolt.*)

The new radicals choose between these two "styles," and what is characteristic is that they choose the path of anti-Establishment Left opposition. This is the thread that runs through the tendency as a whole. Its
defenders and attackers range themselves in battle lines drawn by this
pattern, whatever else they prefer to talk about. (Hal Draper, "In
Defence of the 'New Radicals'," *New Politics*, Summer 1965.)

The Area of Debate

There is great discussion amongst the intellectually creative new radicals about the abolition of private control of the means of industrial
production and distribution, and the substitution of popular control (the
scope and form of this has yet to be defined). The issues debated include:
radical or participatory democracy generating *active participation* in the
decision-making process throughout society and, consequently,
redistributing power and dismantling hierarchical structures; the establishment of various parallel or counter-institutions as small group-oriented
eco-systems challenging the legitimacy of existing mainstream institutions, and thus, creating new balances of societal power while redefining

power, instead of "seizing power"; decentralisation as a political, social and economic process down to the most local level, made possible for the first time in history as a consequence of the human use of a liberatory technology; youth as class and as principal historic agent of social change; the nature of an extra-parliamentary opposition and coalition bringing together the underclass (including its specific racial and ethnic compositions), students, young industrial workers, middle-masses contesting around issues of consumption, radicalised professionals and technicians; anti-militarism, revolutionary non-violence and mass civil disobedience as core elements in a strategy of creative disorder and social dislocation; the abolition of the Nation-State in all its ramifications, creating a radical and genuine internationalism, while at the same time respecting cultural and ethnic self-determination made more possible in a participatory democracy; and new life and work styles including a new sexuality, and human interpersonal relations. In addition, many young radicals are researching the configurations of the liberal corporatism and monopoly capitalism of the Western countries and the contours of the Stalinism, State-capitalism and bureaucratic collectivism of the socialist countries. The New Left continues to place its thrust on action, but at the same time there is a far greater preoccupation with theory then ever before. A score of books have been written on and by the new radicals, and many more are either at the publishers or being written at this very moment. The actions of the youth movements in Germany and the May events in France have also produced an upsurge in critical literature.

> The general pattern of what is happening can be expressed in the following schema: There is a break in the continuity of the radical tradition; the socialist movements waste away; there is no handling on of the torch. But that does not mean the end of the impulsion to revolutionary change. After the interval, radicalism sends its shoots up again, from the seed. It is new, green, inexperienced, unknowledgeable, immature, even bumbling and exists in a welter of question-marks and confusion. In other words, it is a new beginning. Some shoots spring up and die out; others live and flourish and give rise to the new movement at last. But the new movement is not a reduplication of the one that existed before the hiatus: it works out new forms, new phrases, new activities, even maybe new theories, which eventually merge with the old ones and change them and are changed.... (Hal Draper, "In Defence of the 'New Radicals'," *New Politics*, Summer 1965.)

In the opening of this article, it was stated that with reference to the development of a new social movement and ideology, our period has many of the characteristics of the 19th century. In addition, we must keep the following in mind:

> Today, in the last half of the 20th century, we too are living in a period of social disintegration. The old classes are breaking down, the old values are in disintegration, the established institutions — so carefully developed by two centuries of capitalist development — are decaying before our eyes. Like our Renaissance forebears, we live in an epoch of

potentialities, of generalities, and we, too, are searching, seeking a direction from the first lights on the horizon....In a time of such instability, every decade telescopes a generation of change under stable conditions. We must look even further, to the century that lies ahead; we cannot be extravagant enough in releasing the imagination of man. (Lewis Herber, Murray Bookchin, "Ecology and Revolutionary Thought," *Anarchos, I.*)

The new radicals have become progressively aware of the limitations of classical pacifism, anarchism and socialism, and are trying to create a *new synthesis* from the best features of these previously radical ideologies.

From *socialism* come the insights of "historicism," humanist vision, understanding the nature of the socio-economic power structure and its relation to the ownership and control of property, and the need for rational social planning and so on.

Neo-capitalism, with its emphasis on compulsive individual consumption, forms the *economic* basis of the "one-dimensional society" which Marcuse describes so eloquently. It is the historical situation in which, for the first time, a ruling class is forced to organise not only production, but consumption and ideology as well (see Gramsci). It gives rise to certain specific new contradictions and creates both new forms of oppression and new forms of revolt.

Because neo-capitalism occurs at a stage when the level of productivity increases very rapidly and because it demands increased consumption, it requires a break with the "ideologies of scarcity" which had previously justified class society and provided solace for a suffering humanity. In its ideological development, the bourgeoisie can no longer rely on the Church and the Christian religion. Both "simplicity" and "otherworldliness" conflict with the economic needs of neo-capitalist society. Jesus of Nazareth must be replaced by Santa Claus (the patron saint of consumption) in the new hagiology, while Playboy nightclubs become the sanctuaries of the new cult of consumption and repressive desublimation. (Greg Clavert & Carol Neiman, "Internationalism: New Left style," *Guardian*, June 22, 1968.)

From *pacifism* come insights on the nature of international power politics and the arms race, the function of unilateralism, the question of the congruence of means/ends, anti-militarism, civil disobedience or direct action, revolutionary non-violence and resistance, the moral borders of revolution and so on.

We cannot have peace if we are only concerned with peace. War is not an accident. It is the logical outcome of a certain way of life. If we want to attack war, we have to attack that way of life.

Disarmament cannot be achieved nor can the problem of war be resolved without being accompanied by profound changes in the economic order and in the structure of society.

The nation-state is finally based on power-politics, and finally based on militarism, demanding the supreme loyalty of the human being, the ultimate symbol of worship. The significance of this as the basic political structure and symbol of devotion is reflected ironically in the fact that on the one hand there are the two greatest military powers — capitalist

USA and communist USSR, and on the other, communist USSR and communist China. (A.J. Muste)

The radical pacifist scope is large and includes the following:

My background is psycho-analytic, and psycho-analytically, we feel that face-to-face violence, like a fist fight, is natural, and it does damage to try to repress it; that it's better to have the fight out. Therefore, on that level I have no opposition to violence. Naturally I don't like to see people punching each other, but anger is a rather beautiful thing, and anger will lead to a blow, and there you are. When people are under a terrific oppression, as say Negroes in the United States or the Parisians, let's say, during Hitler's occupation of Paris, it seems inevitable that at a certain point they are going to blow up and fight back. And that seems to me like a force of nature. You can do nothing about that, and therefore I don't disapprove. That kind of warfare, guerrilla warfare, partisan warfare, brutalises people, of course it does, but it's human and I would make no moral judgement.
   As soon as warfare, violence, becomes organised, however, and you are told by somebody else, "Kill him," where it's not your own hatred and anger which is pouring out, but some abstract policy or party line, or a complicated strategic campaign, then to exert violence turns you into a thing, because violence involves too much of you to be able to do it at somebody else's direction. Therefore, I am entirely opposed to any kind of warfare, standing armies as opposed to guerrilla armies and so forth. Therefore, all war is entirely unacceptable because it mechanises human beings and inevitably leads to more harm than good. Therefore, I am a pacifist. (Paul Goodman, BBC Radio, January 10 and 30, 1968.)

From *anarchism* come insights on the nature of the corporate state, decentralism, sexuality, progressive education, mental illness, industrialism and technology, human organisation and so on.

Anarchism is not only a stateless society but also a harmonised society which exposes man to the stimuli provided by both agrarian and urban life, physical activity and mental activity, unrepressed sensuality and self-directed spirituality, communal solidarity and individual development, regional uniqueness and world-wide brotherhood, spontaneity and self-discipline, the elimination of toil and the promotion of craftsmanship. In our schizoid society, these goals are regarded as mutually exclusive dualities, sharply opposed to each other. (Lewis Herber, Murray Bookchin, "Ecology and Revolutionary Thought," *Anarchos, 1.*)

If the problem of history is the problem of consciousness, the subsidiary problem of "false consciousness" arises from an awareness of the fact that existing ideologies are inadequate and incompatible. The limitations of such intellectual efforts themselves are a factor complicating our understanding of the theoretical and practical unification of the world which is now proceeding under our eyes. And yet, the very existence of man depends on some solution or advancement with reference to this problem and in which (because of the nature of our times) groups of individuals belonging to the most varied societies and cultures must share.

Consequently, the attempted new synthesis within the modern context of the ecological limitations on human freedom is an effort which is more than an idle play with concepts in the fashion of eclecticism. It represents a response to a practical purpose which in our age becomes more urgent as the globe shrinks, and historically divergent and disparate cultures press against one another threatening to grind each other to pieces. Because these pressures are experienced as largely ideological conflicts amongst people holding different aims, it remains the task of the new radicalism to evolve modes of thought and action which will enable people to recognise the common purpose underlying their divergencies. In this perspective, the development of the concept of ideology itself appears as a barometric reading of the comparative temperatures between actual historical process and critical consciousness. Ideology thus understood regains its ancient pathos, especially as it brings about a new marriage of philosophy and politics.

What will be the intermediary morphology of the new radicalism is not possible to say at this time. The dialectic of this synthesis of which we speak can be a liberating force or, as some students put it, the most important result of this process will be expressed in thirst as the thesis, beer as the antithesis, and the synthesis running under the table.

In this brief and incomplete sketch of the general outline of the new generation's thinking we have been essentially descriptive in our analysis.

In the context of his own analysis of a radical ideology, Alan Haber put our task as follows:

These tasks are difficult. They demand a great deal from the few and young intellectuals who now devote themselves to ideological politics: discipline in pursuing the problems that are important, rather than opportunism in following the current of reformist discontent; patience in developing goals and strategy rather than haste to re-enact the frustration of mass organization where the mass is politically impotent; introspection in examining their own role in society, rather than enthusiasm which leads to submerging personal identity within a collective enterprise; and not the least is courage to stand as opponents within their disciplines and professions against those once-leftists who proclaim the End of Ideology as either necessary or desirable. (R. Alan Haber, "The End of Ideology as Ideology," *Our Generation*, Vol. 4, No. 3.)

Winter 1969

HISTORICAL PERSPECTIVES

Nineteen sixty-eight was as extraordinary a year as 1848. In that year the old empire and absolutism throughout Europe was shaken at its roots. The advocates of the values were at first mostly defeated, but their ideas and actions left a permanent imprint upon the development of that continent and the world. The revolutions of 1848 were part of the political and social consequences of a profound industrial revolution slowly being born.

In 1968 all modern industrial societies, whether capitalist, socialist or social democratic, underwent upheavals under the advance of an onrushing revolutionary technology with the most complex social and political problems arising from it. This movement has jarred the international political and economic systems which have grown up around industrial States. In over *twenty-five* countries youth-led rebellions have left a mark on the social order in 1968. The war in Vietnam, the student revolts and general strikes, the threatened collapse of the Western monetary system, Czechoslovakia, the wars and civil wars in Africa and the Middle East, the manned flight around the moon, China's "cultural revolution," suggest a growing struggle between revolution and counterrevolution.

What is most significant is that events like those that took place in the spring of 1968 have a momentum of their own, and the degree to which individual people appear to be inspiring or controlling them in a significant way is more often times than not an illusion.

North America

In North America, the year 1968 has witnessed an extraparliamentary upsurge in Mexico, the USA and Québec. The major segments of this society engaged in such activity were students, blacks, Québecers, other ethnic and radical groups, and certain sections of the new and industrial working classes. There were more strikes in 1967 and 1968 than in any year since 1947.

College and university students led protests across the continent on an unprecedented scale, joined for the first time by an increasing number of high school students. This extremely significant development beacons new areas for radical organising because high schoolers and their decisions determine not only the tempo of future insurgency on campuses, but also the nature of the future labour force. (This last October, for example, of far greater importance than the 55 terrorist bombings by the Front Libération du Québec, was the general strike of 50,000 students in the technical and junior colleges which lasted in some cases up to six weeks. (This wave of school occupations was a qualitative advance in the forms of direct action used and it inspired the class-conscious working population, — winning nominal trade union support — and the laxer university students.)

Pompous *Fortune* magazine recently reported that approximately 40% of American college students show a "*lack of concern* about making money" (their italics), and tend to "embrace positions that are dissident and extreme."

Fortune hired an opinion research firm to conduct a survey of people in the 18 to 24 age bracket last October to be told that about 750,000 stu-

dents now "identify with the New Left." It added that such radical notions are affecting the thinking and behaviour of the rest of the student
population.

Towards a Revolutionary Youth Movement

Significantly, in 1968 greater clarity was sought by the New Left as to
where it must go and how. The Students for a Democratic Society, for example, moved into the area of a new class analysis on the theoretical
proposition that what must now be built is a revolutionary youth movement. Although the resolution adopted at its National Council meeting in
Ann Arbor was unclear as to what "the working class" consists of, and its
relation to the class character of the proposed youth movement, SDS maintained that:

> Youth around the world have the potential to become a critical force. A
> youth movement raises the issues about a society in which it will be
> forced to live. It takes issues to the working class. They do this because,
> in America, there exists an enormous contradiction around the integra-
> tion of youth into the system. The period of pre-employment has been
> greatly extended due to the affluence of this highly-industrialized
> society and the lack of jobs.
>   Institutions like the schools, the military, the courts and the police
> all act to oppress youth in specific ways, as does the work place. The
> propaganda and socialization processes focused at youth act to channel
> young people into desired areas of the labor market as well as to socialize
> them to accept without rebellion the miserable quality of life in America
> both on and off the job.
>   The ruling class recognizes the critical potential of young people.
> This is why they developed so many organizational forms to contain
> them. Many young people have rejected the integration process that the
> schools are supposed to serve and have broken with and begun to strug-
> gle against the "establishment." This phenomenon has taken many
> forms, ranging from youth dropping out as a response to a dying
> capitalist culture, to young workers being forced out by industry that no
> longer has any room for the untrained, unskilled, and unorganized.
> Both the drop-out and the forced-out youth face the repressive nature of
> America's police, courts, and military, which act to physically and
> materially oppress them. The response from various strata of youth has
> been rebellion, from the buildings at Columbia to the movement in the
> streets of Chicago, to Haight-Ashbury to the Watts uprising.
>   The great strength of the New Left has come from its ability to
> change course when the demands of political struggle indicate change.
> We view the present transition in that light. One great weakness of the
> New Left, however, has often been the failure to implement theoretical
> developments in practice. We hope the youth movement resolution will
> produce more than a new level of rhetoric.

We should add that such a position on youth has been maintained in
Québec for some years now. It was here, after all, where the concept of student syndicalism was first born in North America. This was followed by the
concept of a revolutionary youth movement whose primary objective was

national liberation, supplemented substantially this year by the concept of a libertarian social revolution.

Winter 1969

STALIN IS DEAD, BUT NEO-STALINISM LIVES

Many of us expected the Soviet-led invasion of Czechoslovakia. Years of studying the nature of the super-powers, the history of Soviet socialism, and the contradictions in socialist theory on the questions of nationalism and imperialism could not suggest otherwise. But when three of our editors visited Prague during August 1968, the unbelievable optimism of the Czechs and Slovaks that we met did not allow us to dare to pose the question without being smiled at.

Editors Lucia Kowaluk, Jogues Girard and Dimitrios Roussopoulos met a great stream of people while in Prague. Members of the Prague New Left, of the Union of Czech Journalists, the Union of Writers, the Central Committee of the Communist Party, the Ministry of Education, Radio Prague, Liternary Listy, the Union of Students and so on. We experienced the exuberant feeling of not only being in one of the most beautiful and cultured cities of the world, but also one of the freest. Everywhere there was a spirit of reconstruction, a new sense of purpose, a feeling of experimenting with new forms of "democratising the socialist revolution," and, above all, debate. Debate about workers' councils, decentralisation, new concepts of education, new forms of economy, de-bureaucratisation of institutions and society. Many positions were taken, but it is important to note that while we were there (and we left four hours before the Warsaw Pact troops marched in) the future of Czechoslovakia was not determined. All important orientations were to be determined at the crucial Communist Party congress slated for early September. Therefore, other than the guidelines set down by the Action Programme of April, the currents of the debate, and over and above the newly established civil liberties, it is not possible to speculate as to the outcome or the impact the debate would have had on society. Even so, with *no* "ifs" or "buts", we condemn the Soviet-led invasion of Czechoslovakia by the Warsaw Pact.

What is a Friend?

From an article which appeared under the title, "From Warsaw to Bratislava", in Prague's *Literarni listy* (August 8, 1968) we have the following prophetic insight:

Despite all the propaganda of our "friendly socialist countries," the West did not prove itself our ally when we were in difficulties. Although it has not been publicly admitted, the world is divided into power blocs, and in certain situations, the West correctly adheres both to the secret agreements and to the status quo. If our country were occupied, the same situation would occur as has occurred several times before in Europe. When a group of our students asked a prudent and well-informed citizen of an important European country what his country would do if our country were to be occupied by its allies, he answered composedly: "Gar nichts, liebe Freunde" (absolutely nothing, dear friends). A few divisions perhaps would be flown to our western frontier, but that would be all. As a matter of fact, nothing would be better for the West than the occupation of a territory which they have written off as being outside their sphere of interest. They would achieve an enormous propaganda victory without the slightest effort on their part...

The Rumanian and Yugoslav communists proved to be very useful allies. Rumania and Yugoslavia were the only two countries which publicly supported our cause and "recognized our new regime." Other helpful allies were the communists in many European and other parties who welcomed, or at least tolerated, our post-January development, and the majority of democratic and socialist public opinion throughout the world, which considered the fate of Czechoslovakia to be part of the fate of democracy and socialism itself.

Undoubtedly, we also had supporters in those friendly communist parties and countries which signed the Warsaw letter. We don't know what the citizens of East Germany, Poland or the Soviet Union thought about Czechoslovakia and the danger of a counterrevolution. We are inclined to believe that they were scarcely convinced by the tales of our ruin reported in the official information media, perhaps even less convinced than we were at the time of the propaganda campaign about the fascism of Marshal Tito and his clique. The 1968 anti-Czechoslovak campaign has differed little from the anti-Yugoslav campaign of 1948. In fact, it seems to have been inspired by the latter. In those countries which signed the Warsaw letter, those who know us a little must have found it difficult to believe that the Czechs and Slovaks "have suddenly been seized by the desire to stage a counterrevolution." We can count on sympathies among these people, even if they cannot publicly express them...

The Resistance Grows

In the deliberate, public sacrifice of his own life, 21-year-old student, Jan Palach, has managed to encompass the pain, the pride and the spirit of resistance of the Czechoslovaks under Soviet domination.

He believed that the truth could be most powerfully realised in flames fed by his own body, and his further purpose of encouraging protest against the Russian occupation is being fulfilled as Czechoslovaks are moved from shock and anguish to resistance.

Tens of thousands of Czechoslovaks honoured the young student as they filled Wenceslas Square.

As we go to press, there is news of another self-immolation in Czechoslovakia — this time by a young brewery worker in Pilsen — and in Budapest, Hungary, a 17-year-old boy also set fire to himself.

These acts of protest are not isolated, but represent an almost inevitable development of the remarkably courageous campaign of passive resistance to Russian domination which is being sustained across Czechoslovakia.

Workers and their unions, students and intellectuals, are taking the lead in this resistance movement which seems to be developing independently of the Dubcek Government.

The Czechoslovak resistance will not have wanted these acts of suicide, but will be challenged incalculably to maintain its struggle for dignity and freedom. Jan Palach may yet be a second Jan Hus.

From a variety of reports, some appearing in the *Economist* (Nov. 28, 1968) and *Die Zeit* (Oct. 18, 1968) and from friends in Paris and London, we know that many young people in other socialist countries have been arrested. In the Democratic Republic of Germany, for example, there have been a number of closed trials. For distributing typewritten sheets condemning the invasion, Thomas Brasch, a son of the German deputy minister of cultural affairs, got 27 months. Rosita Hunzinger, a sculptor's 18-year-old daughter and Erika Berthold, daughter of the Director of the Institute of Marxism-Leninism, were given suspended sentences of 20 months. Sandra Weigl, a relative of Brecht's widow, was given two years and Horst Bonnet, Director of the Berlin comic opera, got two and a half years prison, and his wife two years. The two teen-aged sons of Prof. Robert Havemann, the Marxist scholar, have been arrested. Actions of protest against the occupation took place not only in Moscow, but also in the three capitals of the Baltic Soviet Republics, in Charkow and in the Caucasus. In Leningrad, a group of five people was arrested because they collected signatures for a document which called for solidarity with the Communists in Prague. Two of them, the chemist Danilov, and the engineer Studenkov, were put immediately into a lunatic asylum. The other three, the jurist Gendler, the chemist Gladschewskij, and the engineer Schadlenkow, are charged with "anti-soviet agitation."

It is significant that when the SDS in Germany marched on and occupied the Soviet Military Mission in Frankfurt in protest against the invasion, the Russians, caught under-staffed, called upon the American Military Mission to help them evacuate the students. Bertrand Russell, who set up an International Tribunal on Vietnam, is now in the process of setting up a commission on Czechoslovakia.

The world continually convulses with this kind of authority, maintained by a generation that has many of the same instincts throughout the world. The force that sends young Poles and Russians, Germans and Hungarians into Czechoslovakia, is the same force that sends young Americans into Vietnam, that beats up young people in the streets of Paris, Madrid, Chicago, Berkeley and Rome. Systems groping to perpetuate themselves, cause and condone death every day.

COMMUNITY CONTROL

The nature of the workplace, its relationship to society, the primacy of the economic sector, and the crucial importance of workers' control to any contemporary definition of socialism is well known. Unlike most other socialists, we have attempted to move away from a vague concern for workers' control of the production of goods and services to an analysis that related this objective to immediate industrial struggles. We must be equally concrete with the question of community control.

To begin with, we must give the concept of community control certain limitations, and, consequently, a sharp focus. To be sure, community control *cannot* be separated from workers' control. These two objectives are in fact not only interrelated in the context of creating a new society, they are inter-dependent. No fruitful understanding of community control is now possible unless we juxtapose it with the necessity of urban liberation and the political economy of the city.

To contemporary radicals, the general outline of a new society tends to be one in which the great historic splits, to quote Murray Bookchin, are eliminated. These are the splits dividing human beings from nature, human from human, city from country, mind from sensuousness, work from play, individual from society, and the individual from himself or herself. That is, social revolution today means the creation of organic societies where patriarchal family, private property, class domination and the State are forced into oblivion. In order to begin this renovation, the contemporary process of production for the sake of production, consumption for the sake of consumption, bureaucracy and centralisation must be abandoned along with the command of Capital and State. *At the political heart of this process is the modern city*, which is supposed to be the highest achievement of our civilisation. The most acute domestic contradictions are to be found in our large cities. It is these ugly mass *concentrations* of power and alienation that are today boiling with aimless revolt. No consideration of the social reorganisation of urban life is possible without a profoundly decentralised urban socialism which has at its centre the reality of community control. A programme that realised the removal of the present urban-based power structure would not lay the basis for social revolution in the country, unless it envisaged the breaking-up of the urban megalopolis into small self-managing communal units based on a contemporary definition of self-reliance. Such a programme is based on community control.

Compared to its few positive features, we would do well to remind ourselves of the overwhelmingly negative and oppressive features of our urban existence in Canada. Let us recall the appalling contrasts between city and rural life, and the staggering inequality of the distribution of power between the federal and provincial governments on the one hand,

and city governments on the other. The problems of modern poverty, housing, transportation congestion, environmental decay, social alienation, and economic chaos, are all interdependent and they are all centralised in the crisis of our cities. Yet, ironically, we are so immersed in false political consciousness, we are so cleverly distracted from our day-to-day problems by the politicians and their games in Ottawa or in our provincial capitals, that City Hall has the aura of a gothic novel.

We know that our urban centres, including the suburban fringes, have undergone and will continue to have the most rapid population increase. By the end of this century, over half of all the people in Canada will live in the twelve largest metropolitan areas. Of the 16 million people added to our population by that time, 11.5 million, or three-quarters of this increment, will be located in these twelve urban centres. The largest centres will be affected most: Montréal and Toronto alone will accommodate more than half (6.5 million) of all this metropolitan growth, together accounting for one-third of the Canadian population.

All present indications are that neo-capitalism, not simply because of its economic limitations, but also because of its *structural or institutional contradictions*, will not be able to deal with the "urban crisis." Within the next twenty years, this crisis will assume revolutionary proportions. Yet, the Left today still concentrates on taking power at the top of the pyramid — federal or provincial. This crisis is the main weak link in the power chain. With the gigantic increase in the power of the modern State, that is, with the growing need of neo-capitalism for government assistance, we can only foresee a greater acceleration of urban decay and discontent. At the same time, the awareness of the "urban crisis" is primitive, piecemeal and formalistic, and only the most mechanistic solutions are being offered. Only the *complete* reorganisation of our society, that is, a social revolution, can begin to approach this decomposition with the hope of reversing it. Such an undertaking is beyond implementation by the present power brokers because it would mean dismantling *the* political citadel their power rests on. Even the *beginning* of such a process of dismantling is fraught with the most dangerous possibilities for the present oligarchy. The technocratic solutions now offered tend to either involve buck-passing between the various levels of government, or handing down monies to corrupt, confused and chaotically enmeshed city governments. And yet, the demographic factors indicate that the power of political numbers is to be found in the cities.At the same time, we have day-to-day experience as well as impressive documentation which makes it clear that the power elite of this society has done a masterful job of convincing the population that the only real politics are the politics at the national or provincial level. Somehow the urban definition of politics has not been taken seriously, except by the minority that controls urban life and profits from this control. Interestingly enough, the demand for community control began among those who concluded that those other definitions of politics were unreal and meaningless to their daily lives. A return to the "community" began but with a few exceptions it got lost along the way. One reason for the confusion was that community was never defined, and a new intra-community plane of political and social action was never analysed and understood, especially in the large cities. I shall return to this point.

Alongside the demographic facts and their power-political implications, the concentration of economic activity in our urban centres also accentuates their overall domination of the country. By 1966, Montréal and Toronto accounted for over one-third of all employment in Canadian manufacturing, wholesale trade, and finance. So, the economic importance of the large cities is considerably greater than even their demographic weight.

Yet, when we discuss the economy as a whole, and when we analyse workers' and community control, we rarely situate it in the concrete realities and radical political possibilities of the political economy of the cities. Urban-based economic activity moves from adolescence to maturity. The political economy of Montréal and Toronto, for instance, has all the signs of advanced development with their highly structured industrial networks, permitting the subsequent growth of these cities to be self-sustaining. They are fully developed political economies in themselves. For example, the availability of large skilled labour pools provides benefits to the further development of capitalism because inducements to attract labour and costs of training are much less. There is a long list of other advantages which need not detain us further. The point has been made, however briefly. The economic and technological realities of modern North American capitalism force us to take the urban centres, especially the key urban centres, as *the* political nexus out of which will emerge any social revolution, *the* area where power will be diffused, and meet *the* contradictions of urbanism.

Urban demolition and congested construction is an inherent feature of a society based on capitalism and private property. Thus, at this point, there is an element of instability and decay in our cities, which cannot be changed unless the nature of the economy is changed. Community is completely non-existent, when land is a commodity, where everything is measured in monetary terms for the quickest purchase and sale. Thus, the fundamental unit is not the neighbourhood, but the privately owned building and grounds. Central to any movement of community control is the slogan, "Property is theft." The most intense political education on the origin and role of property is such a movement's essential didactic feature. It is not only that economic privilege is most naked in the large urban centre, but also where domination and police repression is most visible.

Let me conclude by surveying that urban metropolis that I am most familiar with. Metropolitan Montréal is the axis of economic growth in Québec because of the concentration of the labour force, industries, and financial institutions. At present, this economy is threatened because of its outmoded industrial structure, chronic unemployment (thirty percent in my area), and numerous factory shutdowns. In brief, Montréal is in an economically depressed situation notwithstanding the politics of grandeur at City Hall.

The volume of population, its pivotal economic, political and cultural position, will make any popular upheaval here *the* crucial determining factor in the future of Québec. One reason why the historic general strike of last May didn't go any further was because Montréal was not ready to move. Eighty percent of the population here is working-class, and seventy-five percent are tenants. Twenty-one percent of the city budget goes to the police department. The City Council is dominated by businessmen, lawyers, professionals. In the elections previous to those of 1970, thirty-three councillors out of forty-eight were elected by acclamation. In 1954, 52 percent of those who could vote, voted; in 1957, 50.2 percent; in 1960, 41 percent; in 1962, 42.6 percent; in 1966, 33 percent.

In Montréal, the most unbelievable chaos exists in the area of housing; the same is true of health, transportation, leisure and culture, economic and social development, education, and working conditions. Where, then, does *community control* enter?

It begins with the self-organisation of block-based communes which integrate radical life styles and work styles within relatively homogeneous communities. That is, city-centre areas that have the rudimentary characteristics of a neighbourhood, with a class composition that is primarily working-class. The commune, as the basic small unit of a revolutionary social movement, affords those qualities of group work and that integration of personal and political change which maximises the characteristics of personal and collective liberation. Several communes in an area begin immediately the revolutionary practice of co-operative sharing, and gradual elimination of private property in the goods that they possess in common. Citizen action groups concerned with particular daily problems like housing, education, and health, are either organised, or the existing ones are invigorated with the spirit of communalism. Political education, complemented by direct action, unfolds around the future of the immediate neighbourhood or community. The various citizens' groups are constantly brought together into supportive actions and combined struggles. Street organisations, primarily based on block-based communes, are helped to emerge out of the single-issue citizens' committees. The street organisations are multi-issued, and composed of thirty to fifty people who initiate political education, cultural and recreational activities, organise street cleaning, day care centres, and work with other groups for the creation of a community centre. They would also undertake various projects of mutual aid, from house repairs to general beautification measures. Meanwhile, a community assembly (the democratic body that decides on intercommunity life) undertakes the establishment of co-operative laundromats, a bookstore, restaurants, variety stores, second-hand shops, a garage, and so on. The political education programme and urban commune organising raise the questions of workers' control from the start, so that people begin organising at the place of work and bringing these experiences back to their community to be shared by other residents. A social dialectic between where people work and where they live emerges. Struggles for workers' control are joined with struggles for community. The street organisations, federated through the local community assembly, and these assemblies coalesced within the bosom of the urban liberation movement, formulate the demands for popular and local (community) control over all vital matters like housing (through community clinics, radicalising the professionals, working with service workers and direct action with hospitals), transportation (through a traffic policy eliminating cars travelling from the suburbs to the centre of town), education, womens' liberation, and so on.

The urban communes, the street organisations, the community assemblies, the workers' councils in the various places of work — all function within the framework of urban liberation socialism. This means that City Hall is not only taken over by the majority for the majority, but that urban government is fundamentally re-organised into a federation of decentralised communities, each developing in co-operation and co-ordination with other community assemblies the process of social reconstruction, by means of grass-roots social planning among other forms. Some of the exciting proposals that FRAP (a coalition of neighbourhood-based citizen's groups involving trade unions, and also a municipal Montréal political party) has as part of its programme would be implemented, such as the urbanisation of all city land, democratisation of the mass media, fundamental rearrangement of taxation along egalitarian lines, free public transportation, abolition of the automobile from the city centre, transformation of "Man and his World" into a popular university, co-operative housing, and even more radical changes would be undertaken. Such a movement sweeping into municipal power would naturally carry out such changes not simply because people's community organisations would begin more and more to interfere in the political and economic affairs of their areas, setting up embryonic liberated zones, but also because workers in various industries and institutions would have begun a takeover process.

Needless to say, such a movement of direct democracy in all areas of daily life *from below*, focusing on local and urban power, would frighten provincial and federal levels of the State. The serious dissolution of the urban power base of capital and State would create tremendous conflicts between them and the new urban liberation movements. But the new cities would begin challenging the entire framework of present-day society.

The nub of this commentary is this: The concept of community control cannot be discussed in abstraction. We must set it within the urban power struggle, and the clear desire among people for a sense of community.

ROOT AND BRANCH: THE POLITICAL ORIGINS OF THE 1960s NEW LEFT AND THE FUTURE

A panel discussion on "The New Left in the 1960s and Socialism for the 1980s" took place during the Learned Societies Meeting in the spring of 1980, at the Université du Québec à Montréal. The text published here is based on the talk given.

The New Left in the 1960s sought to redefine the revolutionary project. The need for such a redefinition became evident to a new generation of activists when it appeared that the old Left socialist tradition lacked the practice or the theory appropriate for the complete transformation of advanced industrial/technological societies.

By the 1950s, one of the two dominant socialist traditions, namely social democracy, was in an even greater crisis than it had been in its past. The other dominant socialist tradition, namely Marxism-Leninism, was by the same decade also in a profound crisis. The old Left was not able to provide an alternative to bureaucracy, to authoritarianism of one form or another, to centralisation, to the continuous growth of the State, to the social division of labour, to militarism and war, all characteristics of bourgeois society but not exclusive to it. Marxism-Leninism did provide a strategy and instrument for overthrowing existing power structures in certain countries, but in the process reproduced a party/State, the bureaucratic centralism of which undermined the growth of a truly socialist society. The graduated reformism of the social democratic parties, and the Eurocommunist parties that have followed more recently in advanced capitalist countries, led to the co-optation and integration of class-oriented politics into the existing structures of these societies and the cherished recourse to the established rules of parliamentarianism. Both of these old left socialist traditions were perceived by the New Left to have actually contributed to the growth and relative stabilisation of neo-capitalism. The Hungarian uprising of 1956, the revelation of crimes under Stalin admitted during the 20th congress of the Communist Party of the USSR, the Suez canal debacle, the general impotence of the British Labour Party in power, the aggravation of the Cold War, the indiscriminate testing of nuclear bombs by all countries which possessed them, among other world events, plus the insights about the old Left responding to these events drove the youth of the 1960s into wanting to recast the revolutionary project. These insights reformulated, constitute important features when outlining a socialist perspective and strategy for the 1980s.

The Basic Division

At the heart of the division between the old and New Left was the organisational question. To be sure there were other related questions rotating around this division, but the fact that Marxism-Leninism and social democracy lack a theory and practice of radical organisation, or association, or social forms that are to replace the bourgeois structures of hierarchy and domination was crucial. Marxism-Leninism and social democracy never really transcend the realm of bourgeois politics, since bourgeois relationships are mirrored in the organisational structures offered as alternatives to those prevailing. Despite rhetorical contrasts, the two traditions rest on many of the same theoretical and programmatic assumptions. With the disintegration of the New Left as a formal expression in Canada and elsewhere, many of the activists gravitated to Marxism of one form or another. The fact that many of these individuals soon became restless in this camp and once again are seeking to re-examine the insights of the 1960s, speaks not only to the usefulness of those insights, but corroborates as well the essential unity of the various expressions of the old Left.

The failure of Marxism to spell out the clear parameters of the organisational question as central to the process of transition cannot be attributed to its so-called temporary aberrations which include Stalinism, revisionism and other "incorrect" readings of Marx and Engels. The absence of such theory is at the core of Marx's contribution, and no collection of partial quotations from this or that book can be taken seriously as theory. We are hard pressed to find useful material on the question of social forms, methods of struggle, and kinds of leadership necessary in the transformation towards socialism. Instead, we have ambiguity and inconsistency which Lenin filled in by distilling from Marx's writings an authoritarianism which he elevated to the central position in the organisation question and the revolutionary project.

Marx did not interest himself with the process or transition towards a new society. Socialist transformation seemed to resemble the passage from feudalism to capitalism. This heritage, the determinism of Marxism which relied on the mechanism of capitalist development to produce crisis, collapse, breakdown, became the cornerstone of a belief in the inevitable demise of capitalism and the birth of socialism. The falling rate of profit, immiseration of the proletariat, the crisis of over-production, concentration of wealth, all were thought to be such contradictions as to spell the end of the capitalist system. This heritage underplayed the means and ends of socialist revolution which were to be automatically determined by the logic of capitalism; therefore, questions of the *how* and the *by-what-means* were set aside in favour of those prevailing answers in the bourgeois order of things. And so, the pre-World War I mainstream of Marxism anticipated a parliamentary road to socialism until the great collapse. Attempts to examine the means and ends of the socialist revolution in detail were considered straight-away as utopian speculation. The unresolved problems of the mass socialist consciousness of a class that was being called upon to fundamentally transform society, hierarchy and domination, bureaucracy and the future of the State, were all matters put off until some other time.

Bolshevism or Marxism-Leninism was principally responsible for not only failing to squarely face these unresolved problems in Marxism, but for offering a theory of organisation which unquestioningly assumes a notion of political revolution which itself presupposes and determines in large measure the nature of a post-revolutionary society. Since its emergence to singular prominence in the Marxist movement, especially after 1917, the Bolshevik or Marxist-Leninist tradition buried all self-emancipatory or democratic tendencies in the contribution of Marx.

Outside Marxism

In the past 130 years, the authoritarian foundation of Marx's philosophy and the Marxism which evolved, has been most directly attacked by the anarchists, including the revolutionary syndicalists, the council communists (such people as Anton Pannekoek, Herman Gorter, the non-political party Marxists), and the New Left. The socialist tradition interacts with social history in a number of ways at various times. It became visible once again in the advanced capitalist world during the ongoing development of a movement which stressed those forms of organisation and accompanying social relations, permitting a process of decision-making and socio-political culture that are one and the same with its end objective. The sharpest features of this socialist tradition, it is important to note, developed *outside* Marxism. Rejecting the idea of political mediation, its critique of exploitation was linked with its analysis of domination, thus reflecting a deeper grasp of the nature of bureaucracy.

The expression of this socialist tradition in the 1960s through the New Left was brilliant but short-lived. It was destroyed by its own innocence. It was rather easily consumed by the State or by various Marxist-Leninist sects on the one hand, while on the other its rhetoric and many of its activists were absorbed by various other established institutions. More will be said on the nature of the New Left's demise as a formal expression further on. What is important for us to distinguish at this point is why this tradition re-emerged in the 1960s after its submergence just before the Second World War, and why it not only persists today, but is growing. This powerful critique of both social democracy and Marxism-Leninism commands the attention of those interested in reformulating for the 1980s a movement for the fundamental transformation of our society, especially in its advanced capitalist industrial/technological form.

Marxism chooses to recognise exploitation and domination as manifestations of only the capitalist mode of production and its class structure. This central weakness in its theory not only explains the absence of a critical understanding of a process which takes no cognizance of domination and hierarchy before the revolution, but undermines its ability to recognise new forms of authority after a change of power structure.

The New Left, however, viewed authoritarianism and its various bureaucratic formations as a particular problem, clearly visible from the start, which must be abolished in the course of the revolutionary process. The early New Left rejected "leadership" as such, later placed emphasis on "participatory democracy", and still later, set as goals the establishment of networks of popular institutions.

The *libertarian* socialist perspective implicit in the New Left at its best — and expressed in a more sophisticated manner in more recent movements — stressed the overthrow of all forms and relations based on domination. This developed the socialist project beyond its basic concern with the expropriation of private ownership of the economy and its wealth. It incorporated with this concern the insights that nationalisation of the economy, central planning of various aspects of society, and new social priorities for the improved material well-being of people, as announced by a new state power, indicate a change in the *form* of control that prevails. But this alone may leave hierarchical control intact by perpetuating an apparatus and continued division of society into a State against people, sex against sex, town against country, people against nature, and old against young.

Thus, the New Left, as a recent manifestation of the classical anti-authoritarian or libertarian socialist tradition, warned against the reproduction of hierarchical social relations presented under a new guise. It found to be wanting the political party and the electoral or power ambitions of its leadership, as an instrument of revolutionary change; criticised the bureaucratic degeneration of the trade unions and their transformation of radical politics into accommodations with the power elite; and chose, instead, to experiment with new social forms or organisational models that attempted to be locally rooted in the community experience of living and working-collective expressions of an anticipated future. The radicalism of the 1960s introduced new substance to the historic anti-authoritarian tradition. All areas of social life and all structures of domination became part of the terrain for struggle. Personal, cultural and what we now call "lifestyle" issues were integrated into politics. This was especially so in the area of feminism which came later — far more extensively than in past radical movements, where few women participated on an equal footing. Questions of personal consistency and integrity became central again: should one own property? should one marry before church or State? should one wear a wedding ring? should one baptise one's children or observe religious or political holidays that are meaningless? what kind of living standard should one seek? and what does one do with a large salary? These kinds of questions were invested with deep political significance. The New Left focused on a spectrum of questions offering a generalised critique of the system as a whole which, it was maintained, must be continuously and generally pressed and not particularised: war, health care, sexuality, culture, ecology, education and community. It was important to meld economic and socio-political concerns by generalising the struggle for a self-managed locus *beyond* the point of economic production.

Departures from the Past

The New Left tended, however, to overreact against the whole of the old Left tradition, including classical anarchism. In North America especially, it was barely aware of the theoretical outlines and history of this tradition as it reacted to the present manifestations of the old Left. The New Left's glorification of spontaneity and subjectivity was often without ballast. Its hostility to official politics and hierarchical organisation often turned into their counter-productive opposite. Its fear of centralisation placed an excessive weight on localism to the point where effective co-ordination of struggles became impossible, and the New Left's understanding of the organisational question hardly included the concept of a federation of autonomous units. In its inflexible abstentionism from mainstream politics, it also excluded an understanding that local institutions from schools to school boards, to community centres and social agencies, were indeed supple structures, vulnerable, perhaps amenable, to radical struggle and influence. Its anti-intellectualism, manifested in an unawareness of the socialist tradition it was carrying, caused it to ignore the fruits of certain important historical experiences of non-authoritarian protests and revolutions. Because of its youthfulness, as with all youth movements in the past, it was unable to give a sustained programmatic and strategic presence to its vision of a new society, involving other social classes in the struggle. In choosing to live its radical goals so totally it did not refine the means of socially attaining these goals. In rejecting the concept of "democratic centralism" or vanguardism of the Marxist parties, and the social democracy of Robert's Rules of Order, it all too readily overlooked as well the complexity of social revolution, and became naively ignorant of the question of power, thus underplaying the importance of mass organisation. And like Marxist-Leninist parties, the New Left failed to develop a comprehensive radical theory of the nature of the pre-revolutionary and revolutionary period for the movement. Indeed, "the movement" itself in large chunks gave way to a "counter culture" of independent groups and individuals, on the whole "doing their own thing."

The Complexity of Radical Social Change

The mercuric and fragile quality of the two competing spheres of power in a society on the edge of important change was not understood. When locally based organisations rise to prominence to challenge both Capital and the State, the possibility of a rapid move towards a federated network of regional co-ordination is necessary. This step alone can translate the ignited popular impulse into a protracted movement that is politically tough and that strikes with revolutionary effect. The genius of the libertarian socialist movement in the 1980s will be, as its historical predecessors manifested, a synthesis of spontaneity and conscious intervention, or economic concern with the socio-political, the combination of struggles for the decentralisation of power and self-management, and a strategy for disabling central authority.

Recent experiences in the new radical movements of the late 1970s, however, still reflected a similar harmful polarity. One need only examine closely the women's movement, the ecology movement, the gay liberation movement, and the new peace and disarmament movements. The romance with the Maoist "alternative" did not last long. It showed itself to be just a different variant of Jacobin authoritarianism distilled through the Leninist filter. Put simply, the party/State continues to be hegemonic, directing society and its development from above. That this relationship is "naturally" arrived at is not only a flaw in Marxism with its lack of a theory of bureaucracy, but with Leninism which builds the party like a State.

This relationship must be completely reversed if revolutionary politics is to have a future in neo-capitalist societies. The political party is quintessentially an instrument of mediated power relations with a logical tendency towards the manipulation of minorities. This is not only a result of its organisational form, but also of the dominant system's definition of politics and its rules. On the contrary, since the outline of freedom and the steps towards self-emancipation can only be worked out in the daily round of work and community life through local organisational structures or social forms, it is these organisms — rather than the party/State — that must be instruments of social revolution. The social forms rooted both in the workplace (as revolutionary syndicates federated into regional unions) as well as in the community (as neighbourhood councils municipally federated) will challenge any centralised structure superimposed on popular struggles. This is an accomplishment to be attained only through the emergence of co-ordinated mechanisms administrating and implementing on the basis of delegated and revocable power. Such popular organisms, painfully emerging from the base of society preoccupied with every sphere of daily life, offer the most fruitful space for the realisation of radical impulses which can fight off the repressive infiltration of bureaucracy and generate collective participation, the bloodline of social revolution.

To the New Left of the 1960s we owe the evolvement of a number of cardinal insights, the importance of which had been verified by social history, but which were now buried by the cracked hegemony of social democracy and Marxism-Leninism in our lifetime. The concept that State ownership was the same as collective ownership was more than dubious. Equally, the idea of collective ownership without clearly marked and consciously understood means of popular/local control was set aside. The "State" was not found to be one with the "public"; indeed, a critical examination of the history of the growth of the State, its present role and function, revealed that its use as an instrument of liberation brought forward only superficial and abstract solutions to the contradictions of capitalism. Through the actual history of social democracy and Marxism, it became apparent, in recent times, more than ever before, that there can be no construction of a radically new society without a revolutionary culture and consciousness, and that this cannot be based upon a political system of representation, a division of labour, a set of ideological institutions, and a technology arising from the material base of capitalism.

Impetus from Below

When workers themselves construct new social forms directly controlled by their assemblies, then alienated labour can come close to being
abolished. Such a transformation is more profound than simply the transfer of formal ownership, for it destroys the all-important authoritarian
structure of the workplace, leaving open the possibility of eliminating the
fragmentation of work-skills, the separation of mental and physical labour,
and the production of commodities for the sake of production. All these
splits arise from the capitalist division of labour which the so-called
socialist societies have not changed since they are considered to be essential for efficiency and productivity. In fact, these features are meant for the
social control of labour. Specialisation and hierarchy in the labour process
do not arise only from capital accumulation and new developments in
technology, but also from the need for social control, which means a
bureaucratically organised and disciplined work force. Specialisa-
tion/hierarchy and the discipline imposed by bureaucratic organisation
cannot be separated.

That this hierarchical form of societal (including industrial) organisation is a contradiction to the revolutionary process was not foreseen by
Marxism until well into the pre-World War II era. The verification of what
the controversies during the First International were all about was made by
history or the historical practice of social democracy and Marxism-
Leninism, and by the history of the anarchist movement. The integration of
the State and the corporate economy, making for the immense expansion of
the public sector, has spelled the establishment of a centralised web of
power that dries up all initiative which does not originate or is not sustained from above. This elitist structuring of society sets in motion its organisational logic which permeates every area of daily life, requiring in
turn, an ideology which creates a culture of passivity, social purposelessness, routine, reformism, and pragmatic self-censorship.

The logic of sanctioned institutional authority precipitates a fatal
process of depoliticising potential opposition by imposing *its* definition of
what is political discourse, by rationalising alienation in the name of
productive efficiency, by posing a series of seemingly "technical or practical" solutions to problems, all of which have a determining political dimension. Once established, the crowning sovereignty of bureaucracy — the
State — no matter how benign and far-flung its apparatus, establishes a
resistance to all fundamental change which it correctly evaluates as fatal to
its continuity. Marxist parties/States have been repeatedly swallowed up
by bureaucratic authority.

A New Critique

The New Left articulated anew this critique, however incompletely.
Even though the dominant homogenizing politico-economic process
seems so overwhelming as it penetrates every pore of human existence,

new breaches appear, new fields of resistance and revolt emerge, as new areas of vulnerability appear on the capitalist power structure. Where social peace was established yesterday, we have loud disturbances today. Anti-authoritarian movements which have left traces throughout recorded history, have, if anything, multiplied in our era. The renewed social explosions of the 1960s — the New Left in Canada, the USA, Latin America, Japan, Western Europe, and elsewhere, rank-and-file insurgency at the workplace, oppositional revolts in Eastern Europe — indicate that the tradition of libertarian socialism has re-entered the historical stage. In retrospect, clearly, the 1960s constitute an overture; and, if we are to witness another period of mass social motion, it will be in historical continuity with that upheaval.

The social forms of the movement are small-scale, local organs directly controlled by the participants — neighbourhood assemblies, factory councils, radical action committees, affinity groups — seeking to transform revolutionary politics in a way that is within the grasp of every person. Often this thrust emerges from traditionally established institutions that open themselves up to notions of direct democracy and find that opening irreversible. Often these social forms emerge from the fabric of community maintained by local folk wisdom, forms such as the collectives in Spain, Hungary, Russia, the Ukraine, Chile or the community and collective forms of self-management recalled and resought by the radical collectives which pepper Britain, Italy and France. Whether dormant in the collective experience, or active but small at present, these social forms often become radicalised at times of crisis, producing large-scale revolutionary forms that could transform society.

The major difference between the practice of these social forms in the past, especially as exercised by the anarchists, as compared to the New Left, was that the former entered into them with a critical and self-conscious perspective. This, of course, makes all the difference, this close scrutiny of the tension between the possible and impossible, the conscious and unconscious, between freedom and licence, for by such critical practice the definition of political reality is expanded.

The Nature of the New Social Forms

In the context of a highly conscious and militant base working through individual and collective self-discipline and self-direction, leadership is organically rooted in the local workplace and neighbourhood, and is thus directly accountable and revocable at all times. Hence, the new social forms incorporate a wide range of questions, demands, and needs breaking the ideological hegemony laid down from above. Out of this rupture comes the possibility for developing a vital intellectual and social potential likely to lay to rest the fatalism, passivity and acquiescence to bourgeois authority and "order of things". The cultivation of this anti-authoritarian rebellion generates a capacity to resist the deradicalisation process which facilitates counterrevolution. These social forms, as they rise, fall and rise again, are part of the fabric of a large social movement, a new source of political legitimacy, a form of foundation-building for the future society. Such a radicalisation stands for the negation of politics as a separate and special area of activity: it stands for the total involvement of society in the control of its development. These, then, are some of the insights and experiences that constitute the heritage of the 1960s at its height.

Beyond the New Left

During the 1970s, many New Left activists entered the traditional organisational modes of the old Left, taking on an existence more appropriate to lobotomised creatures, or refusing to fit altogether the old mould, were expelled by the social democrats as was the Waffle by the NDP; others, ill-adapted, left quietly through the back door, others still remain in the institutional corners of that tradition moving from committee to committee. As this group of people found social democracy and Marxism-Leninism wanting in their own personal experience (in contrast to the rejection of the old Left on intellectual or existential grounds which marked the 1960s), they undertook new efforts to respond to the persistent and annoying anti-bureaucratic critique. One mutation that has emerged is a refined and supple form of liberal Marxism with the flexible manouverability of social democracy — Eurocommunism. Here, the old elitism takes on a new garb, as a more "sophisticated" strategy is unfolded in the name of structural reformation which has a selected way of permeating the State. To be sure, the State is subjected to a more comprehensive, though incomplete, critique than that provided by Marxism-Leninism. Having established itself in some Western European countries, Eurocommunism now has its North American impresarios. Structural reformism, coupled, needless to say, with a chorus of extra-parliamentary rhetoric, still leads to suicide for the powerless class.

Others have passed the last decade verifying, refining and pruning their experiences of the 1960s. Whether this has been accomplished through reflection or through continued militancy or both, the initial insights are now refined and placed within the larger historical tradition of what the Spaniards call *communismo libertario*. At the same time, during the 1970s, contrary to what the commercial media and their uncritical spectators would have us believe, a new crop of anti-authoritarian movements arose. This occurred in the cities over neighbourhood or urban issues, through the social ecology movement, through various radical interpretations of the women's movement, though the anti-nuclear and alternative technology movements, and through the large anti-consumer movement. The same basic insights of the New Left, supplemented sometimes to be sure, are echoed and put to useful service time and again. The old Left has had a predictable ambivalence towards these new movements, as it did in the 1960s. Trying to co-opt them on the one hand, rejecting them on the other, or simply revising the old dogmas once again.

In terms of a recasting, the project to radicalise society is now ready to take on a new vital direction. Its contribution during the 1980s in

Canada/Québec will be as important as that of the 1960s. More conscious of the political parameters of a culture dominated by the US Madison Ave./Hollywood mould of values, of a political economy controlled by multinationals and American capital, a growing State bureaucracy at all levels of society, a country comprising many regions and cultures and several distinct nationalities, the movement for a society of self-managed socialism has begun here again. The twin dimensions of community control and workplace control will be its cutting edge. The tendency towards fragmentation of local initiatives and struggles must be overcome through the conscious emergence of a co-ordinated, but extra-parliamentary opposition, which brings groups and individuals together to make the power of direct action sharper and better implemented. Certainly this cannot come to pass unless the movement of social action takes seriously the heritage of the anarchist tradition and those dissident anti-Bolshevik Marxists who made a major contribution to the theory and practice of anti-authoritarian revolution, and who continue to play an important role in that direction.

Neither the social democrats, the Marxist-Leninists nor the Eurocommunists can point to any more success in the last two decades than can the New Left. And, since the redefinition of the revolutionary project keeps coming from outside these traditional political groupings in the industrialised societies, history is trying to tell us something. We should listen.

Chapter 4

POLITICAL ANALYSIS AND POLITICAL THEORY

Spring 1968

THE POLITICS OF CREATIVE DISORDER

Christian Bay argues very persuasively the need for civil disobedience. Oscar Wilde once said: "wherever there is a man who exercises authority, there is a man who resists authority. Disobedience, in the eyes of anyone who has read history, is man's original virtue. It is through disobedience that progress has been made, through disobedience and through rebellion."

Only ten years ago, people were extremely pessimistic about the possibilities of fundamental social and political change in North America, indeed in industrial/technological society per se. One of the most important factors in unfreezing our society to various options for change has been direct action or civil disobedience in its many forms. People, especially youth, existentially took social questions into their own hands instead of just pleading with authority or symbolically and politely protesting and moved into confrontation politics. First this was done by individuals and small groups and that lead to mass actions such as the recent October 26 Pentagon action.

In any area of human concern against injustice, be it work in organising the poor, democratising the educational system, gaining the human rights of ethnic or racial minorities or creating an awareness over the threats of war, when the time is opportune to use direct action, the tone and style of the protest dramatically and qualitatively changes.

History is full of examples of mass non-violent direct actions. The form of action is not new, but with time, new skills and new insights have been gained. Nicolas Walter touches on a few examples: the mass exodus, the boycott, the political strike, non-co-operation and general resistance. He substantiates this as follows:

> The most obvious method is the mass exodus, such as that of the Israelites from Egypt in the Book of Exodus, that of the Roman plebeians from the city of Rome in 494 B.C. (according to Livy), that of the Barbarians who roamed over Europe during the Dark Ages looking for

somewhere to live, that of the Puritans who left England and the Huguenots who left France in the Seventeenth Century, that of the Jews who left the Russian Empire in the Nineteenth Century and Nazi Germany in the 1930s and 1940s, that of all the refugees from Fascist and Communist countries since the 1920s.

Or, there is the boycott, used by the American colonies against British goods before 1776, by the Persians against a government tobacco tax in 1891, by the Chinese against British, American and Japanese goods in the early years of this century, by several countries against South African goods today, and — in a different sense — by the Negroes who organised the bus-boycotts in Montgomery in 1955 and Johannesburg in 1957.

Then there is the political strike, such as the first Petersburg strike in 1905, the Swedish and Norwegian strikes against war between the two counties in the same year, the Spanish and Argentine strikes against their countries' entry into the First World War, the German strike against the Kapp putsch in 1920, and dozens of minor examples every year — in fact most strikes are examples of a familiar form of non-violent resistance. The syndicalist general strike and the pacifist general strike are both ideas derived from the ordinary industrial strike, which is after all the basis of the strength of the Labour Movement.

There is also the technique of non-co-operation, as used by the Greek women in Aristophanes' *Lysistrata,* by the Dutch against Alva in 1567-72, by the Hungarians against the Austrians in 1861-67 (consider how their leader Ferne Deak is much less famous than Lajos Kossuth, because he was much less romantic — and much more successful), by the Irish against the English in 1879-82 (until Parnell made the Kilmainham Treaty with Gladstone), by the Germans in the Ruhr against the French in 1923-25. When this technique is used against an individual it is called: "sending to Coventry"; the people mentioned above sent their oppressors to Coventry.

General resistance to oppression is often non-violent, not because of principle but because violence is for some reason unnecessary or useless. This sort of resistance, without violence was used by the Jews against Roman governors in First Century A.D., by the English against James II in 1686-88, by the German Catholics and Socialists against Bismarck in 1873-83, by the English Nonconformists against the Education Act of 1902 and the English trade-unionists against the Trade Disputes Act of 1906, by the Finns against the Russian introduction of conscription in 1902, by the Koreans against the Japanese and the Egyptians against the British in 1919, by the Samoans against the New Zealanders in 1920-36, by the Norwegians and Danes against the Nazis in 1940-43, and by the Poles and Hungarians against the Russians in 1956.

The greatest contemporary shortcoming of radical politics in Canada is the fact that we are trapped in limited and sterile forms of social action. These undynamic, non-confrontation politics have a depressing effect on us — on our staying power. Most radicals in this country still hover between electoral politics and traditional protest. Very few of us want to put ourselves on the line. Some small and badly organised experiments were tried, but not followed through. It is this lack of real gut commitment which exists in Canada (although less so in Québec) which will destroy our potential in the end. We need a form of action which profoundly motivates us subjectively as well as cerebrally. No wonder American radicals turn to us and say with half-scorn: "You Canadians are not for real."

In the last six to eight months, civil disobedience has been used as never before on Canadian campuses. Hopefully radicals will begin to use direct action in anti-poverty work, anti-war and anti-colonialist activities. it is easier for people to dismiss another petition or a moving picket line then to disregard the commitment of people who are taking real risks with civil disobedience.

What is needed in Canada, if people are to believe in a qualitatively different future, is our version of a *politics of creative disorder*. A peace and freedom movement must understand the instrument of direct action which can loosen the grip of conventional thinking at the base of our society introducing a turbulence, a passion, an excitement, a commitment, a militancy which clearly is non-existent now Once our society enters such a period of creative conflict, solutions and options envisioned now only in the salons of intellectuals will become real.

Direct action is only a part of the politics of creative disorder, although quite central to it. A.J. Muste, Arthur Waskow and the rest of us have understood this. But at our point in history in this country it is a most elemental necessity. In my mind it must be a key part of a peace and freedom movement both in a tactical and strategic sense. It is also true that much has to precede this movement (which will be an alliance of many forces and many kinds of action) as it generates new kinds of power in new centres while it resists injustice and builds the future in the present. But when will this new beginning of which we speak start in earnest, within what has begun? Hopefully Christian Bay has helped readers legitimise civil disobedience in their minds, and hence contributed to the social and political consciousness of radicals in Canada.

Spring 1969

TOWARDS AN EXTRA-PARLIAMENTARY OPPOSITION IN CANADA

Where Does a Radical Analysis Begin?

It is of fundamental importance to us where an analysis of a political situation begins. If our political analysis begins with an election, and what is necessary to win it within the present framework and definition of politics, we have taken as central a particular fact which determines all subsequent analysis. Our central interest and what we as a consequence wish to project decides in fact what we discuss and how

Alternatively, we can start from Canada's general condition: its overall statistical record, its total productivity. We can look at this country as if it were some single entity to be amended by this percentage or improved by that average. But this description can hide as much as it shows; it can show a nation-wide income but not how it is distributed; or total productivity but not what is produced. What appears like a neutral analysis has in fact been prejudiced by a camouflaged political assumption: that we are all in the same situation and have an equal stake and interest in it.

Or, again, we can start an analysis from some particular personal careers: the prospects of A in his new administration; the developing rivalry between B and C; the character factors in this speech or that television appearance. The assumption here is that these careers are all important and that policies are merely an aspect of these careers.

We are all very familiar with the above approaches; they surround us daily through the commercial press and mass media. In fact, between them, they dominate orthodox discussion, serious and popular. To be interested in contemporary politics is to be interested in these particular approaches. One indication of these approaches is what passes for political commentary on *Viewpoint* every weeknight on the CBC. It is quite difficult to see how things might be otherwise and how one could start differently. This is how our particular culture imposes its orthodoxy on a politically illiterate society before any detailed arguments begin. You may go on to differ at this or that point, but if you accept these approaches to Canadian politics, there are certain things you can never find time to say or say reasonably and relevantly.

The key to a political analysis is always indicated at the point at which it starts.

We believe we have been dominated for too long by other approaches and definitions and the consequent politics are both pointless and destructive. We think we have to make a break in order to see the world in our own way, a radical way that will go to the roots of the crisis in this country. Then we can offer this way to others, to see how far they can agree with it, how closely it connects with their lives.

We start our analysis from our situation as revolutionaries amid the present contradictions of radical motion now taking place in Canada and Québec. These contradictions are out in the open but we must draw attention to them. We say, here and elsewhere, that current definitions of radicalism and socialism have failed. We are in fact asking what it means to live in Canada today amid disappearing political landmarks, immersed in an urgent reality which we are trying to understand — that of a particular people in a particular country.

We wish to overcome the unsystematic and fragmented approach to understanding this country and gain an organic overview. What has happened up until now is a bringing together into a general position the many kinds of new political and social responses and analyses around which essentially local work has been done. We stopped talking and writing about "national" work a long time ago because of its very rootless nature. It was work more often than not without a base. Its "usefulness" was a fiction our society maintains. The consequences of this failure has become apparent to many. The positions taken on various questions were fragmentary. They could be taken without real commitment into the simple rhetoric of the "liberally-minded" progressive party of Canada, the NDP, while the other parliamentary parties used them at will as political footballs. But that NDP rhetoric becomes cant for we are constantly told that nothing can happen without a parliamentary victory.

In the meantime, the fragmented social questions we are concerned about are thrown back at us. So a failure in solving one question is referred to another in an endless series of references and evasions, the staple of all politicians. As a result, the character of the general crisis in Canada within which these failures are symptoms, can never be grasped or understood or communicated. Clearly then, what we need is a description of the crisis as a whole, in which not only the present mistakes and illusions but also the necessary and urgent changes can be intelligently linked.

It is our basic contention here that the separate campaigns in which we have been active, e.g. against nuclear arms and the Cold War, the Vietnam war, Biafra, the recognition of China, the anti-poverty movement, student power and the other separate campaigns with which we have been concerned run back, in their essence, to a single political system and its alternatives. We believe that the system we oppose and its injustices can only survive by a willed separation of issues and the resulting fragmentation of consciousness. The fundamental pivot of our position is that all social and political questions — structural and industrial, international and domestic, economic and cultural — are deeply connected; that what we oppose is in fact a system; and that what we want to work for is a qualitatively different society. An end must be put to the fact that the problems of whole men and women are habitually relegated to specialised and disparate fields where society offers to manage or adjust them by this or that consideration or technique.

We have had close experience with the different single-issue campaigns. We know and appreciate the dedication and energy that is given to them. We understand the impatience of those who say, "…but let us at least change this small area…." It is from just this kind of experience in repeated campaigns that we set out on this new perspective. We have learned in the course of following the campaigns, though from our different initial priorities, that a new total analysis, however preliminary, is now indispensable. The first stage of this new perspective was gained when we developed from the Campaign for Nuclear Disarmament into a student movement concerned with social change as a means of changing Canadian foreign and defense policy and now have the realisation that we must go still deeper into the nature of change in our kind of society. Against the inherent power and speed of the system we oppose, only a systemic position can effectively stand.

Against a discontinuous experience, our immediate political decision is to make new connections between issues which means a development in awareness. This is necessary before we can solve the problems of political organisation. This may be dismissed by some as merely "intellectual" work: a substitute of thought for action. Our political culture continually prompts this response: "action, not words." But we reject this separation of thought and action, or of language and reality. *If the people interested in social and political change are conscious in certain ways, they will act in certain ways and where there they are not conscious they will fail to act.* Of course it is not enough to simply describe and analyse a general crisis and its particularities; but unless the New Left does, other descriptions and analyses prevail and the most relevant political life in terms of radical alternatives is pushed back into the margins and the precarious unwritten areas. Among all the flapping about on the Left in Canada, we asked ourselves the question: what action can we take with this journal in the next little while? Our answer was to try to establish this practical and alternative view of our world and our society.

We are quite conscious of the fact that describing the connection between social questions within the system we oppose is not making the connections, nor is it the praxis we support. As a first step, we are identifying the facts of and reasons for the existing process of incorporation, homogenisation, absorption and hence discontinuity. But in spite of this process, an unprecedented number of people in Canada and Québec, in many different ways, are still opposing the system. It is clearly not for us as a group of editors but for all people now in various kinds of opposition to consider the practical consequences of a radical systemic political analysis. We have tried to initiate the process of political analysis afresh which, if successful, would go far beyond ourselves even though we should still belong to it.

What Is Neo-Capitalism?

Our society has many dimensions, some more central than others. We shall begin at the most central with an analysis of the socio-economic framework of this society and its significance.

We are in a transitional phase between the old and new capitalism. Often, those seeking fundamental change belabour the old definition of problems without understanding their new underpinnings. Radicalism is a tool which allows us to understand the nature of the transitional process. What we will describe further on, under the label: neo-capitalism, should not suggest that all of the old classical contradictions have disappeared. Rather, it should be made clear, that in order to solve these contradictions, we must be aware of the fact that, although the system's point of gravity has not changed, the fulcrum has.

We must first describe that unfamiliar but now crucial phenomenon — called in official circles: post-capitalism or the mixed economy — that is in fact a new kind of capitalism, the political dimension of which is referred to as liberal corporatism. It presents crucial problems of recognition and description and leads our society to political problems of a new kind.

Canada and societies elsewhere have adapted and changed in order to survive. This process of change has been the main task of the post-war governments. The leading role of the State has been to initiate the reshaping of an economy in relative decline, structurally imbalanced, backward in many regions, paralysed by a slow rate of growth, by inflation, recession and payment balance problems and to create instead a political economy based on organised rapid expansion. An essential part of this strategy has been the containment and ultimate incorporation of the trade union movement and other sections of the infra-structure as well as the political opposition parties. An essential pre-requisite was the redefinition of what is progressive and what is socialism and the internal adaptation of the agencies of change — including the New Democratic Party and Communist Party — within some broad range consensus. The current crisis is then a phase in the transition from one stage of the political economy to another. It is the crisis which occurs when a system, already beset by its own contradictions and suffering from prolonged entropy, nevertheless seeks to stabilise itself at a more "rationalised" level.

Neo-capitalism, though a development from free-enterprise capitalism, is — in terms of its essential drives and its modes of operation and control — a distinct variant. It is an economic system dominated by private accumulation where decisive economic power is wielded by a handful of very large US industrial mufti-national corporations in each sector, emulated by those remaining Canadian enterprises. The bureaucratic complexity of corporate structures, the size and scale of operations, the advanced manipulative techniques required to man and control such units, and their pervasive impact upon society at large are so immense that the allocation of human and natural resources and the creation of compulsive consumption can no longer be left to the play of the market place. What is required, according to the prevailing public philosophy, is a further rationalisation that would enable our kind of society to consciously go over to an administrated price system, wage negotiations within the framework of agreed norms, managed demand and efficient, effective transmission of orders from the top the bottom. The attempts to rationalise injunctions in the Rand Report, for example, is only one such effort dealing with one aspect of the production process. This integrating and harmonizing authoritarianism is among the constant themes uttered before meetings of the Manufacturers Association and the Chambers of Commerce. These efforts would represent, without doubt, a major stabilisation of the system. The market place, once the focus of capitalism, is progressively bypassed for the sake of greater management and control and the consequent rewards of growth. Within this context, it is this shift which makes some kind of planning imperative.

Planning in this sense does not mean what socialists have understood: the subordination of private profit (and the direction which profit-maximization imposes on the whole society) to social priorities. The fact that the same word is used to mean different things is extremely significant. It is by this semantic sleight-of-hand that the NDP has mystified and confused its supporters, taking up the allegiance of may to one concept of planning while attaching quite another meaning to what it understands in reality.

What does planning of an economy mean today? It means better forecasting, better co-ordination of investment and expansion decisions, a more purposeful control over demand. This in turn enables the more technologically equipped and organised units in the private sector to pursue their goals more efficiently, more "rationally." It also means more control over the trade unions and over labour's power to bargain freely about wages. This involves another important transition.

In the course of this rationalisation of capitalism, the gap between the corporations and the State is narrowed. The State, indeed, comes to play an increasingly critical role. It makes itself responsible for the overall management of the political economy by fiscal means. It must tailor the production of trained manpower to the needs of the economic system — hence the active influence of this system on the educational apparatus. In the political field, it must hold the ring within which the necessary bargains are struck between competing interests. It must engineer the public consensus in favour of these bargains and directly take on the task of intervening to whip it into line behind the norms.

The Canadian work force, of course, can only be expected to co-operate with the system if it regularly gains a share of the goods produced. The first promise held out is that the State will be in a better position to manage the inflation-recession cycles which have beset the post-war political economy. The second promise is that a stable system will be more efficient and productive and that, so long as it works, labour will win its share in return for co-operation. When productivity rises, it is suggested that labour shares the benefits. On the other hand, when productivity slows down, labour cannot contract out since it has become party to the bargain. This looks on the surface like a more rational way of guaranteeing rising standards of living; it is in fact a profound restructuring of the relationship between unionized labour and capital.

We noted already how the word "planning" has been maintained but how its meaning has been redefined. Equally, the word "welfare" has been given a semantic somersault. Free-enterprise capitalism was, for a long time, the enemy of the welfare State. This has now undergone certain changes. Why? The welfare State in the US, Britain and Europe has been introduced as a modification of the system. Like wage increases, it represents a measure of redistribution and egalitarianism, cutting into profits, imposing human needs and social priorities on the profit-oriented system. The various welfare States in the Western world vary in comprehensiveness. In Canada, the comprehensive welfare State is in the foreground of the NDP's political programme.

There is one central difference, however, between this aspect of a neo-capitalist economy and its alternatives. Rising prosperity — whether in the form of higher wages, increased welfare or public spending — *is not funded out of the redistribution of wealth from the rich to the poor.* Redistribution would eat into the necessary mechanisms of private accumulation, internal reinvestment and the high rewards to management on which the whole system rests. Rising prosperity for the powerless class of our society must therefore come out of the margin of increased growth and productivity.

The existing distribution of basic wealth and power remains the same. It is no wonder that the quality of our lives has not changed and, in fact, has deteriorated. The new wage claims can only be met by negotiation, out of the surplus growth, and controlled by a framework of agreed norms. The norms, however, are not the norms of social justice, human needs or claims of equality; they are arrived at by calculating the percentage rise in productivity or growth over a given period and by bargaining what proportion of that is the "necessary" return to capital and what proportion is left over for wage increases and welfare costs. In effect, within this new system of bargaining, wage increases must be tied to productivity agreements (not to egalitarianism) and welfare becomes a supporting cast for modern capitalism — not an inroad into or a modification of the system.

This is one of the crucial dividing lines between neo-capitalism and the old and between organised capitalism and the demands of revolutionary socialism. it means that the rising prosperity of the industrial working class, for one, is indissolubly linked with the growth and fortunes of the multi-national corporations, on the one hand, since only by means of the productivity of this industry will there be any wage or welfare surplus at all to bargain for.

Therefore a successful neo-capitalist political economy is one in which the people may enjoy a measure of increased abundance and prosperity — what is loosely called "affluence" — provided there is growing productivity but it is by definition not an egalitarian society in terms of real income, wealth, opportunity, authority and most importantly, therefore, power. There may be some levelling of social status within classes; nevertheless, "open" capitalist societies, where stratification is not so marked, are still closed systems of power. Free enterprise capitalism created the modern hostile conflict relations of class-society; neo-capitalism, where successfully evolving, seeks to end these conflicts, not by changing the real relations of property and power, but by suppressing all the human considerations of community and equality in favour of the planned contentment of organised producers and consumers. In this task, the system is aided consciously or not by the New Democratic Party in Canada. By continuously avoiding an organic political philosophy or ideology that goes to the root of our crisis, that is radical in that it deals with the new problems of our post-scarcity society which include questions of the quality and meaning of our lives, the NDP helps to perpetrate a fragmented view of where we are. Nobody profits from this condition other than those who continue to have power in all its centralised, bureaucratic and military sense.

All these factors hinge on a decisive reality in Canada and that is our relationship to the USA. Our practical dependence on the US, expressed in political and military alliances, confirmed by various forms of economic penetration and supported by diverse kinds of cultural and educational colonisation, makes any attempt at disengagement a struggle from the start. Radicals should not rely, in such a struggle, on the counter-force of nationalism and certainly should not toy with any "social nationalism." We have noted with encouragement in the past few years, the emergence of a revolutionary movement throughout the US which works towards the same internationalist objectives as we do. The élan and courage of this growing movement presents an urgent claim upon us not only for our solidarity but for an active strategy of collaboration in the pursuit of this new international radicalism. The development of a similar movement in Québec is also a factor to be celebrated and encouraged.

But it must be stressed again that no critique of Canada is valid unless it recognises from the start the fact that this country is a "branch-plant country" or a "client State." Slipping into the cosy embrace of Moloch, we have developed the fine art of a client politics, a client militarism and a client culture. As the old stiffness of the British-embroidered class structures of recent times fade, this client apparatus, extensively established in every field with most of the national communications system safely in its hands, confronts us as an enemy who is very difficult to recognise because his accents and appearance are "Canadian" although his decisive agency runs back to the corporate powers of the USA.

What Is the Nature of Liberal Corporatism?

Towering over the socio-economic structure of our society is a political super-structure surrounded by a chorus attempting to legitimize its values. in the face of the system's twin process of maintaining and developing our powerlessness and our meaningless lives, how does our political super-structure respond. Clearly to us, the elaborate procedures and structures of "representative" or parliamentary democracy born in the Nineteenth Century and embroidered on since, stand as ossified caricatures. We live in a society where the majority of people passively consent to things being done in their name, a society of managed politics. The techniques of consultation are polished but they remain essentially techniques and should not be confused with participation. This "passivity" or "apathy" is officially decried ritualistically but in fact is generated by the very structures of our society.

It is a fact that in our type of society, any conventional opposition group inevitably assumes the values of the system it opposes and is eventually absorbed by it. In Canada, as elsewhere, this is the fate of socialists and social democrats, supporters of this country's political party of the Left and the NDP. the whole point is that in opposition, there is a profound gap between consciousness and organisation, partly because of real changes achieved through industrialism and technology and partly because the familiar institutions of the Left have been pressed out of shape and recognition by the society we have been describing.

The perspective of Canada's power elite and its supporting institutions is clear to us. It is to muffle real conflict, to dissolve it into a false political consensus; to build not a genuine and participatory democracy, a community of meaningful life and work but a bogus conviviality between every social group. Consensus politics, integral to the success of neo-capitalism, is in its essence manipulative politics; politics of man-manage-ment and deeply undemocratic because of its basic, non-negotiable premises. Governments are still elected to sure, M.P.'s assert the supremacy of the House of Commons but the real business of government is the management of consensus between the most powerful and organised elites.

The ruling elites can no longer impose their will by coercion as they used to but neither will they see progress as a people organising itself for effective participation in power and responsibility in a society that can be de-bureaucratised and decentralised by modern technology.

The task of the politicians is to build consensus around each issue by means of bargain and to compromise through a coalition of interests, and especially to associate the large units of power with their legislative programme.

Consensus politics is thus the politics of incremental action; it is not intended for any large-scale structural change. It is the politics of pragmatism, of the suc-cessful manoeuvre within existing limits. Every administrative act is a kind of clever performance, an exercise of political public relations. Whether the manoeuvres are made by a Conservative, Liberal or a social democratic party like the NDP, it hardly matters since they all accept the constraints of the status quo as a framework.

The circle of politics is very narrowly defined in Canada and thus has been closed — this in a very special way. In all societies there are always separate sources of power but, in our own, the consequences of the negotiations are disastrous. The whole essence of this system is an increas-ing rationalisation and co-ordination of these sources of power. The State within the State — the high commands in each sector —the banks, corpora-tions, the federations of industrialist, the Canadian Labour Congress — are given a new and more formal role in the political structure and this, in-creasingly, is the actual machinery of decision-making — in their own fields as always but now also in a co-ordinated field.

This structure, which is to a decisive extent mirrored in the ownership and control of the public and private media of communication, is then plausibly described as "the national or public interest" To the extent that the "public interest" is defined largely to include the very specific and damaging interests of the banks, insurance companies and combines, it also excludes what, on the other side, are called "sectional" or "local" inter-ests of the poor, low-paid workers, youth in general and backward regions. The elected sector —the vote which is still offered as ratifying — gets redefined, after its passage through the machines, as one interest among others; what is still called the public interest is present now only as one — relatively weak and ill-organised — among several elements involved in effective decision-making.

All this has thrown socialists into profound confusion. They have, in effect (those who have not turned ideologically to the East or those who have not accepted a libertarian perspective), been absorbed by the system. For neo-capitalism, in the very process of "surpassing" socialism, in fact takes over many collectivist forms — though none of the content — of freedom. Thus socialists have always believed in planning — and now organised capitalism needs to plan and does. The NDP supports a strong trade union movement — and now organised capitalism needs a strong, centralised trade union movement with which to bargain. It seems easy to turn and say, as does the NDP leadership: we are making socialism in fact, only we call it something else and we are all in it together.

What in has happened is quite a different matter. Long before the present evolution began in earnest, its leaders and intellectuals translated these aspirations into narrow economism — expert planning — and a minimum welfare standard. With the whole end of the spectrum of democratic recovery and power left out, this meant a critical redefinition. In this transition period, the NDP leadership, already wedded to a to a very particular concept of socialism, sees its opportunity for power. It is thus making a bid for the job of harnessing and managing the new system but only partly because of its exhaustion and more importantly because of its faulty perspective. It has been itself taken over from both outside and inside by a very subtle process.

"But democracy means parliament," "Elections are politics." Isn't that the usual answer? At a very formal level it appears that parliamentary democracy is the democracy of today but it is not. It offers, in fact, a congress of representatives more loyal to their political parties than to their constituents. These elected representatives will, of course, often quarrel among themselves, and the rest of us may be asked to take sides. But all actual choice will be directed towards the resolution of conflicts within that specific machinery. We then confront a whole system which is foreclosing upon democracy and which is robbing the people of any political culture and identity. *What we face is not simply a question of programmes and ideologies, what we face primarily is a question of institutions.* Consequently, we can add a footnote that, as long as the present order prevails, even a political party with a "revolutionary programme" contesting from within the electoral system is doomed.

Can we then challenge our political institutions and the political economy and culture that depends on it, given our systemic analysis, by entering that pre-defined area in order to contest it? The answer of the New Left is an emphatic no! and it is not a yes and no. It is a principled no. Otherwise, as radicals, we will delude ourselves again, for what will looks like confrontation turns out to have been another bargain; changes of the system reappear as change in the system and the quality of our lives remains the same while the cardinal questions of humanity persist.

The traditional agencies of political change are failing and so have the older definitions of politics. The political voting machines, once considered the means by which humanity would be emancipated, have been bypassed in importance and indeed seek to expropriate us from any political identity. Is it not farcical to hear the Conservative leader of the opposition or the Union Nationale government or social democrats talk about the need for participatory democracy? All of a sudden, the politicians who have discovered participation talk glibly about the need for an extra-parliamentary opposition. The capacity of the establishment to absorb the language of the New Left while leaving the essentials unchanged is horrific and only deepens the cynicism of the young.

We have no alternative but to withdraw our allegiance from the machines of the electoral process and from the institutions of "representative democracy" like parliaments to forego the magical rite of voting for our freedom and resume our own initiatives before liberal corporatism asphyxiates us. We are now in a period of transition like the system itself, in which we will seek to unite radicals in new common forms of resistance and counter-institution building. As we have explained elsewhere, we wish to create a political movement of people with the capacity to determine their own lives but one that has a cultural reality to it. For this we need common opportunities for education, for agitation, for building, for international discussions and for mutual consultation and support in all active campaigns against injustice.

What Is an Extra-Parliamentary Opposition in Canada?

The idea of the Extra-Parliamentary Opposition (EPO) arose as a result of a lot of people arriving at much of the analysis above. EPO is not a formal organisation but rather a critical concept or a political term of reference. We shall describe what EPO should be like in Canada and this is based on the political experience of many people here and in other industrial countries.

The idea of EPO is that a coalition of individuals and groups with a common critique of liberal democracy and a minimum programme choose to act together and separately within such a framework. The range of the coalition is focused on a similar although not identical critique of the institutions of political representation in this country. At one end of the coalition, the EPO includes individuals and groups very critical of the function and representation of parliament and electoralism. This part of EPO, although it recognises the necessity of generating a movement for social change in Canada, still believes it useful to "utilize" electoralism by supporting certain candidates on their own merits who, while campaigning, would also criticise the inadequacies of both electoralism and parliamentarianism. This would constitute the moderate wing of EPO.

At the other end of the coalition, people in EPO would have a principled position against electoralism (especially at the federal and provincial level) and against parliamentarianism and would seek to create revolutionary alternatives to this definition of politics. At the head of this wing of EPO would be the New Left student and youth movement which demand that producers should control what they produce using the operational principles of "self-determination," "*autogestion*," "workers councils," "participatory or direct democracy." This section of EPO would consist of individuals and groups ranging from revolutionary socialist parties to other revolutionary groups that reflect involvement in party politics, electioneering and voting in our prevailing political institutions. They seek to organise new centres of power among ethnic and racial minorities, urban and rural workers, youth, the poor and other groups on a neighbourhood and work level.

The two wings of EPO would thus share a basic critique of the political institutions of Canada but would

differ as to the implication and application of this critique. There would be a "creative tension and dialogue" between them.

Our programme for the EPO would include the following:

- The decolonisation and liberation of Canada from the American Empire.
- A stand against all Great Power Imperialism and Chauvinism — East or West.
- The self-determination of the people of Québec and for that nation's independence if its people so choose.
- The creation of a broad movement for social and political change in Canada to implement the human rights of all people. Further, EPO recognises that Canada's basic foreign and defense policy will not change until certain key institutions and values are also changed which includes a disengagement by this country from American imperialism on the one hand and the decolonisation and democratisation of Canada on the other. This task is the burden of a movement for social change.
- The cultural autonomy of ethnic and racial minorities and their right to self-determination and the struggle against current attempts of assimilation and institutionalised racism.
- For the self-organisation of new constituencies presently without a political voice, i.e. the poor, ethnic and racial minorities, youth and students, farmers and industrial workers. This can be done by creating a movement with a cultural reality based on counter-institutions.
- The encouragement and help to focus the need for research into Canada's colonised past and present.
- The principle of legal mass action as well as civil disobedience where necessary.
- A minimum action programme which is under continuous study and evolution. EPO is not a formal organisation but a common political term of reference for those in Canada who seek genuine change and a qualitatively new society. EPO will have specific positions on specific issues, i.e. with reference Vietnam — US GET OUT NOW! or with reference to Czechoslovakia — USSR GET OUT NOW! etc.

These positions are common denominator positions but what is important is common action. Supporters of the concept of EPO in Canada and in other countries will sometimes act both together and separately.

There is no doubt that there is much to be discussed in this proposed EPO programme. It is significant, however, to note that many groups across the country individually include many aspects of what is suggested above. The striking difference will be having a common campaign on many of these questions which will begin a systemic approach to change in Canada and allow us to emerge out of our fragmented existence.

The EPO and its supporters are brought together because of a new awareness that

- The present system cannot solve the major problems of our society. It pretends that our difficulties are temporary. The present system is not geared to give to the majority of our people: real social security; meaningful and humane education; peace and disarmament.
- The present system cannot identify or solve the problems of our society. It drifts against social change and substitutes its rising curve on existing lines and inequalities. As a consequence, it must absorb or deflect new kinds of demands in a rapidly changing world. It cannot affect the quality of our lives and thus cannot provide for the growing demands for meaning in work and leisure, for participation in actual communities, for an urban environment shaped by human priorities, for equality of women, for personal liberation from the routines of living inside the machine. All it can offer is compulsive consumption and its fashionable gimmicks and "entertainment" and these feed on themselves. In the face of dissent, alienation, apathy and a growing social and personal violence, it can offer only new manipulation, new forms of control and force, for it cannot conceive what indeed would end this.
- The present system cannot operate with genuinely conflicting political parties and movements and so it must try to drain these of meaning which, in practice, involves taking significance, legitimacy, values and participation away from many thousands of actual people.
- The present system cannot, finally, stand the pressure of the contemporary world. It is the last dream of a myopic local group; a way of preserving its structures of minority power against a world revolution with which the needs of its own people for peace and freedom must be eventually ranged. Centred in its dying concepts of what the world should be like, it is being driven to conflict and war, to massive armaments and dehumanisation even while it proclaims its own version of life as an endless, mild, hand-to-mouth paradise. This contradiction is already bending it and will continue to bend it. It is the weak link in its otherwise glassy facade. It is the point where change will begin and where we must be ready to push change right through until the system as a whole is dismantled.

In the coming years, the failures of the present system will provoke repeated struggles on particular issues, representing the urgent needs and expectations of million of people. We must see each conflict as a opportunity for explaining the basic character of the system which is cheating us and as a way of helping to change consciousness; to follow our needs and feeling through until they reach the kind of demands which the system can neither satisfy nor contain. What has been the characteristic weakness of those in this country who have sought radical change, namely running separate campaigns in so many different social and political fields, through the EPO can become our strength. We are present in a society where the system and its political leadership have a diminishing legitimacy.

The existing political institutions and party structures are under great strain and the pressure can be expected to increase. This system and we who have worked within it up until now, were not able to prevent nuclear bombs from entering Canada, not able to disengage ourselves from the Cold War and the arms race, not able to stop American imperialism in Vietnam, were unresponsive to the aspirations of the people of Québec, to the poor, youth and oppressed minorities in our society; unable to do much about the immense human suffering in the world.

We do not intend to made any premature move which would isolate people interested in radical change or confuse our actual and potential supporters. At the same time, we mean what we say when we declare an end to tactics and organisational forms. If this analysis is right, then radicals must make their voices heard again and again among the growing majority of people who feel no commitment to these forms. Already, thousands of young men and women who share many of our objectives and whose internationalist conscience and immediate personal concern indicates more alertness than their predecessors and elders, stand outside the NDP and refuse to give it the kind of allegiance it demands. The other organisations of the Left represent, in most cases, the same hardening shells of old situations, old bearings and old strategies. *What matters now, everywhere, is movement.* In the context of such a new awareness, a movement for fundamental social change has a greater chance of emerging; a movement that will have the capacity to both resist injustice as well as build the new society by means of building the institutions and system of institutions of that new society now, thus giving a cultural reality to the new politics. We have indicated elsewhere what the scope and orientation of such a movement as a part of an EPO should be.

To those who say that there is no future without changing the NDP, we reply that we shall only influence it by refusing to accept its machine definitions and demands and that the real change required is so large and so difficult that it can only come about as part of much wider changes of consciousness and as a result of manifold struggles in many areas of life. In a seminal sense, we must begin afresh.

This statement asks for a response. There are may people who share this general analysis and who have come to a similar position. We invite their active initiative.

Spring 1970

THE RADICAL IMPLICATIONS OF THE ECOLOGY QUESTION

Do-good liberal have been trying to find a *cause célèbre* upon which to bear their souls without being pursued by radicals. There are more than three hundred ecology-conservation organisations in the greater New York area alone. Most of these, like their Canadian counterparts, have names like The Riverdale Civic Association to Promote a Better Landscape. They are hopelessly impotent in the midst of the present ecological catastrophe. Probably less than a dozen groups are spontaneously activist, radical or revolutionary freak green guerrillas. These latter groups are now in hot pursuit of this important social question.

Up until this point, most "radical" ecology groups across the continent had in reality adopted a liberal outlook, not unlike their early days. They did not make the connection between violence on the environment and the society that perpetrated that violence. They attacked only the effect, not the root causes. They joined in pleas to government leaders and in campaigns to influence legislation. If anything is evident about the present ecological crisis, it is that human energy spent in those directions can only delay the final catastrophe; it can never prevent it.

For our part, we do not believe that the wielders of political power are "uninformed" or that changing "attitudes" will solve the problems.

We do not find useful: movements of pollution reform that act as mere safety valves for a system of natural and human exploitation and domination.

We cannot believe that the fundamental cause of the ecological crisis is the fact that scientists have too little (or too much) political power. Nor is the fundamental cause technology. Nor is it population growth. Nor is it merely the "profit system." It is our position:

- that the ecological crisis is fundamentally a social problem, deeply rooted in the structure of society and in the cultural values that this society generates and reinforces,
- that the present structure of society, a product of material conditions is based on our domination and exploitation both of nature and our fellow humans,
- that this domination is a result of the concentration of power created by the centralisation of energy, material and human resources and social administration,
- that, therefore, the cities must be decentralised into regional communities,
- that the earth's resources must be utilized on a regional community basis of mutual aid and be determined by the life carrying capacity of the ecosystem in which the communities are located and,

- that all social institutions of domination and exploitation, from the patriarchal family to the modern Nation-State, must be dissolved,
- that the life-style revolution of the hip culture that expanded experience, eroticism, freedom and consciousness is inseparable from the radical ecology movement,
- that the creation of this life-value society is impossible within the present death-value social system and therefore the ecology movement is also inseparable from the liberation movements of colonised peoples, black and brown people, native people, working people, gay people, women, youths and children,
- that direct action is the only effective means that people can take to gain control of their environment, their lives and their destinies,
- and that revolutionaries must become hip to ecology and the ecologically hip must turn on to revolution.

Fall 1972

THE STATE

We would like to maintain that the liberals and the political Left in Canada and Québec have no coherent theory of the State. The present poverty of "political science," as taught in our schools of "higher learning," need not surprise us but this attitude on the part of establishment academia has important social consequences. The current orthodoxy in "political science" has turned on the claims (which have become unexamined articles of faith) of a pluralist-democratic view of society. Therefore the State is not a special institution whose essential purpose is to defend and perpetuate the present class structure.

On the other hand, "...Marxist political analysis, notably in relation to the nature and role of the state, has long seemed stuck in his groove and has shown little capacity to renew itself." In The State in Capitalist Society, Ralph Miliband not only shatters the myth of pluralistic democracy, he goes on to admit that Marxism has made no substantial contributions to our understanding of the State for a very long time. Indeed, we might add that the cancerous growth of the State, both in capitalist and "socialist" societies, as well as the new relevance of the anarchist critique of the State, has forced many radicals to re-open the question in a fundamental way. Miliband adds, "Marx himself, it may be recalled, never attempted a systematic study of the state." He goes on to say:

> For the most part, Marxists everywhere have been content to take this thesis as more or less self-evident; (referring to the thesis in the *Com-*

munist Manifesto — D.R.) and to take as their text on the state Lenin's State and Revolution, which is now half a century old and which was in essence both a restatement and an elaboration of the main view of the state to be found in Marx and Engels and a fierce assertion of its validity in the era of imperialism. Since then, the only major Marxist contribution to the theory of the state has been that of Antonio Gramsci, whose illuminating notes on the subject have only fairly recently come to gain a measure of recognition and influence beyond Italy. Otherwise, Marxists have made little notable attempt to confront the question of the state in the light of the concrete socio-economic *and* political *and* cultural reality of actual capitalist societies. Where the attempt has been made, it has suffered from an over-simple explanation of the interrelationship between civil society and the state. Even though that "model" comes much closer to reality than democratic-pluralist theory, it requires a much more thorough elaboration than it has hitherto been given; Paul Sweezy was scarcely exaggerating when he noted some years ago that "this is the area in which the study of monopoly capitalism, not only by bourgeois social scientists but by Marxists as well, is most seriously deficient."

Our analysis of the State is far from complete and is only a beginning. We do not, for instance, deal with the question that Miliband raises in his book about whether we can speak of a "ruling class" in relationship to countries of advanced capitalism as contrasted with the existence of economic elites which, "by virtue of ownership or control or both, do command many of the most important sectors of economic life." An investigation of this question is crucial if we are to understand the degree to which the State has an independent and separate institutional role and function in our type of society. We do not deal with the whole range of institutions related to the "state system" — public corporations, central banks, regulatory commissions; that is, the vast administrative function of the State which reaches way beyond the traditional bureaucracy associated with government. Nor do we deal with the social composition of the "state elite." We also do not deal with the role, function and enormous growth of the civil service, the judiciary (including the police and prison system) and the military and para-military. We have not dealt with the role of the State in the competition between different "interests" in capitalist society. Finally, we have not dealt with the mass media and the extensive educational system as the central agencies that legitimise the system along with the political parties and legislative assemblies. In a word, what we have done is to survey the major economic and social characteristics of the State in our advanced capitalist society and submitted to detailed analysis the pattern of economic power and relationship of the State to the political economy. Without, however, continuing the study of the role and function of the State in "socialist" countries, not only will our understanding of the processes of centralisation, bureaucracy and authoritarianism be limited, the revolutionary alternative well itself be limited as well as its programmatic and strategic potential.

The growth of the State apparatus in capitalist society has not escaped the attention of radical observers. Yet, while it is universally admitted that

Western economies are characterised by a form of State capitalism, the theoretical and strategic conclusions to be drawn from this fact have often not been made. Too frequently, we act according to an outmoded conception of the structure of capitalist society and the means of transforming it, even when we know that structure has been substantially changed.

A major cause of our weakness in this area of research is that not enough detailed material has been gathered describing the extent and form of the role of the State in capitalist society to analyse its origins and pattern of development. This has been particularly the case in Canada and Québec.

From the kind of analysis presented, a new strategy and concept of organising a socialist movement must be fashioned. Our theoretical inadequacy grows more apparent every day; and as militancy among governmental and para-governmental workers spreads and manifests itself in strikes, wildcats, takeovers and other forms of political opposition, it becomes more and more intolerable. And as we all know, these are not matters which affect only an isolated group of workers; the government sector, as we shall see, is immense and major labour management disputes in it inevitably become political crisis.

Because of the lack of an ongoing socialist critique of the State in capitalist society, a social democratic liberal view still prevails far too widely. This view associates the State as the tool of reform, the redistribution of wealth and services. The State is the path to the "just society"; so, the further we are along this path, the nearer we are to socialism. (Note that this is how the American Communist Party regarded the New Deal.) Liberals point to the growing bureaucracy, the expansion of an industrial "public sector" and other government initiatives as portents of the good society tomorrow. Because the Left lacks a profound empirically based understanding of the State in Canada and Québec, our critique has not overcome the left-liberal assumption that the resolution of the contradictions of capitalism lies in the gradual enlargement of the "public sector."

We set the term "public sector" in quotes on the basis of facts which show that the role of the State is to serve private capital and those segments of the economy that are owned by the State are nevertheless private in their fundamental purpose and thrust. Socialists know this; they know that an enlarged State under capitalism means only a strengthened capitalism; if they do not know, then they are blind to the developments in the industrialised world in this century.

To render this theoretical understanding critically useful to a movement whose goal is to negate the prevailing capitalist system, what is first required is concrete data of a particular sort. First, what is this public sector? What parts of the economy are involved in it? How has it grown? What is its relation with private capital? Second, what does it in fact do to serve the public as compared to what it claims to do? Third, who pays for the services provided by the government bureaucracy and through what mechanisms? Finally, how is all of this justified by the propaganda services of the capitalist State, i.e. the media?

First, it is now clear, if it was not before, that the growth of the State has been, liberal myths notwithstanding, to the benefit rather than the detriment of the corporate rich. While a few anachronistic businessmen object here and there, the State they fear has grown and expanded directly in response to their own corporate needs in areas such as transportation, education, resource development, communications and scientific research, to name just a few.

The second point is that the growth of the "welfare State" which in theory redistributes services and wealth to those at the bottom of the capitalist order has been exaggerated and misrepresented. In relative terms, as compared to GNP or government expenditure, the social services of the State have, more often than not, remained constant. Third, the additional State revenues needed to pay for the growing State bureaucracy and increased activity has been disproportionately raised through increases in personal income taxes and sales taxes; corporation income taxes now provide a less significant share of State revenues. Thus the great majority of salaried employees in Canada has paid for the creation of a vast State machinery, the basic role of which is to serve the needs of the small class of corporate owners.

The fourth element is the growing importance of the State employee. Analysis shows that the very existence of the sector serves the economic needs of the private corporations. The general population, encouraged by the media, expects the public employee to show greater "responsibility." Furthermore, it assumes that the employer, i.e. the government, has the public interest at heart while the workers are pursuing selfish interests. (This is in large part a result of the failure of socialists to educate themselves and the public on the role inevitably played by the State under capitalism.) At the same time the State finds itself often in the most unproductive sectors of the production — those most subject to stress in periods of economic downturn. Added to this is the normal policy of capitalist governments to extend tax and other reliefs to corporations in times of economic difficulty so that the government revenues are even further depleted.

In times such as now, with high unemployment and lagging productivity — a situation, say some observers, which is likely to continue under present day capitalism long into the conceivable future — governments thus confront a political choice. They must either freeze wages, reduce fringe benefits or reclassify in this already underprivileged sector or further raise personal income and sales taxes. In this political battle, the public employee almost inevitably loses (except for the police, on whose backs State power finally rests). At the same time, it becomes the government, rather than private corporations, that crush the most militant labour insurgencies, thus enabling the corporate directors to discretely follow suit in their general attitudes to the demands of their workers out of "public duty." Of course, the most powerful corporate capitalists, because they have relegated low or no-return fields of the economy to the government, can appear comparatively generous since they can transfer added costs to the public through price increases. In this rather complex way, the public sector provides a safety valve — channelling discontent among government employees which is turned towards the public it is supposed to serve, turning public sentiment against unions and allowing corporate executives to present themselves, not as the exploiting, privileged few, but as unusually public-spirited citizens.

In total, using public instruments to serve private ends in the complex ways outlined above, while at the same time laying claim to the liberal/social democratic ideology which associates the State with a socialist or just society, has been very effective in maintaining and screening the basic inequality of wealth and power inherent under capitalism. It has led to the diffusion of popular discontent so that it could be defeated when necessary, but more often directed into harmless channels.

Yet that discontent is there and has raised its head too often among certain groups and in certain areas for government as sophisticated as that in Ottawa not to devise schemes to meet this problem. So we get DREE's (Department of Regional Economic Expansion initiatives) that promise economic recovery to depressed areas and OFY's (Opportunities for Youth) and LIP's (Local Initiative Projects) that hand out government money to young people and other citizens to solve their own and other people's problems. What is provided, in fact, is but the image of economic and social change; the programs, in fact, serve to strengthen the system and confirm the power of the dominant class which is the real source of the problem.

LIP and OFY were designed to deal with a discontent that was unformed and unfocused and to assure people that any suspicions they might have had that their government was not really on their side were mistaken. Here was a government that was hip, that understood. Even the employees were chosen to project that image, one they too often believed. So an already unfocused protest loses its impetus. Such government programs then, are innovative but not really new, merely the latest step in the pattern of the developing role of the capitalist State.

Two concrete examples, both in the field of housing, might be briefly explored here. The first is the leaking of the CMHC's (Central Mortgage and Housing Corporation) Dennis report. The events surrounding this report present an incredibly lucid illustration of what has been said. The task force hired young middle class intellectuals to assess low income housing. They submitted a report, after the expenditure of a great deal of public funds, exposing the role of the CMHC since World War II. This role of the CMHC was one of aiding a few large developers to take over Canada's cities and artificially raise property values through speculations, thereby earning extremely high profits while constructing a totally inadequate number of moderate and low income housing units. The report was shelved. Three thousand copies it seems were actually shredded and would have been completely forgotten were it not for a disgruntled researcher spilling the beans to David Lewis.

The second example concerns the struggle of the Milton-Park Citizens Committee in Montréal against Concordia Development. Here was a concrete example of the kind of collusion the Dennis Report reveals, though in this case, mainly at the provincial and municipal levels. Through legislation and financial aid, the governments supported a private company to build a huge expensive development of elite housing and hotels, destroying the area against the will of residents and the advice of architects and town planners. In Milton-Park, the citizens learned something in the process about the State and its relationship to the economic drives of a capitalist system — lessons they will apply in the future. The government, especially Federal, has been trying to keep these lessons from being learned. The goal is to make it appear that what is good for the State (and therefore for General Motors) is good for Canada (and therefore you and me).

This we must not allow it to do. Events have shown that the "public sector" has become the focus of working-class radicalism and hence, a socialist strategy must concentrate on (rather than ignore which has been the practice too often) this ever growing segment of society.

When confronted with the call to public responsibility, the State employee must refuse to accept the prevailing definition of "public." This employer does not speak for the public. In fact, the "general public" is a creation of the mass media. The only "public" that exists in reality is that public which is actually served in the work performed by the particular group of State employees. Thus, hospital workers must seriously begin to work at involving the patients and others who use their services in the very definition of their role and seek them as allies in their demand for improved working conditions. Teachers must similarly regard students and parents; bus drivers must work together with commuters, etc.

The kinds of demands that must be raised must be more than those traditional ones of bread and butter although these cannot be neglected. Forming coalitions with users and consumers necessitated that public employees organise themselves around the quantitative aspects of their work: exactly what they do, who sets the standards, whom they serve. The takeover by workers both non-professional and professional at the Albert Prévost Psychiatric Hospital in Montréal during the Québec Public Service Strike is an important precedent. It allied public employees from all categories directly with the needs of the patients and against the government-appointed administration. The patients, it was evident to all, benefited from the change to self-management. The reaction of the Castonguay social welfare ministry, the most progressive part of the Québec State, to the Prévost insurgency should convince any remaining sceptics about the primary function and ultimate loyalty of the State. The ministry unequivocally supported an obviously autocratic and unfit handful of bureaucrats against the desires of the entire staff, ignoring the effect this would have on the staff. It suspected, with good reason, that workers' insurgency in support of self-management was a threat, not only to the hospital or even the ministry, but to the entire system.

While Prévost was defeated, the possibilities it raises are indeed exciting. What if public service unions began increasingly to raise qualitative issues? What if they demanded a new system of management for their institutions combining self-management by the workers with participation by that segment of the public affected by the service? What if the workers of Hydro Quebec began to determine who got the contracts, how much power was to cost consumers, where new power installations would be created and what kinds of institutions were to be given priority in the allocation of power, all in consultation with the people directly affected? What if...? To sum it up, what if the public employees began to ignore the State and directly serve the public? Perhaps this is what "the withering away of the state" looks like.

The kind of analysis and strategy outlined here is a personal challenge to those radicals who accept working for the government as a legitimate channel for bringing about real change. Whether employed by the State indirectly and temporarily with LIP, OFY or a task force of some kind, or directly with CMHC, Hydro Quebec or whatever; each government employee must rethink his or her position.

Can the State be used or is it not more likely that the State is using us? Of course none of this precludes organisation among State employees in the direction suggested above; in fact, we maintain this to be a very important area of activity.

The point is that an acceptance of such a strategy requires a total change in the attitudes that exist among most Canadians and (even) Québec radicals in relation to the State. The capitalist State is not a means of meaningful social change; it is a subtle and powerful means of preventing it. We must organise against it from without and within.

Fall 1979

STATE POWER AND POLITICAL PARTIES OR, WHY THE PQ LOST THE BY-ELECTIONS

For months State functionaries and the trade union negotiators of the Common Front (of the Québec Federation of Labour, the Confederation of National Trade Unions, and the Centrale des Enseignants du Québec) were getting nowhere in their attempts to agree on new contractual demands. Finally, the Common Front called for a general strike of its more than 200,000 workers, for November 13, 1979. This was not supposed to happen. Purportedly, the trade union bureaucracy had been permeated by PQ nationalists who would not want to confront the State. But the social question, in 1972 and again in 1976, cannot be capped even in a period as intensely nationalist as the one we are in now. Many in the trade union movement tend to place class interests before national sentiments.

Meanwhile, given the dynamics of State power in our society, the techno-bureaucrats and private capital interests pressed the PQ very hard to limit the offer made to the Common Front. Under the PQ, as under all previous political parties, the State continues to be an instrument for the private accumulation of capital. And so, with consummate cynicism, in the November 14, 1979 by-elections the PQ sought to shore up its chances by passing a legislative act which attempted to prevent the general strike by making it illegal, and imposing prison and heavy fines for civil disobedience.

As the call for civil disobedience against the State grew in other parts of the Common Front, it was weakened, notably among the teachers and the public service unions associated with the PQ-leaning QFL. Only the social service and hospital workers, who belonged to the CNTU (some 75,000), defied the legislative law. Many arrests were made and heavy fines were imposed. In the meantime the State, on the collective agreement, made more concessions to these direct-action insurgents than it intended - at the relative expense of the conforming teachers, who abstained from striking.

Over the past three years the myth of the PQ as a pro-labour party became somewhat dissipated as the cold realities of power began to set in. The promised major reforms of auto insurance, tenants' rights legislation, women's rights, decentralisation, municipal democracy and taxation turned into patchwork "reformettes" that fell short of the expectations of many who had supported PQ. After an initial clumsy swipe at the Drapeau regime in Montréal, the government displayed no interest in breaking down the Mayor's autocratic power structures; and the PQ, particularly its non-progressive elements, allowed the Liberal-tied Civic Party machine virtual free rein in their East End "strongholds," thus sowing the seeds of their own defeat in Maisonneuve a year after the latest Drapeau landslide.

But it was in the field of labour relations that the PQ government showed itself. Never regarding themselves as leaders of a "workers' party," and imposing upon themselves the contradiction of providing "good" (read "routine") government while aiming at radical changes in the very structure of the State, the government also tried for "evenhandedness" in its labour policies and succeeded in pleasing nobody. They banned electoral contributions from corporations and unions as well. After the shooting of strikers at the Robin Hood mills they introduced an "anti-scab" law, but by the time it was adopted it had been considerably watered down. The government's much vaunted industrial health and safety bill came under fierce attack from many unions, who saw it not only as inadequate but as an assault on acquired rights. And finally, as the negotiations in the public sector dragged on for month after weary month, it became apparent to the union rank-and-file that despite the large number of former public sector union negotiators on certain ministry staffs, the government not a "workers' government" but the good old-fashioned employer-State in a new guise.

In the name of budget constraints and the "broader" public interest, the government sought to impose a restrictive wage policy that did not include full cost-of-living indexation, on both the Québec public sector and, indirectly, such agencies as the Montreal Urban Community Transportation Commission which were only too glad to do its bidding. At first the government took a more subtle,"velvet glove" approach than its predecessors, though later its spokesmen would try to turn the union rank-and-file against their leaders. But to the workers who were affected, this approach could be seen clearly for what it was, despite the PQ sympathies of many. The government, in fact, was backing up the local institutional administrations whom the workers had been fighting for years in the hospitals and colleges. It was refusing to give the workers enough money to cover their needs; it was maintaining areas of discrimination and unequal pay for equal work, and continuing the Liberal policy of cutbacks that cost them jobs, overloaded workers who remained and caused services to deteriorate even further.

But all this, despite its disillusioning impact, was being accepted with a certain degree of fatalism. Leaders of the public sector Common Front found they had trouble getting united actions off the ground, and militant action was restricted to a few union locals. Bill 62 changed the picture. This law, which made any strike or slowdown illegal until November 29 and even stipulated the deadlines and reporting procedures for union strike votes, flew in the face of one fundamental PQ promise: that they, unlike Bourassa and the others, would never implement a *"loi-matraque,"* a "bludgeon law," against the workers. They respected this promise for eight months of a crippling transit strike in Québec City. But now, from the narrow standpoint of political opportunism and with an unlimited general strike called for the day before the crucial by-elections, the government felt it had no choice. After all, the Montréal public, having suffered through two bus strikes and a 24-hour hospital walkout, was presumably growing impatient. And, after all, while the PQ needed the non-union vote to carry the by-elections, the referendum and the next elections, the workers couldn't very well vote for the Liberals, could they? Having decided to play to the hilt its role as the employer State, having failed to negotiate on a satisfactory basis in the preceding months, the government had walked into a trap of its own making.

The Common Front, as it had in 1972 and 1976 against Bourassa, decided on civil disobedience as its only option. Strike votes were called in public institutions around the province, in some cases with up to 98% voting to defy the government. High school students and parents in the English Protestant schools and some French schools, organised to support the teachers' unions against the government, taking a leading role as they had against Bourassa and Bill 22 in 1976.

In the working-class riding of Maisonneuve, a PQ stronghold since 1970, the Liberals swept into office. They benefitted from a well-financed machine, from squabbles within the PQ over Lévesque's effective imposition of an outside candidate, from the absence of any third party,and from a certain working-class disillusionment that led to abstentionism or vote-switching and resulted from the government's foolish failure to take steps to cancel the latest transit fare increase, which had hit hardest at senior citizens and low-income families.

The old history lesson has been repeated. We cannot trust the State, under anyone's "guidance," no more than we can trust the technobureaucracy and economic elite. In the final analysis, it is *direct action*, costly as it sometimes is, that bares the facts and brings in results until profound changes can be undertaken by those associations of people that are democratically controlled and to be found at the base of society. The labour movement in Québec has a taste for civil disobedience or direct action. In Québec it has been used more frequently, and on a larger scale, than anywhere else in North America. And it works! Once again, as we have done in the past, we can only encourage the powerless class of our society, to move forward united and speak truth to power.

Spring 1983

THE STATE AND THE MOVEMENT FOR CHANGE

"The modern State is a compulsory association which organises domination...the State is a relation of men (sic) dominating men, a relation supported by means of legitimate (i.e.: considered to be legitimate) violence." This analysis of the State by Max Weber, pinpoints the key element in understanding the threat of nuclear annihilation that we now face: the nature of the modern State as the organising and sustaining force of domination. The major weakness of the peace movement is its failure to recognise that nuclear weapons are not primarily a question of technology and policy, and that the fact of their existence is located in the very structure of social relations as organised by States.

It is a mistake to isolate the issue of nuclear weapons from its social context. What is required is an analysis of organised domination, within society and also within the context of imperialism, as we see, for example, in the present U.S./Central America and Russia/Poland situations. If we fail to understand the complexity of the present nuclear crisis, our strategic efforts to reserve the situation might well be doomed.

There is a danger that the peace movement will restrict itself simply to the fact of nuclear weapons (assuming a preference for conventional weaponry in times of war), which fosters the illusion that with the removal of nuclear arms everything is right with the world and we can carry on as usual. This is a dangerous assumption because nuclear weapons are merely symptomatic of a much deeper problem.

Domination, that desire of the master to control the slave, of men to possess women, and of States to subdue and conquer each other — this power that expresses itself in authoritarian social and political structures — is the core of militarism. The sustaining and reproducing force of militarism is the State. Within the given social and political structures of domination, the possibility of nuclear war makes perfect, logical sense. To be effective the peace movement must be clearly aware that this threat, as well as the presence of nuclear arms, is inextricably linked to the major social concerns of today, one of which is disarmament. The peace movement must also become a movement for social change.

When it began in 1961, the journal founded was titled *Our Generation Against Nuclear War*. In those early years, it focused on the disarmament movement and related issues. The scope of the magazine soon broadened into other areas and attempted to cover other social movements of the 1970s: feminism, ecology and the urban question. In branching out this way, *Our Generation* developed a more coherent perspective on the necessity of social transformation. We realised that without struggles for the transformation of existing power structures and social relations, these movements could only hope for very limited success. We saw, for instance, that the emancipation of women, and efforts towards peace could not come about in a society that remained impervious to ecological concerns.

In recent months, *Our Generation* has published a series of articles on disarmament. The members of the editorial board, as well as many friends and supporters of the magazine, have been involved in various ways with the disarmament movement. In the present editorial we will make an effort to help strengthen the disarmament movement by raising what we perceive to be some of the central themes of discussion and debate.

At the basis of this debate is the question of whether the disarmament movement will continue to limit itself to a single issue and specific related demands, or if it will attempt to analyse its objective — the end of nuclear arms — in terms of a larger perspective. The creation and proliferation of nuclear weapons, the gearing up for "winnable" nuclear warfare by the U.S., the development and deployment of the Cruise Missile with its deadly first-strike capacity — all this is happening and will continue to happen *against our will*.

How can we reverse this drift toward inevitable destruction if we have no power over the decision-making power of States? Unless we challenge the capitalist State at its heart, the power and authority which enable it to maintain itself as a "compulsory association which organises domination," militarism will continue to be the bedrock and ultimate expression of the State. Domination must be challenged at every level of encounter, which is why other social movements inevitably intersect with each other: the women's movement, workers' struggles, and the ecology and disarmament movements. The interconnections of these movements are constituted by their autonomous local structures, their understanding of the power and domination that makes them vulnerable to men, bosses and the industrial process. These movements have tremendous potential to develop as self-mobilised, non-centralised forces capable of mounting strong resistance to the present social structure.

The strategic implications of a perspective that recognises these inter-connections, are that people who are active in different social movements will begin to act in solidarity and mutual support with each other (i.e.: sharing of resources, mutual participation in public actions). The decentralised character and potential of these movements should help them preserve their diversity while enabling them to agree on ultimate concerns. We will outline some ways in which different groups with their specific concerns might come together for the common purpose of disarmament and peace.

Labour

The production of nuclear weapons is highly profitable for the arms industry. This is one of the major reasons why more technologically complex and precise weapons are built every day. Rank and file workers must begin to find a way to help stop arms production, and the only way they can do it is to control the production process.

Autogestion, or self-management, is not likely to occur via the present labour relations system in which the centralised unions bargain with the employers. By definition, self-management must be struggled for locally; self-management cannot be other than autonomous workers' councils. Local self-managed production is our best hope for the creation of conversion projects because these projects would focus on production for need, and would help ensure job creation, rather than job loss, through conversion. The Cruise Missile Conversion Project group is struggling to educate and persuade workers at Litton Industries in Toronto that conversion is directly in their interest, both as workers and as socially responsible human beings. Production for need and use will not come from the employer. The owners of production in a capitalist society will never begin to take social priorities into account in the production process. The pursuit of ever greater profits is not compatible with social justice and responsibility.

These issues concern not only workers but also the unemployed. They must take up these issues and must form a strong movement for jobs that is linked to social need, and particularly to disarmament. There are more jobs related to the pursuit of peace and community well-being than there are jobs whose main reason for existence is the material wealth of a powerful few. The owners of production, along with the State and the military, will surely plunge us into nuclear war. This is why the peace movement is also a workers' movement.

Ecology

Over the last years, *Our Generation* has run a number of articles on the ecology movement. One of the most important of these was "The Ecology Manifesto" by the Regroupement Ecologique Québécois. It read: "The disastrous pillage of our environment must cease. The only way to stop it is to fight the material and social base which sustains it; that is, the system of capitalist production based on profit."

It is not only the social system of domination and capitalist production that leads us to dominate and destroy our environment; it is also the industrial system of capitalism that threatens the life of the natural world. Industrialism as it now exists, be it in a capitalist or a socialist State, is an increasing danger to the environment. The contemporary ecology movement has begun to articulate the links between the industrial system, its military spearhead, and the entire social and political structure.

Unless we strive to transform the whole social system down to its material *and* cultural foundations, the most we can hope to gain is minor modifications to our present condition. The arms race will continue to escalate unless we challenge it with a larger vision that understands nuclear weapons as a coherent expression and integral part of our whole society. According to Rudolf Bahro: "The whole question of human emancipation has taken a new form. The insight that the impulse to obliteration, to the self-extinction of humanity, lies in the very foundations of our industrial civilization and pervades every structure of its economy, science and technology, its political apparatus and its sociology and psychology, is today of such immediate importance that the socialist perspective takes second place, and in any case must be re-defined."

The questions of ecology, like the question of women's and workers' rights, are deeply connected with all other social questions. In order to confront that domination which is the source of human oppression, it is imperative that all these movements link up in a way that preserves their difference from one another. The ecology manifesto recognises the place of the movement in the broader struggle. "Our demands are many and ambitious, but they are absolutely essential. They are just stages toward the egalitarian and participatory society of the future. Each specific victory concretely diminishes the centralisation of power and carries us one small step toward the society we want."

Feminism

Our Generation, published an article on the first Women's Pentagon Action in Washington, November, 1981, along with the Unity Statement by the women who participated in that demonstration. In part, it read:

We women are gathering because life on the precipice is intolerable.

We want to know what anger in these men, what fear which can only be satisfied by destruction, what coldness of heart and ambition drives their days.

We want to know because we do not want that dominance which is exploitative and murderous in international relations and so dangerous to women and children at home — we do not want that sickness transferred by the violent society through the fathers to the sons.

In addressing the war producers of the Pentagon in this fashion, these women recognise the interconnectedness of violence against women and violence between nations. They recognise that the same impulse to mastery and destruction that leads to the exploitation of women, workers and native peoples, also leads to militarism. In societies where some groups dominate others, where the minority exercises power over everyone else, where the wealth of the few grows in proportion to the poverty and im-miseration of the many, in this kind of society deadlier weapons and larger-scale wars become unavoidable.

Many feminists are painfully aware of the relationship between the rape of women, destruction of the environment and imperialism. These are deeply connected realities. They know that power which creates myriad structures of domination is the basis of both misogyny and militarism. It is no accident that invading armies always rape the women of the conquered country: imperialism and rape have the same roots.

It is important, however, to understand these issues through an analysis of power rather than simply in terms of biological determinism. If one argues, as some feminist do, that war must be explained by the relation between a genitally-based male ethos with its concomitant urge to destroy, one lapses into a dualism that views the world as split between the forces of good (women) and the forces of evil (men). We are thinking in particular of feminist writers like Mary Daly, who vastly simplifies reality with her biological deterministic view of men and women. We hope that female powers of nurturing and love are not simply located in gyn/ecology. We ob-ject to that dualistic thinking that sees the world in terms of "us" and "them," friends and enemies. Such an in-group/out-group mentality of an-tagonism allows the dehumanization of the other. The journey from psychological to physical annihilation is frighteningly short, as history has repeatedly proven.

What feminists must realise is that simplistic associations between patriarchy and war on the one hand, and feminism/female life-giving creativity on the other, are themselves based on a split mode of being that is inherently violent. Rather, the problem of violence within social relations and between States must be analysed in terms of domination and its reflec-tion in culturally mediated social relations. In this way feminists can more effectively struggle in a context of potential solidarity with men to build a better *human* future.

The Contemporary Peace Movement

The conclusion to the Ecology Manifesto cited earlier, raises a crucial question for the peace movement: how to interpret the gains it may win? If, for instance, the Canadian government abandons its proposed treaty with the U.S. to test the cruise Missile, should we view this as a great victory? Would such an event mean that we are solidly on the road to disarmament? It would be dangerous to assume that disarmament can only happen via the State. Our fear is that some people in the peace movement might allow concrete, specific gains to obscure the deeper and more troubling social and political reality within which nuclear arms exist; this would contribute to the weakening of the movement. We urge that the peace movement focus its efforts toward the ultimate objective of social transformation. This will only happen if the movement develops a larger political analysis and perspective.

Demonstrations on Parliament Hill, letters to Trudeau and local MP's, petitions — all of these methods of protest are important, particularly as ways of drawing into the movement people who have never participated in acts of resistance before. In themselves these kinds of actions are based upon the false conviction that if only we speak out or appeal to reason, our political leaders will realise the error of their ways and capitulate to the will of the people. We do not suggest that these types of actions be abandoned but that a more profound and complex understanding of the situation will lead to more effective strategies.

According to E.P. Thompson, what the peace movement must construct is "a new internationalist constituency and one capable of acting urgently and with effect." An internationalist peace movement cannot be built through a centralised party or organisation. What must be created is an international movement composed of federated local bodies from all countries. There is no prior blueprint by which to fashion such a movement; it can only develop through action. Says Thompson: "We cannot write our recipes at leisure in the drawing-room...we must improvise our recipes as we sweat before the kitchen fires."

Our task is indeed a formidable one, but not impossible. The internationalised peace movement will arise if it is self-mobilised — it cannot wait upon the "High Command" of any party or centralised body, or it will surely fall.

Chapter 5

THE URBAN QUESTION — THINK GLOBALLY AND ACT LOCALLY

Fall 1974

THE FUTURE OF CANADIAN CITIES AND THE LIMITS OF THE CITY: THINK GLOBALLY AND ACT LOCALLY

In *The Future of Canadian Cities,* Boyce Richardson puts the urban question in its only correct Canadian context. On page 20, he states:

> These cities are coming under intense pressures of growth, and if we do not change, we face the prospect that in ten years our cities will be almost uninhabitable. Certainly we will not be able to control the growth of our cities if we cannot take command of the disposition of our own resources, and if we cannot have a say in the distribution of the wealth created by Canadian workers.
> The problems described above will require a range of solutions at every level of government. We cannot regain control of our destiny as long as millions of people are excluded from participation in the tasks, and enjoyment of the fruits, of our social and economic system. The current stance of Canada does not promise well. We have allowed ourselves to drift into the position of being an American-owned colony for which our masters have established a very clearly defined role: to produce the raw materials for the American industrial-military machine, and to consume the goods produced by that machine.

Thus, Richardson links the urban question with the national question as being inseparable. By doing this, he established himself as the only prominent published critic of the urban crisis in Canada who does not shy away from reality. Nothing that we discuss or undertake to do politically can be separated from the question of American domination and how we are to combat it.

> So long as Canadians sit calmly and permit this to happen (as we have done for twenty-five years), there is nothing much to be done. The whole country will continue to slip into American control, until our independence becomes a total sham (if it is not already so). If that happens, not only will we have unemployment, but we will not have the political weapons necessary to deal with it.

The problem in our society now is that the economic system feeds on itself; the government has never found the strength to insist that the economic system must serve the people, and not the other way around. Our economic institutions are interested only in their own growth. The number of casualties from this blind devotion to economic growth for its own sake is growing every year, yet people seem to have been brainwashed into believing that this an acceptable form of existence for a civilized community.

From this perspective Richardson goes on to attempt an integration of the urban and social questions.

Having set this as the framework of his book, he elucidates the horrendous facts constituting the urban crisis, in reality the crisis of our civilization.

The solutions that Richardson offers are curiously "common sense" social democratic ones. And here we enter into the limitations of this book: its analysis and offered solution. In spite of the fact that the book stands out from other Canadian books on the urban question, this is not a laurel for the author but a shocking recognition of the poverty of the existing literature. The book under review offers "progressive" solutions, not revolutionary ones; that is, they touch on the root causes of the crisis but shy away entirely from real programmes for social change needed to move away from the present abyss. This weakness, which makes the book "soft" or "light weight" is compounded by the fact that the author typically draws (good NDP social democrat that he is) so heavily from Sweden and related experiences. Furthermore, there is an absence of any serious discussion of *strategy*. So that what remains after reading the book is "progressivism" and an absence of revolutionary perspective and strategy, which in effect reveals a kind of blend of Ralph Naderism and populism. The absence of a revolutionary socialist suggestion leaves this mixture brewing dangerously. In the end, it's the same old put-on. The problems are analysed radically, but the solutions offered are short-term and realisable strictly within the system. Nowhere in the book is there a discussion of mass action and organization, nor the need for urban extra-parliamentary oppositions, nor the use of direct action (in spite of the fact that the Provos and Kabouters are mentioned); no discussion of social relations, the role of working-class organisations, block organising, revolutionary socialist government, the decentralization of all power. Read this book with great caution.

On the other hand, Murray Bookchin in his *The Limits of the City*, presents revolutionary analysis and perspective. What is the difference?

The "book" is in fact a powerfully constructed essay of 137 pages analysing the historical development of the city. This history is indispensable knowledge, not only to avoid the pitfalls of the past, but also to map the future wisely. Bookchin rediscovers with us buried traditions of urbanism which have contemporary relevance. He makes clear on the first pages that no solutions are presented from *within* the system. "My purpose is…to emphasize as strongly as I can that the roots of the urban crisis today lie not merely in poor designing, bad logistics, neglected neighbourhoods, and inadequate material support, but in the social system which has created these problems in the first place — and produced the modern metropolis."

The author maintains a precise focus by dealing with key aspects of the relationship between town and country, the historical evolution of the city, and the growth of that social deterioration synonymous with contemporary urbanism. The chapters cover "Land and City," "The Rise of the Bourgeois City," "The Limits of the Bourgeois City" and "Community and City Planning." A later edition includes "The Myth of City Planning."

In the first chapter, the author describes the emergence of what Marx called the "Asian land system." This was a form of agriculture in which land was worked communally, but where management was controlled by a central political apparatus — the State. It was possibly the most ancient of class societies, and its features evolve whenever tribal society begins to disintegrate in the face of the economic development of society. This system emerges where exploitation of one human being by another arises *before* private property of land and resources has been established. In Egypt, Mesopotamia, India, and China this system remained the basis of social relations for thousands of years. When irrigation was introduced, it also brought co-ordinated communal labour which in turn led to State centralisation and bureaucratisation. Within such a system, capital accumulation was virtually impossible, unlike in Europe where an independent bourgeoisie and an industrial economy arose.

Then Bookchin traces the rise of the city, drawing some basic contrasts.

> In the polis, the community achieves unity and flourished spiritually as the material being of man achieves relative freedom, independence, and roundedness. In bourgeois society, the commodity, which mediates all human relations, not only "unites" society in a cash nexus and minute division of labor, but at the same time separates man from the instruments of production, labor from creativity, object from subject, and eventually man from man. In the polis, the relative independence of the individual makes it possible to see the true dependence of man on the community, completely identifying the Athenian with his society.

How did "the Rise of the Bourgeois City" take place? What stands out as a principal factor in this history is again the influence of geography on agrarian relations. "Wherever the forest cover was removed, the agriculturist found large areas of arable land — a notable contrast with the Near East and North Africa, where substantial surpluses and food could be gleaned only from narrow strips of alluvial lands." In Europe, on the other hand, "in the absence of any need for extensive irrigation works, no need existed for the elaborate bureaucratic and monarchical apparatus which drained the commercial life of the ancient world." "Classical European feudalism was nourished by the geography and climate of the continent with the result that European urban communities achieved a degree of independence unknown, apart from Greece, to ancient society." Bookchin adds "all cities emerge in varying degrees from the division of labor among food cultivation, crafts and commerce, the extent to which they rest on this division of labor often distinguishes one city from another." The revolutionary historiography continues:

> The most important material step performed by feudal society was not the discovery of any single corpus of new inventions that presumably made capitalism possible, but rather the opening, clearing, and settlement of the European continent itself and adaptation of the Mediterranean technology to the heavier soils, climatic rigors and sparser populations of the North. And the greatest social advance scored by Europe was the development of commodity production in towns founded without decisive interference by agrarian interests — that is, urban centres with their own law of life, a law of life that found its expression in the development of commodity production.
> With the growth of international trade, commodity relations began to subject the entire fabric of European feudalism, undermining traditional relations in the countryside as well as in the towns. From the thirteenth century onward, European society became the theatre of social and economic developments hitherto unprecedented in history. (pp. 40-41.)

The crucial thing to understand about the early history of the city is the dialectic between community relations and the modes of labour. The most advanced form of commodity production exists under capitalism, but this truism requires extensive comment.

> No major technological innovations were needed to achieve this profound transformation. Although the capitalist system later produced the most far-reaching technological advances know in history, the bourgeoisie initially used the tools and materials of the craftsman to promote the new mode of production. Capital simply altered the traditional labor process by hiring workmen to produce for exchange without appreciably changing the industrial practices of the time. Labor-power was converted into a *commodity*. All the decisive technological advances achieved by the capitalist system thenceforth centred around the adaptation of natural forces and energy to this mode of labor. Technology became an extension of labor conceived not merely as a *human* activity, but as wage labor, a resource for immediate exploitation. Economic activity began to subordinate the satisfaction of concrete human needs to the abstract goals of exchange and capital accumulation. Production, in effect, occurred for its own sake. This marked a fundamental change in all the values of previously existing societies, however exploitative their natures.
> We must focus more sharply on this unique economic transformation and its social consequences. Whatever else may be the principal functions of the early city, certainly in an advanced urban society the authentic nexus of the city is the marketplace — the arena in which the necessities of life are exchanged and in which urban contact has its workaday centre. The nature of the marketplace in any given period of history depends largely on the prevailing mode of labour.

What bears repetition is the fact that labour-power was transformed into a commodity, a purchaseable object like any other object, and that technology became an extension of labour not as human activity, but as economic exploitation or wage labour.

Now we come to the modern city. Bookchin pushes further the revolutionary analysis.

> With the increasingly problematic abstraction of labor from its concrete forms, all relations, objects, and responsibilities acquire a monetary equivalent. Natural life shrinks from the community to the individual: the city becomes a mere aggregate of isolated human monads — a grey featureless mass, the raw materials of bureaucratic mobilization and manipulation.

And further still,

> If the mere extension of commodity relations can be said to have transformed the medieval commune into the bourgeois city, the factory may be singled out as the agent which gives this city its structural form and its social purpose. By the word "factory" I mean more than an industrial enterprise: the factory is the locus of mobilized abstract labor, of labor power as a commodity, placed in the service of commerce as well as production. Accordingly, the term applies as much to an office building and a supermarket as to a mill and a plant. Once the factory becomes an element of urban life, it takes over the city almost completely. Here, a very important historic contrast must be emphasized. In the medieval commune, the workshop was a home: it was the locus not only of highly individuated technical activities, but also (as Mumford has already stressed) of complex personal and cultural responsibilities. With the emergence of the factory, home and work place are separated. The factory is a place to which the worker goes in order to expend his human powers — powers that are steadily degraded to the degree that they are abstracted and quantified as mere "work time" — in the service of increasingly anonymous owners and administrators. The factory has no personal or cultural functions; it is merely the collecting and mobilizing centre for alienated depersonalized labor...
>
> Conversely, the factory transforms the city into a commercial and industrial enterprise. It negates the role of the city as a personal and cultural entity and exaggerates its economic functions to the point of urban pathology...The factory degrades the city to a centre of production for the sake of production and consumption for the sake of consumption.

What Bookchin has done is not, like Richardson, simply link the urban and social question; he has, by contrast, thoroughly integrated the two, demonstrating to us the difference between a radical and a revolutionary analysis. Unless these social relations which are germane to neo-capitalism are changes, nothing changes. Thus, we enter the urban liberation movement with a strategy understanding its full implications. It is these social relations which are, on the one hand, reflected in the rusted cans, broken glass and debris strewn about in the city, and on the other, reflected in the ravaged forests, polluted waterways, shorelines, and communities. In a word, the "growing metropolis," far from showing "urban revitalisation" now demonstrates our arrival at a historic apex, that of urban exhaustion.

What is, in other words, our fundamental criticism of the bourgeois city? It is not that certain historic buildings are being destroyed, nor that we have too many cars in our streets, nor that there is not enough low-rent housing for the working class, nor the fact that property taxes and water taxes are too high, nor the fact that there are not enough green spaces. All these limitations on urban life are quantitative problems and symptoms of fundamental causes. If we are to undertake an urban liberation movement which is revolutionary and will stress the qualitative questions, how do we define our criticism? Bookchin aptly addresses this.

> The integrity of the individual ego depends upon its ability to integrate the many different aspects of human life — work and play, reason and emotion, mental and sensuous, the private and the social — into a coherent and creative whole. By no means is this process of integration a strictly private and personal activity…the possibility of integrating one's ego depends enormously upon the extent to which society itself is integrated existentially in the course of everyday life. The clan, village, and medieval commune were humanly sealed and personally comprehensible totalities in which the individual satisfied all facets of life.

Therefore, we say:

> The bourgeois city separates these facets of life and delivers them, one by one, to institutions, denuding the ego of the rich content of life. *Work* is removed from the home and assimilated by giant organizations in offices and industrial factories…*Play* becomes organized and unimaginative. Faculties of the individual are pre-empted by mass media that define the very day dreams of the ego…*Reason* and intellect are brought under the technical sovereignty of the academy and the specialist. *Political life* is taken over by immense bureaucratic institutions that manipulate people as "masses" and insidiously try to engineer public consent…*Social life*, as embodied by the massified city, rears itself about personal life, reducing the individual from a microcosm of the whole to merely one of its parts…Almost every aspect of urban life today, particularly in the metropolis, fosters this ego impoverishment…*It creates a feeling of insignificance* (my emphasis).

This feeling is most sharp in that ultimate refuge for privacy and intimacy — the home — and in the case of the high rise, it is the equivalent of the office skyscraper. What has to be avoided in all this is a conclusion which suggests that changing life qualitatively makes the project of social change incomprehensible, and too complex. Such a position only suggests a greater degree of social decomposition than is admitted to now. It's nothing new to meet "radicals" who propose that almost every civic problem can be resolved not by action that goes to its social roots, but by legislation that further holds back the rights of the citizen as an autonomous being and enhances instead the power of bureaucracies. These larger "complex" problems are not even recognized as political problems, but referred to vaguely in philosophical asides.

Out of this position emerge "the planners" who are predictably social democrats. What we are saying here is that in addition to the solid principles as to why we should organize a "localist" movement in Montréal, we now also have concrete tactical reasons. A single Montréal political party in opposition to Drapeau under these circumstances is a sitting duck during such a repressive campaign.

Our conclusion then in making a comparison between Richardson and Bookchin can be phrased as follows: Any urban liberation movement that does not present a revolutionary critique of contemporary society and does not make clear that the "urban crisis" is not separate from the "crisis of capitalism" and more importantly, does not demand and work for *the revolutionary transformation of existing social relations*, amounts to reaction in disguise, and is an accomplice to the very society that is producing the mess in which we live.

What does this mean exactly?

1. After many years of community organising on a variety of issues — housing, welfare, education, etc. — an attempt should be made to bring activists and citizens' groups together in various neighbourhoods. The process of bringing together should be undertaken from the bottom rather than the reverse.

2. The purpose of bringing together should be to continue the development of the anti-authoritarian left trend in consciousness, to consolidate it, to integrate it into a systemic analysis and programme to change the social system. This is a process of ideological and political integration, of existing consciousness as well as its further development. The process will naturally include a sorting out of contradictions from a radical perspective. In contrast to "progressivism" this means an open socialist declaration and analysis based upon a class perspective.

3. In a continuing move to the Left, a position must be developed on the question of electoral politics at the municipal level. As libertarian revolutionaries, we reject electoralism at the federal and provincial levels of government as both a fraud and a trap, the generator of false consciousness. Urban politics, however, *may* offer a different dimension. To begin with, urban life is the politics of everyday life. Urban politics may be more vulnerable to mass action. Urban government may be more responsive to direct action.

4. The essence of a strategy, a revolutionary strategy, is to build a consciousness based upon the transformation of existing power into the sphere of daily life. All existing power structures must be challenged, and the demand must be to decentralise established power to the local, urban base. Such a demand cannot be separated from a transformation of social relations. This, in turn, must be based on a *class-analysis*. Class struggle and socialism must be in the forefront of the programme of such a movement.

5. Urban politics is not conceived as an opportunity to allow the social democratic left to penetrate and to gain yet one more sphere of influence. Urban politics is seen here as the crucial microcosms of social revolution.

6. Such a revolutionary perspective implies a nuclear movement, deeply rooted in every neighbourhood of the city, in every block and, if possible, literally in every home. All major social questions must be brought from the stage to the audience, from Ottawa and Québec City to Montréal. This

perspective centres not around the false consciousness of "higher forms of politics" but everyday life.

7. Ottawa and Québec City is *their* capital, not ours. Our "capital" is the locality in which we live our everyday lives: our city, our neighbourhood, our schools, factories, offices and streets — the world their capital dominates and exploits and which we seek to liberate. We are not parochial provincials who jealously guard our own "turf," but rather active participants in the large social, cultural and ecological tableau of our time.

8. A true grasp of social reality requires that we assimilate the local arenas of private life so that those arenas form the basis for dealing with major social questions of the day.

9. We speak here also of the development of a new type of organised politics — of political action on a qualitatively different level from the kind that exists today. Together with the breakdown of the traditional bourgeois institutions such as the patriarchal family, the school system, the church and the army, we are also witnessing a historic cleavage between *local* forms of political administration and the centralised State. Profound institutional contradictions are emerging throughout. People from all walks of life sense that the federal, provincial and metropolitan governments have not permitted the development of popular control over political and civic life. The so-called "common people" scarcely have any say, much less direct control, over the management of their neighbourhoods and municipalities. People are denied any determination over the planning of their towns, over the building of highways, roads, parks, schools, over the siting of power plants, indeed, over the most supine bureaucrats who are supposed to service their needs. By extension therefore, it is no wonder that there is no popular control over foreign policy, or industrial development.

10. We are asserting here the profoundly revolutionary principle of local self-management, the confederal principle, in sharp contradiction to the centralistic political principle required by a monopolistic State capitalist society.

11. We propose a *qualitatively* different level of political activity: the confederal or, if we like, the "Communard" concept of institutional organisation that also found expression in the Paris communes of 1793-94 and 1871. This "communard" approach, so closely in accord with the confederational approach of the early American revolutionaries, essentially called for a confederation of municipalities as opposed to the development of a centralised State.

12. What is needed, therefore, is the formation of local coalitions or neighbourhood councils of a non-party group bringing together the best of the student groups, working class, women's groups, ethnic groups. The local coalition would act concertedly in choosing and presenting candidates for city council. These coalitions must be non-hierarchical, must be rooted in their local communities and act openly with each other in a consistently democratic manner, eschewing any form of bureaucratic or manipulative behaviour, however much they may differ on many issues.

BEYOND REFORMISM: THE AMBIGUITY OF THE URBAN QUESTION

This essay is written in two parts. The first is a criticism of the article by Henry Milner, "City Politics — Some Possibilities," published in Our Generation, (Vol. 10, No. 4, Winter 1975). The second part deals with events in Montréal during the fall of 1975.

One can have no less an objection to the article in question by Henry Milner than to disagree with its premises and consequently, with the groundless speculations he calls "possibilities." It is important to present a criticism of this article because if its assumptions are followed, in spite of appearances, we will be led to a new reformism.

1. The first important premise in Milner's article is stated as:

> The basic contradiction of modern day capitalism, *the process whereby* the decisions that directly shape the lives of all, are determined on the basis of the profit of few,...(my emphasis).

No radical socialist can take seriously Milner's premise. This is not only simplistic but also misleading. The basic contradiction in capitalism is no mere "process." Our society is characterised by the fact that it is organised along authoritarian lines caused by the unprecedented massification of political institutions through bureaucratic centralisation in the form of the State. It is also caused by the ownership and control of the economy by a small ruling class leading to huge organisational monopolies on the one hand, and growing monopolies on the other. It is finally caused by the creation of socio-psychological conditions which re-enforce repression and passivity, reducing people to spectators. Put succinctly, we live in a class society which operates on the basis of both exploitation and domination. The underlying principle is that of authority, which it is important to note is reflected in the economic, political, social and cultural spheres of life. The basic contradiction then, is the fact that we live in a society based on class divisions while it claims the contrary. These class divisions have certain general characteristics differing little from those of the past, while certain specific characteristics are particular to our period.

At the bottom of any social analysis must be a class analysis. Readers will have noted the absence of a class analysis in Milner's article. The nature of both the ownership and control of the economy gives rise to a form of authoritarian organisation — the factory system — based on wage labour which is the heart of exploitation and domination. If the nature of the economy does not change, simply put, nothing significant in the revolutionary sense, changes. Ultimately, all social relations are rooted in this factory system. The system is not simply the industrial unit commonly associated with the term.

...the factory is the locus of mobilized abstract labor, of labor power as a commodity placed in the service of commerce as well as production. Accordingly, the term applies as much to an office building and a supermarket as to a mill and a plant. Once the factory becomes an element of urban life, it takes over the city almost completely. (Murray Bookchin, *The Limits of the City*.)

2. Another important premise in Milner's article is as follows:

When studying urban politics, it is legitimate to consider the city as a specific social entity...there is a similar pattern of technological, geographical, economic, and social development that unites cities. Furthermore, the city more than anywhere else (except perhaps the school) today manifests the most basic contradictions inherent in the very structure of monopoly capitalist society...
    It is not entirely accidental that it has been cities that, since the Paris Commune or perhaps even earlier, right up to the present day, have been the scene of mass protest and revolutionary manifestations...

Milner tries to situate the importance of the city and urban politics, but his formulation is ambiguous, and can become misleading because it is so incomplete. If we further Bookchin's analysis of the extension of the factory system into urban life, we must not set aside the basic system itself. In trying to comprehend the social factory system, we begin to realise that industrial society must be interpreted as the preparatory stage of urbanisation. Industrialisation finds its apogée in urbanisation, which is now dominating industrial production and organisation. Industrialisation, once the producer of urbanism, is now produced by it.
    The pioneering work of Henri Lefebvre is important to cite here:

When we use the words "urban revolution" we designate the total ensemble of transformations which run throughout contemporary society, and which serve to bring about change from a period in which questions of economic growth and industrialisation predominate to the period in which the urban problematic becomes decisive, when research into the solutions and forms appropriate to urban society takes precedence...The urban problematic imposes itself on a world-wide scale. Can the realities of urbanism be defined as something superstructural, on the surface of the economic basis, whether capitalist or socialist? Or as a simple result of economic growth and the increasing power of the forces of production? No. The reality of urbanism modifies the relations of production without being sufficient to transform them. Urbanism becomes a force in production, rather like science. Space, and the political organisation of space, express social relationships, but also react back upon them. (*Henri Lefebvre, La Révolution Urbaine,* and developed again in *La Pensée Marxiste et la Ville*.)[1]

The subordination of industrialism to urban society implies changes which are the basis for severe conflicts. As the world becomes urbanised under the dominant world system of capitalism, transforming more aspects of daily life into commodities, there begins to emerge nevertheless, a basis for resistance at the very core of the urban process where it is most advanced. According to Lefebvre, it leads to the "creation of distinctively local habitats" of resistance. It is at this local level in the city where the seeds of the countermoves are nurtured and where the basis of a movement against global urban homogeneity will be produced.

The point of all this is that the urban question has both different and deeper roots and causes than Milner suggests. Because of this, other strategies and social forces must be called upon to make advances that avoid reformist degeneration.

3. Milner goes on:

> Paradoxically, however, there is another aspect of radical urban activity that, at least in North America, can only be described as under-developed. This might be termed the sphere of *public politics*. In my view, politics is that part of social activities that involves and affects people not as individuals but as citizens — productive participants in a civil collectivity...
>
> ...politics is not to be confused with administration; a political struggle can never be merely administrative. For instance, the nationalisation of some private enterprise by a far removed level of government is not itself a political act...

The paradox that he points to is not paradox to anyone but himself. It is perfectly plain that given how politics are conditioned by our society, including politics as defined by the old Left, people are simply too wise to take the game seriously. Bourgeois and old Left politicians sing the praises of the importance of electoral politics and the changing of governments. If one examines the positions on this question at all, the current parties on the ideological spectrum from conservative to Marxist-Leninist, they remain the same in essence. One part of the spectrum accepts the political system of electoralism (after all, it was created by the bourgeoisie), while the other claims it wants "to use the system," as if it is both more clever and more powerful than the system, and as if this is an important way to reach the people.

The people's response to the voting ritual, to the extent that they vote, is purely defensive. They try to prevent what in their judgement is the worst from happening, and often the system is powerful enough to fool them altogether. At the same time, voting is a self-deluding act by people struggling for self-esteem.

Milner's effort to create some new terminology in political science is just obscurantism. The problem is not with finding an additional or new definition to the word "political" and distinguishing between "political change" and "administrative reform." Any revolutionary would laugh at the suggestion that nationalisation of a private industry is not a political act. It is, in the conventional sense of the word, a political or State act. But what it is not, is a social or revolutionary act, which over one hundred years of socialist history has shown us. Nationalisation is not the same as socialisation under workers' control. Nationalisation takes place in both private and State capitalist societies. These acts are part of the tradition of "socialism from above." The old slogan read, "all wealth is created by labour, all wealth should belong to labour." Nowhere does this exist, because nowhere have we seen social revolution. What we have seen are political revolutions which have transferred State power from, in some cases, a ruling class to a State bureaucratic caste.

Milner places high hopes on "mobilisation." So does Mario Soares. Mobilisation is far from sufficient, indeed it begs the key question. Nothing short of the creation of the autonomous self-organisation of the new proletariat will do. *Autonomous,* so that such a movement cannot be co-opted by either the State or some political party. *Self-organisation,* so that such a movement is built from the bottom and relies on its own strength. *New proletariat,* so that it is built on class consciousness, and advances class-struggle based on a contemporary definition of the exploited majority of society.

Milner's example of mobilisation is suggestive of what he really has in mind. He cites the case of the "health care question." As we know, in Saskatchewan a "political struggle over health care in our society (going) beyond medicare to community controlled clinics and the like" did take place. The mass political campaign was organised by the CCF. What happened? It led to a CCF government with the political State apparatus in hand, legislating medicare and doing little about community-controlled clinics. Why? Because such parallel institutions as community clinics threatened to dilute the authority of a medicare bureaucracy, and indirectly, the authority of the State. To suggest, as does Milner, that mobilisation leading to a change in government is different somehow from other kinds of changes in government, is to avoid the question of the nature of political and economic power and its traps. There is no alternative to the people themselves having direct power through their own social forms, which only a profound social struggle can bring about. As Bakunin noted more than a century ago:

> It is not enough that the people wake up, that they finally become aware of their misery and the causes thereof. True, there is a great deal of elemental power, more power indeed than in the government, taken together with the ruling classes; but an elemental force lacking organisation is not a real power. It is upon this incontestable advantage of organised force over the elemental force of the people that the might of the State is based.
>
> Consequently, the question is not whether they (the people) have the capacity to rebel, but whether they are capable of building up an organisation enabling them to bring the rebellion to a victorious end — not just to a casual victory but to a prolonged and ultimate triumph.
>
> It is herein, and exclusively so, one may say, that this whole urgent problem is centred.
>
> Therefore, the first condition of victory by the people is *agreement among the people or organisation* of the people's forces.

Mobilisation is not enough. The people must be organised into their autonomous organisations, and remain so.

4. The fourth premise of Milner's politics follows:

The prime focus of the public aspect of politics has been, is, and must be the traditional one, namely the selection, role and decisions of those who represent the collectivity and govern its institutions. There is no way around the association of politics and government. Government, if anywhere, is for the assertion of public authority, for the definition of just what the citizens in the collectivity have in common, the locus of their common will as expressed on a lasting basis...

Here then, we have it plainly stated, a veiled attack on libertarian socialism. Without any analysis or evidence we are told that "It is mystical to assert that government will wither away into simple administration..." The hypothesis is that a society of mediated social relations is essential for our continuation as a technological society.[2] What more mediated relations are there in politics than "representative democracy"? We are asked to take the road of liberal and/or social democracy. The premise here is that we are not capable of self-management. This makes Milner's position on neighbourhood councils either ambiguous or the old liberal model of Montesquieu of checks and balances.

Two students of neighbourhood power put the matter thus:

...Past political emphasis always has been on "how" citizenship would be exercised. From that preoccupation has grown the entire system in which citizenship is exercised by representation. Citizens elect others to perform their civil or political chores. That is said to be efficient. It is said also to be a solution to how citizenship may be exercised by millions of people. It presupposes that it is necessary for them to exercise that citizenship all together, towards united goals. It is the prime requisite of the big-nation-state and, in fact, it requires that people be more like residents...than actual citizens. The citizens do not debate and propose, they simply ratify or reject. And, no matter how lustily the rhetoric...may proclaim the equality of all citizens, it is obvious to anyone's common sense observation that some citizens are far more equal than others. The class of citizens whose work is politics exercise citizenship on behalf of all the rest. They *are* political citizens. The others in society are simple political constituents.

It is impossible to say that such a system does not work. Of course it works. It works to support a very particular structure of politics, one with national goals and with national power. All other levels of interest are subordinate to those goals and power and, once again, the preoccupation of politics is with how to mesh the citizens into the structure. (Morris and Hess, *Neighbourhood Power.*)

The analysis of representative government applies to any level of government wherever. Milner's defence of "the assertion of public authority" in no meaningful way differs from Schumpeter's,

Democratic government will work to full advantage only if all the interests that matter are practically unanimous not only in their allegiance to the country, but also to their allegiance to the structural principles of the existing society. (Joseph Schumpeter, *Capitalism, Socialism and Democracy.*)

We have pioneered in this country an anti-electoralist critique as well as an anti-parliamentary form of politics and have consistently argued for an extra-parliamentary basis for social change. While we have rejected the relevance to fundamental social change of "national" or "provincial" parliamentary politics, we have at the same time presented an alternative position on the national and social question in Canada. We rejected parliamentary politics not simply where these apply to remote levels of government, but also because of the contents of these politics and because they imply the acceptance of the primacy of bourgeois political institutions and bourgeois legitimacy. We refused to accept social change in this way, and through the rules set down by the ruling class. It is after all their system, their rules, and it serves their interests rather well.

In pursuing our theory and practice to its logical consequence, and being ever attentive to new insights and experiences, we have moved towards what is called "the politics of everyday life." The natural evolution from our New Left perspective on community organising brought us closer to what we now call the urban setting of the social question or the urban question. We have been searching for new liberatory social forms and content in our striving for a new politics. Some of us concluded that what the Italian revolutionary Left called, "Take over the city" was what the New Left called, "taking control of your daily life."

Not being against elections in principle, but electoralism in their system and in *their* political institutions, we have had to explore the role of electoral politics at the city level and in its specific circumstances. The force of localism and the direct access of city politics *may* very well make city hall the political institution most vulnerable to people's rage. In a context which places a priority on building an independent mass movement, on mass direct actions, and radical social struggle both in the neighbourhood and the workplace, elections to city hall may have a role to play as a *secondary* form of activity. The tentative nature of this thesis must be stressed.

Having accepted a strictly defined form of electoralism on the city level, and for a limited period of time within the context of a revolutionary strategy, we must indicate the specific role and objective of "city council politics." The objective set down by Milner is wholly unacceptable. An urban social revolution must have the objective of the dissolution of authority and not its reconstitution under a more benign guise. Once elected to city hall, the strictly mandated and revocable delegates of a radical movement have the task of helping in the decentralisation of all power back to the people in the neighbourhood councils that will have emerged in the course of social struggle. The remaining function of a profoundly transformed city hall would be largely that of the co-ordination of the political economy of the city to be undertaken by strictly mandated delegates from the districts or neighbourhoods. City hall would "administer things" and not "administer people." State authority at the urban level as we know it would be dismantled, as the political economy of the city would be socialised and self-managed by the working people. This

then, is the essence of the social struggle, the essence of the urban libertarian socialist project, of which the "public political struggle" is but a part.
This is the tradition of the Paris Commune.[4] Needless to say, all this cannot
happen in a vacuum. It is certain rather obvious developments will have to
take place in society as a whole, outside the city.

Milner then backtracks, and in an aside which he does not develop,
proposes that what he just put forward with respect to "the public aspect
of politics"[3] as a justification for Statism at the urban level, should not be
taken as a defence for "any particular government nor level of government." Other than the city. And why not? It is after all a rather traditional
definition of authority and the State, in spite of the fact that he places it on
the urban level.

At this point, Milner turns to the Chinese National People's Congress
as a paradigm of delegated authority. Not wishing to suggest that Milner is
an apologist for a totalitarian society, it is nevertheless a characteristic of
some people these days to point to certain aspects of Chinese society as instructive to us. But a slice is part of a whole and a reflection of it. To suggest
that we should look to the Chinese National People's Congress, representative of an ideologically monolithic society, and that in January, 1975
met for the first time in ten years, raises questions. If we wish to learn from
examples in the history of decision-making bodies which used the principle of delegates, the history of revolution is full of them in societies and
times where people were using such bodies as instruments of social revolution. The Chinese "communists" are indeed masters of mass mobilisation
(Milner's assertion of "the collective") without, needless to say, creating a
society of workers self-management, or a society where there is direct
democracy and the State is dissolving.

5. The second part of Milner's article attempts a review of the evolution of urban politics in North America. It is an interesting review as far
as it goes. It is the omissions from this historical review that again raise
questions about Milner's approach to the urban question. He spends no
time on the fact that there were many socialist administrations in city
governments in the USA for instance, especially at the turn of the century. These governments existed in both small towns and medium-size
cities. Socialists came to power in Milwaukee — an important centre of
radicalism — in 1912 when they received 30,000 out of 43,000 votes.
They were also in power in Schenectady, New York, and among the
radicals who gave them crucial support at the time was Walter Lippman
who stated: "Reform under fire of radicalism is an educative thing;
reform pretending to be radicalism is deadening." These words hold
true today. In other words, what Milner is neglecting is an assessment
of the significance of socialists in local governments, but even more importantly, he neglects an examination of their programmes and activities. Avoiding this examination is to set aside a critical look at
whether a new urban liberation movement today is making advances in
the theory and practice of radical social change. A radical historian of
American socialism reflects:

Complete socialism required the public ownership of all the means of production and distribution. To this end much could be done on a local basis. The municipal socialism programme of the Social Democrats aimed at extending the power of the municipality to ownership of all public utilities, particularly gas and electric lighting plants, street railways, and telephones. It would seem, therefore, that the Social Democrats envisioned a gradual socialization of America through piecemeal nationalization of trusts and municipal ownership of public utilities. (Ira Kipnis, *The American Socialist Movement, 1897-1912*.)

Does this sound familiar? We should not avoid this critical look at socialists in local governments in the USA or in Western Canada, for we need to arrive at a complete analysis of how and why they failed, and how and why any new movement can go beyond the approaches of the old Left. Indeed, if contemporary urban socialists in this society want to go beyond social democracy no analysis of "possibilities" is serious unless we also examine the role and effect of socialists in local governments in countries like England, France, Italy, Germany and the Scandinavia. Socialists have been in power in these countries for decades with municipal programmes, and have contributed not to fundamental social change, but to reformist improvements. If this is what certain people want, then let them not have pretensions to the contrary.

All of these administrations, past and present, have certain features in common. None were or are revolutionary, in spite of rhetoric to the contrary; they all serve the capitalist order and are all Statist. In none of these instances were the mass of people encouraged to construct their own independent economic and social institutions in the neighbourhoods and the workplace on the ruins of the bourgeois political structures.

What is needed is to admit the following: socialists of various hues have been in socialist city governments in several industrial countries for decades. Why have none of these cities moved beyond reformism? What was/is missing from these socialist city programmes and actions? Milner does not even acknowledge these questions, and it is this fact that is troubling about his historical review. It is not surprising, therefore, that he ascribes "a moment of great celebration by the Left in Montreal" when the Montreal Citizens Movement (MCM), a municipal political party, made electoral gains. What Left does he have in mind? The scores of anarchists and Marxists in Montréal who are working in community politics, in the trade unions, in the educational system? His statement is singularly untrue, but it also shows that his position places immense importance on the fact that the bourgeois political order accorded the MCM a part of its mantle of legitimacy. Are we not back to the urban reform politics of the past, albeit of a left social democratic strain? To be sure, it is very difficult to distinguish social democratic and populist rhetoric from the radical and revolutionary strategies which alone can change the established order.

As in private life, one distinguishes between what a man thinks and says of himself and what he really is and does, still more in historical struggles must one distinguish the phrases and fancies of the parties from their real organism and their real interests, their conception of themselves from their reality. (*Marx*)

6. We can now comment on Milner's assessment of the MCM programme and the organisation's activities. He leads us with a sense of adventure into the party's commitment to the idea of neighbourhood councils. In a sense his projected outline of what constitutes the councils ("It gives rise to possibilities such as a decentralisation of services so that each of fifty or so neighbourhoods might have its own small bureaucracy") is clearer than the party programme. He admits this by saying: "While this kind of administrative decentralisation is not explicitly spelled out in the program..." What we have to ask is, why not? After almost two years of existence the MCM has put little effort into (a) a serious clarification of what neighbourhood councils should or should not be, and (b) the grass roots organisation in the neighbourhoods that alone will lead to the formation of these councils.

One reason may be that the political consciousness and commitment of MCM members is quite low, and that it is a body of people who are primarily attracted to change through electoral work. Not being a mass movement, and not reflecting mass activity, the MCM is in large part the design of its architects who deliberately chose, in putting together the Progressive Urban Movement (a precursor of the MCM), a "broad progressive coalition of PQers, Communists, NDPers, and trade unionists, etc." One reaps what one sows. Such a coalition will bear bitter fruit, and sharp contradictions. The MCM programme is a mixture of populism and implicit social democracy, with some very important decentralist notions. PUMists however insisted, and continue to do so, that their programme is socialist in a radical sense. Time will tell whether the MCM membership will agree.

Milner's political naiveté knows no bounds. He points out how pleasant an experience it is to work within the MCM, and contrasts this to the experience in other left groups. He believes that the MCM has discovered some new formula to avoid bitter internal conflicts. He treats us in a footnote to a homily on how to avoid conflicts. As long as members are outwardly mobile, "when the political struggle is abdicated and replaced by...private activities..." we are told, there will be no conflicts over basic principles within the MCM. Every political group goes through a honeymoon period. The average honeymoon lasts six months. This will happen to the MCM also, otherwise it will dry out. The MCM, if it is going to have any potential for making a contribution to radical social change in Montréal must develop an open radical socialist left-wing within it in the very near future. Before and after the elections, the majority of the commercial press lavished praise on the MCM. They did so for their own reasons and in doing so did not depart significantly from the basic values of the establishment media in this country, or the values of the dominating ideology of capitalism. Is this not some indication that the ruling class does not consider the MCM a problem? Sooner or later more opportunists and careerists will flock to the MCM. What will hinder this process is an honest coming to terms with and resolving the many ambiguities in the urban question as it is being currently addressed by many reformists.

The kind of myth-making that Milner generates when he deals with the particular status and importance of the St. Louis district is dangerous. This district or ward has had the longest history of community-oriented activity in the city. Nevertheless, it lacks today working-class unity of any sort, and it certainly lacks an autonomous self-organising movement of this class. On the contrary, there is a high degree of competitiveness among the numerous charity, social work, and social action groups. There is a marked absence of a social and political consensus beyond populism. It is a district where countless sincere people have been co-opted by the system by a windfall of OFY (Opportunities for Youth) and LIP (Local Initiatives Project) projects (in some parts of the district unemployment is as high as 30% of the workforce). This is the stark reality that Milner does not even mention.

This is not to say that St. Louis has not been the site of some very militant and important struggles, and some base-building organising reflecting some sense of social direction. But to be honest, these examples are few and far between, in spite of the tremendous social potential of the neighbourhoods of St. Louis.

The objective situation of the district however, and some of its past political traditions, have forced a certain left-wing rhetoric to be quite popular in St. Louis. But rhetoric which rationalises our limitations in this case is one thing, and the task of building a co-ordinated mass movement solidly based on the proletariat is quite another. This task has barely begun.

Milner uses to support his case, the hypothesis that if the three MCM City Councillors elected in St. Louis had been in office during the famous Milton-Park struggle of some years ago, and if they had been arrested along with the militants, the outcome would have been different. At the time of the presentation of his article, serious criticism was raised over such speculations. This criticism was largely borne out by subsequent events. Within a few months of the publication of his article another important urban struggle concerning housing broke out in the area on St. Norbert Street.

The property was owned by the City of Montréal, and the government wanted a row of houses destroyed in order to build a large garage area for snow removal equipment — this in a city with an acute shortage of low-rent housing. This conflict had certain advantages over the Milton-Park struggle. Any social action fighting the State as compared to a private developer can expect greater room for manoeuvre and many more tactical options for its pressure campaign. A unique opportunity presented itself in Montréal, an opportunity with the advantages of a vocal opposition inside City Council. The opportunity was missed. Milner states: "...one can really expect analogous occurrences over the next few years with MCM elected officials using their access to the political arena to collectivise and thereby politicise popular struggles." This did not happen, why?

Families and other residents were forced to evacuate the housing scheduled for demolition. The *Comité Logement St. Louis* (the principal group in the area concerned with housing) took the initiative in organising the popular opposition along with *Save Montréal* (a collection of groups concerned with housing and green spaces). Small demonstrations took place, petitions circulated, and an occupation of the empty houses was undertaken.

The role of the MCM? It has been argued by some that the presence of the MCM, especially because of the "broad progressive coalition" it brought together, would lead to "an opening to the Left in Montreal." Indeed, even references to the effects of Allende's Chile were evoked to justify the strategies of some of the leading MCMers. But the events of St. Norbert St. stared them in the face. Where was the commitment behind all the talk about "mobilisation" and "collectivising popular struggles"?

Instead of helping in the organisation of a massive city-wide mobilisation to "Save St. Norbert Street," instead of organising large scale public demonstrations (by systematically calling upon its more than 3,000 members to work and join in), instead of organizing a large-scale occupation of the housing, instead of organising mass picketing outside city hall, what did the MCM do? The MCM City Councillors showed their support by symbolically coming to the small occupation and sit-in, while one St. Louis City Councillor put up a valiant fight by helping as much as a single person could have. The St. Louis MCM which claimed 400 members, did not or could not call upon its members to help organise action and demonstrations either.

In other words what we are saying here is that the emergence of the MCM since the Milton-Park struggle has not meant very much in terms of radical urban politics, that is mass action and organisation. As a matter of fact, the St. Norbert St. struggle had far less of an impact and significance than the Milton-Park fight. Fewer people were involved in the action and fewer popular organisations offered their concrete solidarity. If Milner was correct, it would be logical to assume that this struggle over the St. Norbert St. houses should have been a much bigger and important conflict.

The Milton-Park campaign was against a private developer. The St. Norbert St. one was against "public authority." A mass mobilisation of Montréalers around this issue could have been a turning point for radical urban politics. The MCM certainly showed no particular understanding of the importance of defeating the Drapeau regime over a popular question, in-between elections, and most importantly, in the streets.

These are some of the questions and problems arising from the Milner thesis. The urban question is far too important to allow such woolly thinking to add to the complexity of the revolutionary project.

August 1975

During the writing of the commentary above and since its completion, a number of important developments have taken place that shed new light on the potential of the MCM. Many of the preceding criticisms were being echoed inside and outside the MCM.

1. There were two long and bitter strikes in the public transportation sector. The bus and metro drivers, followed by the garage and maintenance

workers of the transportation commission went on strike. Although the MCM made statements in support of the strikers' demands and a call for a fare strike was being considered at one point, the MCM's weakness at the base made it helpless in terms of either organising solidarity for the striking workers or creating a wide-scale public education debate on transportation among the people. This made some people within the MCM aware that an analysis of the relationship of the struggles at the workplace and those in the neighbourhoods was missing. The absence of such an analysis meant the absence of a full understanding of the urban question and the importance of a dialectic between transforming the city and moving to radical socialism.

2. Within the MCM an open socialist current was surfacing. Over the last year, a number of members, especially those with an overview on the executive, were obviously agonising over the internal contradictions within the MCM. Out of this experience, an executive committee report was submitted to the MCM district committees for consideration before the annual congress of November 7-9, 1975. The report consisted of a discreet evaluation of the MCM during the preceding months, and proposed ten resolutions to the congress. The first two were the most important:

1. The programme of the MCM stems from a socialist analysis of the city which implies:
a) that the capitalist mode of production is the principal cause of the urban crisis;
b) that consequently, our strategy of political action must stem from this socialist analysis of the city;
c) that in the public stances of the party at all levels, we link our immediate demands to this socialist critique of the city.
2. The first priority to emerge from this analysis is grass roots mobilisation: electoral and parliamentary activity must be situated within this perspective.

3. Following the public transportation strikes, the city government used the prevailing anti-strike mood to impose a fare hike. In a week's time the MCM called a public protest meeting. One of the MCM speakers, Stephen Schecter (a member of the executive) spoke out clearly for direct action and civil disobedience against the fare hike. A *Comité de Lutte Contre la Hausse* was quickly formed in which the students took the leadership. There followed a vigourous campaign of door to door public education in some of the districts, Metro stations were occupied and thousands of people were let in free, a "penny campaign" was organised where people were encouraged to pay the new fare of 50 cents or the old fare of 30 cents in pennies in order to fill up the ticket boxes and render them useless. There was also a massive demonstration of 20,000 people, mostly students, which ended at City Hall. This was one of the most widespread campaigns of direct action in Montréal's history. After the initial call to action, the MCM played a marginal role in the Comité de Lutte. The MCM City Councillors however, played the role of a very vocal opposition.

4. The publication of "Urban Politics in Capitalist Society: A Revolutionary Strategy" by Stephen Schecter (*Our Generation,* Vol. 11, No. 1) aggravated the crisis within the MCM created by the executive committee report. This outstanding article clarified many points only touched on in the report. The commitment to radical socialism by its author was not only clear, but the article's lucidity advanced the debate on the urban question considerably.

The individuals and factions who opposed the executive document were the Stalinists (members and ex-members of the Communist party), the social democrats (NDPers and PQers), and those who were either fellow travellers or who were nervous at opting for an explicitly socialist perspective.

The publication of the Schecter article helped consolidate the support for the executive committee report both inside and outside the MCM. But in adding fuel to an already passionate debate, it exposed the real position of certain people. When the article began to circulate, some City Councillors opposed to the executive document took the matter to the bourgeois press and helped orchestrate a press campaign against the nascent MCM socialist current. The debate had some unbelievably primitive and opportunistic dimensions.

5. The MCM congress itself turned out to be a significant meeting at which the ideological lines were sharply drawn. As predicted, the honeymoon period was clearly over. A social democratic and populist wing, as well as a radical socialist tendency played themselves out in the workshops and plenary sessions. There was no possibility that the majority of the MCM delegates would vote to adopt the report, in spite of the fact that five or six district MCM committees out of eighteen had voted for it at mini-congresses before the annual congress. The bourgeois press of course added its divisive blows, especially through the reform-oriented *Le Jour* and *The Gazette,* lambasting the executive and its socialist position. *Le Jour* and the PQ were particularly unhappy at the prospect of having any political movement of substance emerge on their left.

Nevertheless, the congress reflected some extremely interesting dynamics, indicating that many outstanding questions are still at a formative stage.

a) Out of eight workshops, one narrowly accepted the socialist clause, two voted to table this part of the report, and the rest voted for a "compromise" resolution presented by the Snowdon district committee, which was in fact a populist position. All workshops accepted the important second resolution, and without opposition.

b) The plenary session, as expected, defeated a motion to table the socialist resolution, but by a very narrow margin of seventeen votes indicative of a rather even split among the MCM delegates. This in itself was a positive reflection on the congress and impressed radical observers outside the MCM.

c) Other important positive reflections of delegate consciousness included:

- a clear subordination of the caucus of City Councillors to the MCM General Council of district delegates. It remains to be seen however what this will mean in practice. What must be overcome here is the proverbial contraction between the professionals (the City Councillors who work on their roles almost full-time), and the volunteer-members (who find it difficult to keep up with every development and keep abreast of important information);
- electoralism and the prominence of the parliamentary politics was placed in a secondary slot by the congress which was the hope of the MCM Left;
- the continuous defeat during the plenary sessions of resolutions presented by the Cotes des Neiges district committee in favour of more hierarchy and centralisation within the MCM. This committee was the spearhead for the anti-executive committee report campaign.
- the defeat of a well-known social democratic City Councillor who ran against a radical candidate for an executive post;
- the passage of a resolution that all persons holding an official position in the MCM, including City Councillors, cannot have an official position in another political party. This has already led to the resignation from the MCM of one PQer who was elected City Councillor from the low-income district of St. Jacques. He now sits as an independent, but before parting he denounced the MCM as being in the hands of revolutionaries. Indeed, as equally important as the adoption of this resolution was a widely applauded and eloquent statement by one City Councillor who insisted that urban politics were the most important, and must not be used as a springboard for provincial or federal politics;
- election as party vice-president of Schecter, the acknowledged intellectual leader of the socialist tendency, in spite of a concerted campaign to isolate him. Schecter made his position clear in his nomination statement which, along with his published article, added to the significance of his election;
- the position of six radical socialists on an eight-member executive.

It should be noted, however, that the socialist Left in the MCM is very much a mixed bag ideologically, in the sense that there is no identification with any particular school of socialist thought per se. Many outstanding issues have to be debated and resolved, but for the moment there is a strong implicit direction towards a kind of libertarian socialism — one that rejects social democracy on the one hand and Marxism-Leninism on the other.

d) On the negative side the congress revealed that:

- There is an overwhelming anti-intellectual/anti-social theory atmosphere in the MCM, reflecting the dominant mind-set in our society. This separation of practice from theory is produced by our educational system. It is fertile ground for opportunists and careerists. It is an atmosphere which discourages the asking of fundamental questions in order to avoid reformism, but also to avoid activity for the sake of activity. And it leads to an avoidance of the need for a systematic analysis of reality.

- The combined Stalinist and social democratic stance of the "coalition of progressive forces" was on the one hand defeated, but on the other hand remains strong. It will re-emerge again.
- Another danger for the radical socialist wing is to continue to delude itself that the MCM programme as it stands now is a radical socialist one. It is this delusion that led the executive members into believing that their report would be accepted by the congress in the first place or, failing that be tabled. Neither happened and as a consequence, the MCM acquired an anti-socialist image.
- Finally, in spite of a commitment to mobilisation of the grassroots, there is no clear indication of what this means exactly. No progress was made in the clarification of this in either the executive committee report or in the Schecter article.[5]

What is important, however, is that a radical socialist wing within the MCM be committed to class politics, and that this commitment be reflected in work, both in the workplace and the neighbourhoods. Also important, is its commitment to place a secondary importance on electoralism and top priority to the urban struggle. It is not some isolated fringe group, but represents a substantial sentiment within the MCM. Coupled with a commitment favouring decentralisation of power, the way is open to further refining the libertarian socialist project. The objective, as well as the subjective conditions, exist in Montréal to propel an urban movement or party which develops a distinctive type of urban socialism. Libertarian socialists should now join the MCM and help this development. But this work must be undertaken with these paraphrased words of David McReynolds in mind from parts of his recent article, "Revolution: The Politics of the Impossible."[6]

> If we seek a social revolution, it is necessary to know before we begin how weak we are, how enormous the job. It has been said that politics is the art of the possible — revolutionary politics is the art of the impossible, the willingness to accept a series of defeats in order to win the war. We do not preach a doctrine of "impossibilism," of utter inflexibility, or the glory of defeat but a doctrine of reality. Socialism may not come. In fact, it can come at all only with great struggle. But *where nothing is inevitable, everything is possible.*
>
> Let's look at the concept of revolution, itself a fairly new notion. Historically, there were palace coups, civil wars waged by opposing contenders for a throne, religious wars, and the tragic rebellions of slaves and peasants. The possibility that *people* could, in their collective self, intervene in history in any conscious way is a recent concept. How strange the concept first seemed when it was advanced as an ideology — that *the people* had the capacity not simply to rebel, but to carry through a revolution against the old order and *govern themselves,* to organize themselves in their own name; to establish their own structures, and to retain for themselves the power to change those social structures.
>
> One reason the Establishment does fear us, even in their strength and our weakness, is because although we are very interested in power, it is not in terms of assuming that power for ourselves but distributing it to the people. Therefore, we cannot be dealt with, absorbed, or bought

off, and such individuals or groups becomes a problem. It is particularly disturbing to have a group emerge which suggests to people that, since the game of politics as it is played is a lousy one which dooms most of the players to be losers, we stop trying to win this game and invent a new one altogether. And social revolution is that new game.

NOTES

1. To fully grasp the revolutionary implications of the urban question it is useful to also turn to the works of M. Castells, D. Harvey, R. Peet — the work of the Union of Socialist Geographers. Indeed, the area of urban political geography as a whole is becoming an area of research to watch carefully.

2. Milner evokes technophobia to justify his Statism. On the other hand, some of the more perceptive modern writers on social and economic matters, such as Lewis Mumford, Murray Bookchin, Paul Goodman, Theodore Roszak, have suggested that the eventual result of technology may well be a breakup of the monolithic structures of today's capitalist industry, paralleled by regional decentralisation, a dissolution of megalopolis, and a return to an organic social order in which the individual will be more free. Hardly the ranting of mystics.

3. In the article, Milner develops a distinction between "the collective" and "the public" "spheres" which, together, comprise the political, according to his definition of it. It is apparently in terms of the former criterion, the collective, that Milner affirms that "a strong case can be made that any level above the local level can never be the locus of politics, being instead an administrative convenience." The matter is not clarified further either at this point or in the lengthy development where he deals with politics as "the collective." In spite of the qualifications above, Milner's position justifies authority and Statism.

4. Our goal should be nothing less than what Kropotkin reflects in approvingly quoting an interesting passage from Sigismond Lacroix's *Actes de la Commune:*

> The state of mind of the districts...displays itself both by a very strong sentiment of communal unity and by no less strong a tendency toward self-government. Paris did not want to be a federation of sixty republics cut off haphazardly each in its territory: the Commune is a unity composed of its united districts...But side by side with this undisputed principle, another is disclosed...which is, that the Commune must legislate and administer for itself directly, as much as possible. Government by representation must be reduced to a minimum; every thing that the Commune can do directly must be done by it, without any intermediary, without any delegation, or else it may be done by delegates reduced to the role of special commissioners, acting under the uninterrupted control of those who have commissioned them...The final right of legislating and administering for the Commune belongs to the districts — to the citizens who came together in the general assemblies of the districts.

5. The Schecter article is outstanding, and represents a sharp contrast with that of Milner's. However, the one important question that is no clearer in the Schecter piece is the question of "mobilisation" and its meaning. Schecter states on a number of occasions, that it is not the purpose of the MCM to "swallow other organisations." In another context he asks "...should the MCM await the independent formation of workers' councils or should it press for them as a parallel organisational base *within* the MCM?" (my emphasis). In yet another instance, he states "...a mobilised and radicalised population will provide a socialist administration with the necessary backing to wrest power from the ruling class."
   Let us draw on the important experience of the radical Left in Italy. Lucio Magri, reflecting *Il Manifesto's* re-reading of Gramsci, states categorically:

The party inevitably becomes an authoritarian and bureaucratic apparatus if it co-exists with a disorganised mass. Its strategy will necessarily oscillate between parliamentarianism and putschism. The only way to overcome the schema is to not merely or mainly "change the party" (democratisation of internal life, right of tendencies, mass recruitment), but introduce a new element altogether: workers' councils. Between the party and the masses, there must be a third term, which mediates the relationship between them: *autonomous and unitary political institutions of the working class*. These institutions must emerge right across society (factories, offices, schools), with their own structures — *in which the party then acts as an element of stimulus and synthesis* (my emphasis).

There should be no question of having workers' councils *within* the MCM. When such new social forms appear, as in the case of neighbourhood councils, they should be autonomous of the MCM, with the latter's militants active within them. There should be no question of regarding a mobilised population's principal role as providing a socialist administration the necessary muscle to wrest power from the ruling class. Only a passive population would allow this to happen. The task of wresting power is the task of the people, and it will be done in the workplace and in the neighbourhoods through direct action, and only within this struggle will a socialist administration play its secondary role.

Revolutionaries are not for a mobilisation in which "the masses struggle and the politicians decide." They are for the self-organisation, and self-activity of the people. This means organisation, solidly based, street by street, bloc by bloc, neighbourhood by neighbourhood, workplace by workplace, federated and co-ordinated by popular assemblies. Within such situations, City Hall will have a role described elsewhere in this commentary. This means clearly — socialism from below, and not socialism from above.

Finally, a remark on the continued existence of organisations like *Citizens on Cycles*, or *Save Montréal*. In spite of the fact that many activists in these and other such organisations are members of the MCM, it obviously gives them the impression of a political party in the narrow sense and not also a movement where social action can be organised. The NDP and social democratic parties have the same image. So long as the MCM plays the half-hearted role it played during the recent St. Norbert St. struggle, militants will go elsewhere to organise action. When *Citizens on Cycles* recently called for demonstrations against the Montréal Auto Show to protest the automobile's use in the city centre where was the MCM? Passing resolutions against the automobile's use in the city centre at the MCM general council was not enough. There should have been hundreds upon hundreds of MCMers at this demonstration. When the MCM undertakes to organise its own mass street actions, and gives active support to the initiative of other groups, many more of the conscious radicals in the city will work within it, and look to the MCM as perhaps the most important focus of urban social and political action. When this happens, and everyone should strive to make it happen as soon as possible, these actions will have greater meaning and impact because each issue attacked will be part of an overall radical analysis and programme for social and political change.

6. *WIN* Magazine, Dec. 23., 1975.

Also from

BLACK ROSE BOOKS

YEAR 501
The Conquest Continues
Noam Chomsky

In Noam Chomsky's characteristic style, *Year 501* offers a succinctly written, logical analysis, firmly grounded in the documentary record. Noting that the current period has much in common with the Colombian age of imperialism, during which western Europe conquered most of the world, Chomsky focuses on various historical moments in this march of imperial power, up to an including the current axis where the United States, Germany, and Japan share world economic control with the United States, revelling in a virtual monopoly of military might.

250 pages
ISBN: 1-895431-62-X $19.95
ISBN: 1-895431-63-8 $38.95

REMAKING SOCIETY

Murray Bookchin

Remaking Society is a primer on Murray Bookchin's thought. It provides a clear synthesis of his ideas for his faithful readers, and serves as an excellent introduction to anyone new to Bookchin's work.

...an intellectual tour de force...the first synthesis of the spirit, logics, and goals of the European "Green Movement" available in English.
Choice

208 pages
Paperback ISBN: 0-921689-02-0 $16.95
Hardcover ISBN: 0-921689-03-9 $35.95

WRITERS AND POLITICS

George Woodcock

The author critiques such international figures as Alexander Herzen, Peter Kropotkin, Ignazio Silone, Arthur Koestler, Kafka and Proudhon...The book indeed provides a good background to the intellectual development of one of the most prominent Canadian humanist voices...a bracing reading for humanists...Well worth the read.
The Humanist in Canada

260 pages
Paperback ISBN: 0-921689-82-9 $17.95
Hardcover ISBN: 0-921689-83-7 $36.95

BLACK ROSE BOOKS

has published the following books of related interests

Mutual Aid, *by Peter Kropotkin*
The Great French Revolution, *by Peter Kropotkin*
Urbanization Without Cities, *by Murray Bookchin*
Language and Politics, *by Noam Chomsky, edited by Carlos P. Otero*
The Political Economy of Human Rights, Vol. 1. The Washington Connection and
   Third World Fascism, *by Noam Chomsky and Edward S. Herman*
The Political Economy of Human Rights, Vol. 2, After the Cataclysm: Postwar
   Indochina and the Reconstruction of Imperial Ideology, *by Noam Chomsky and
   Edward S. Herman*
The Real Terror Network: Terrorism in Fact and Propaganda, *by Edward S. Herman*
The Iran-Contra Connection, *by Jonathon Marshall, Peter Dale Scott, and Jane Hunter*
The Politics of Euro-Communism, *edited by Carl Boggs and David Plotke,*
The Modern State: An Anarchist Analysis, *by Frank Harrison*
Post-Scarcity Anarchism, *by Murray Bookchin*
Toward an Ecological Society, *by Murray Bookchin*
Bakunin on Anarchism, *by Sam Dolgoff*
The Cuban Revolution: A Critical Perspective, *by Sam Dolgoff*
Germany East: Dissent and Opposition, *by Bruce Allen*
The New World Order and the Third World, *edited by David Broad and Lori Foster*
Voices From Tiananmen Square: Beijing Spring and the Democracy Movement,
   edited by Mok Chiu Yu and J. Frank Harrison
Nationalism and the National Question, *by Nicole Arnaud and Jacques Dofny*
World Inequality, *by Immanuel Wallerstein*
The State, *by Franz Oppenheimer*
Anarchist Organization: The History of the FAI, *by Juan Gòmez Casas*
Indignant Heart: A Black Worker's Journal, *by Charles Denby*
Mexico: Land and Liberty, *by Ricardo Flores Magon*
The Bolsheviks and Workers' Control, 1917-1921, *by Maurice Brinton*

Send for our free catalogue of books
BLACK ROSE BOOKS
C.P. 1258, Succ. Place du Parc
Montréal, Québec
H2W 2R3
Canada

Printed by
the workers of
Ateliers Graphiques Marc Veilleux Inc.
Cap-Saint-Ignace, Qué.
for
Black Rose Books Ltd.